Praise for

THE CONVERSATION BEGINS

"A revealing yet comforting overview of the generational passage of feminism that discloses as much about elemental family conflicts as about the future of the women's movement . . . As a collection of discrete stories of a social movement and of the eternal bond of mother and child, this is an impressive book."
—*Kirkus Reviews*

"Compelling . . . Through individual stories, the reader begins to see, in subtle and not-so-subtle ways, how each mother's politics caused ruptures in the daughter's world."
—*New York Newsday*

"A provocative series of narratives . . . [These] stories are ripe with challenges, frustrations, rage and love."
—*The Kansas City Star*

"A unique and intimate examination of the mother-daughter bond."
—*Lawrence Journal-World*

"A reflective and hopeful dialogue about the past, the present and the future of feminism."
—*Bangor Daily News*

Join the conversation! *Christina Baker Kline*

THE

CONVERSATION

BEGINS

Mothers and Daughters
Talk About
Living Feminism

Christina Looper Baker
and
Christina Baker Kline

Bantam Books
New York   Toronto   London   Sydney   Auckland

The Conversation Begins: Mothers and Daughters
Talk About Living Feminism

A Bantam Book
PUBLISHING HISTORY
Bantam hardcover edition / May 1996
Bantam trade paperback edition / April 1997

ISBN 0-553-37524-5

Published simultaneously in the United States and Canada

PRINTED IN THE UNITED STATES OF AMERICA
BVG   0 9 8 7 6 5 4 3 2

To Cynthia, Clara, and Catherine—
the other voices in our conversation

I say this conflict is hard for me. You say it is
hard for you. I say there is respect between us,
you say so too, that we stand here on our own
two feet, alone in a room together, and that only
then can we begin to name the tempest, the
dissent, only then are we prepared to risk
mother's love, to coexist without a cord to bind
us, to risk the persuasion of safety and take our
chances. I say you hurt me. You say I scorned
you. We say we care. It begins. The conversation
begins.

—Louise Bernikow
from *Among Women*

Contents

Acknowledgments

This book could not have become a reality without the wise counsel and generous support of many people. Our agent, Beth Vesel, was the first to hear our idea in the spring of 1992. She believed in the project from the beginning and helped us give it form. Anita Kurth, Deborah Rogers, and Bernardine Connelly read the proposal and made helpful suggestions, challenging us to sharpen our focus. At the 1993 National Women's Studies Conference in Washington, D.C., Judith Arcana and Arlene Fong Craig brainstormed with us to develop as broad and inclusive a list of participants as possible. Kay Trimberger suggested others. Several of the women they mentioned, whom we might never have found without their help, ended up in the book. Gail Hasey contributed her wisdom and insight at crucial times along the way.

In the spring and summer of 1993, a research grant from the University of Maine and writer-in-residence fellowships to the Virginia Center for the Creative Arts (VCCA) enabled us to work on the book together for concentrated periods. Using the grant, we traveled across the country from New York to Washington, D.C., to New Mexico to San Francisco, interviewing participants at every stop. The five weeks we spent at the VCCA in Sweetbriar, Virginia, gave us a chance to make sense of the thousands of pages of transcripts we'd amassed; by the time we left, the book had begun to take shape. We are grateful to the director, Bill Smart, and administrators Sheila and Craig Pleasants, who fit us in at late notice and even extended our stay.

Special thanks go to Leslie Meredith, our original editor at Bantam, who saw the book's promise and conveyed to us her enthusiasm about it, and to Linda Gross, who took over the project when Leslie left and shepherded it through to completion with skill and intelligence and good humor. Her assistant, Samantha Howley, kept track of endless details and patiently assembled all of the disparate pieces of the manuscript into a coherent whole.

Throughout this project, Bill Baker and David Kline provided many kinds of support, literal and figurative. Without their help, our work would have been harder and much less fun. Perhaps their most tangible contribution was in reading and commenting upon drafts of the proposal and the introduction to the book. Peggy Danielson, Jerry Nadelhaft, and Sandra Haggard also generously critiqued the introduction. Clara Baker and Kim Holman were invaluable transcribers and critics. Cynthia and Catherine Baker joined us for some interviews, read material, and offered advice. In the middle of it all, Marcia Mower organized our files, created labels, and generally kept chaos at bay.

Finally, we would like to thank the many women we interviewed for their willingness to let us into their lives. They met us at sidewalk cafés and noisy restaurants, welcomed us into their offices and homes and apartments, provided us with directions and transportation, fed us meals and even offered lodging. Most important, they opened up to us about personal and sometimes painful material. We made mistakes; we weren't always as tactful or as sensitive as we could have been; we sometimes pushed too far or asked too much. But almost always they were willing to give us the benefit of the doubt. It is a testament to the strength and fortitude of the women we spoke with that most of them appear in these pages. We are proud to present such a strong and diverse array of voices from across the country—voices that reflect, examine, and critique the personal and political implications of being a woman in America today. If not for their honesty, openness, and insight, this book would not exist.

Like the women we interviewed, we the authors have laughed and cried and gotten angry with each other. We have also loved each other intensely, grateful for the privilege of working together in conversation with these women who have so generously shared the stories of their mother-daughter relationships against the backdrop of their lives.

Introduction

As the bus lurched around a busy Manhattan corner, Christina leaned over to Tina and said, "If we're going to do this project together, we'll need to have money for therapy built into the contract." It seemed a reasonable proposal for such a risky venture. Was it wise, we wondered aloud, for a mother and daughter to attempt to coauthor a book about feminist mothers and daughters? Could we negotiate the twists and turns of our own relationship as we explored the dynamics of others'? Pausing under the weight of these questions, we sat together in silence until the bus came to a stop. Outside in the warm sunshine on a spring day that seemed filled with possibility, Tina turned to Christina and said, "Why not? It will be an adventure."

This was not the first of such conversations, nor would it be the last. The idea for this book germinated from two separate experiences in the spring of 1992. While teaching at the University of Maine, Tina was helping to create a feminist oral history project designed to retrieve the early experiences of second-wave feminists—founders of the modern women's movement. Meanwhile, in New York City, where she teaches and writes, Christina attended a one-day colloquium, "Women Tell the Truth," featuring Anita Hill as the keynote speaker and introducing a new group calling itself Third Wave: younger feminists—movement daughters—intent on designing an identity of their own. "Why don't we put the two ideas together?" Christina suggested.

Initially we planned to interview symbolic mothers and daughters—those who shaped the modern women's movement and the younger activists who are their heirs. From the older generation we would learn what it was like to have been on the cutting edge of contemporary feminism; from the younger we would ascertain the variety of ways they are reshaping feminism for their own purposes. Along the way, however, we discovered that many prominent second-wave women have daughters of their own. By interviewing real-life mothers and daughters, we could examine whether and how the feminist legacy is passed from one generation to the next and, at the same time, explore the ways women have combined motherhood with a passionate commitment to a broader life. This approach promised to make the project twice as interesting—and doubly complex.

The movement toward equality for women has been a continuing struggle—a struggle discussed often in the United States in terms of cresting and receding waves. What is now referred to as the first wave, began around 1830 as part of the attempt to abolish slavery and heightened by Elizabeth Cady Stanton's call to women to convene at Seneca Falls in 1848, culminated in the winning of the vote in 1920 and Alice Paul's introduction of the Equal Rights Amendment in 1923. During the Depression the first wave began to ebb as women turned their attention away from individual advancement to the struggle for survival. Although in World War II they demonstrated their competence in the workforce by filling jobs vacated by men, in the war's aftermath most women retired to the private sphere of the home.

In 1963 Betty Friedan's *The Feminine Mystique,* encouraging women to reach beyond the "comfortable concentration camp" of the home to find added fulfillment in careers, marked the genesis of feminism's second wave. Subsequently, young women, fresh from the civil rights and antiwar movements and freed for the first time in history from compulsory childbearing by the birth control pill, began calling for equality in the workplace and in the home. Images of protesters at the 1968 Miss America Pageant, waving signs declaring "I'm a woman—not a toy, pet, or mascot" and unfurling a banner announcing "Women's Liberation," were beamed across America, introducing an entire nation to the feminist movement. With the publication of three landmark books in the early 1970s—*Sexual Politics* (Kate Millett), *Sisterhood Is Powerful* (Robin Morgan), and *The Female Eunuch* (Germaine Greer)—second-wave feminism gathered momentum. Focusing on sisterhood and the politics of personal liberation, the movement encouraged women to postpone or avoid pregnancy, experiment with their sexuality, and establish careers.

During the next decades, women mobilized to transform America. New organizations and publications, such as the National Women's Political Caucus, the National Organization for Women, and *Ms.* magazine, pushed women's concerns to the forefront. The Supreme Court legalized abortion, Congress passed the Equal Rights Amendment (as yet unratified), and the Equal Employment Opportunity Commission mandated equity in the workplace. Ushering in a new era of political and personal freedom, contemporary feminism changed forever the way women think about themselves.

Yet in this fundamental re-visioning of women's role in society, many second-wave feminists saw little room for motherhood. Reacting to a not-so-distant past when women were valued primarily for their reproductive role, feminist leaders frequently devalued motherhood and sometimes actually opposed it. Some saw childbearing as a heavy yoke inhibiting women's pursuit of equality; in an extreme example, Shulamith Firestone's *The Dialectic of Sex* (1970) called for artificial wombs to free women from the restrictions of childbearing. To these feminists, having children represented collaboration with the patriarchal system they were trying to change. Given the movement's ambivalence toward the subject, a discussion of motherhood, wrote Letty Pogrebin in 1973, would "shake sisterhood to its roots." Small wonder, then, that motherhood was relegated to the margins of feminism. In *Of Women Born,* published in 1976, Adrienne Rich cited motherhood as "a crucial, still relatively unexplored, area for feminist theory." And so it remains.

Feminist motherhood has been a topic deferred because it complicates the role of the emancipated woman. "Feminism is infinitely easier when you take motherhood out," says Arlie Hochschild, a feminist sociologist and author of *The Second Shift,* "but then it speaks to fewer women." Bearing and nurturing children remains a fact of life for most women; eighty-five percent of American women and over 90 percent of women worldwide give birth. At best, the second wave's antinatalism has been shortsighted; at worst, the movement's "radical bias against making babies," as journalist Gina Maranto phrased it in a 1995 *Atlantic Monthly* article, excluded millions of women. "Women's Liberation makes me feel defensive about being a mother," said a young mother in a 1973 *Ms.* interview. "I think feminists are looking at me and thinking: Is that all she can do?"

Even today, the women's movement has a hard time reconciling motherhood with sisterhood. According to Joan Walsh in a 1993 *Vogue* article entitled "The Mother Mystique," ambivalence about motherhood remains at the heart of today's feminism: "The feminist daughters of Friedan's desperate housewives have been hard put to reckon with motherhood—the institution that imprisoned their own mothers—either personally or politically, to agree on its proper place in a woman's life." The 1995 edition of Sheila Ruth's widely used women's studies text *Issues in Feminism,* for example, allots only a handful of its 536 pages to issues surrounding motherhood. Many feminists now acknowledge that until it addresses the ambiguities involved in reconciling one's work and one's personal life, the women's movement will never succeed on a larger scale.

The 1990s have seen a renewed commitment to exploring issues of particular concern to women. The Senate Judiciary Committee's treatment of Anita Hill, the issues surrounding child care raised by the Zoë Baird and Kimba Wood confirmation debates, the sexual harassment exposed by the Tailhook scandal, a series of abortion-clinic murders, and the graphic depiction of domestic abuse that appeared in the O.J. Simpson trial outraged millions of women. Faced with the erosion of civil rights and abortion rights, a new generation is emerging, bringing energy and focus to the women's movement.

In rejuvenating the very cause once advanced by their mothers, young feminists are in a unique position to critique it. Aware of the gains their mothers made and determined to extend those gains into the twenty-first century, these daughters also know the costs and the pitfalls. Having witnessed firsthand the conflict between a woman's following her own path and being present for her child, they themselves must now grapple with the question of whether and how to combine motherhood with dedication to career and social issues. Several recent books, including *Mother-Daughter Revolution* (Elizabeth Debold, Marie Wilson, and Idelisse Malavé) and *Daughters of Feminists* (Rose L. Glickman), have begun the process of linking motherhood and sisterhood by focusing jointly on feminist mothers and daughters. *The Conversation Begins* introduces the mother-daughter relationship itself into the discourse by exploring the dynamic interaction between the two.

In inviting real-life mothers and daughters to tell the story of their relationship to feminism and to each other, we sought to explore how women who have profoundly affected their own generation have influenced the next at this most personal level. The main criterion for participants in our study was that either the mother or the daughter (or both) has made a public contribution to the contemporary women's movement. Some involved at the national level have widespread name recognition; those working at the grassroots level are known mainly in local communities. Initially we planned to interview eight to ten mother-daughter pairs, but early participants suggested others ("Have you contacted so-and-so? You can't do the book without her"), and our list gradually expanded to include a more broadly representative group of American feminists. All told, we interviewed nearly thirty sets of mothers and daughters, nearly half of whom identify themselves not only as Americans but also by their Native American, African, Latin American, Asian, or East European ethnic heritage. Countless other mothers and daughters qualify for this project, but time and space have limited the number we could include.

Though their language and work are congruent with feminist beliefs and attitudes, not all of our participants call themselves feminists. Some, younger women especially, are reluctant to use the label because of its perceived negative connotations. Others, particularly working-class and minority women, feel out of place in and emotionally disconnected from a movement that does not always speak for them. African-American women's advocate Nkenge Toure describes feminism as a middle-class white women's organization indifferent to her concerns. Instead of calling herself feminist, she calls herself womanist. For many years Asian-American activist Miriam Louie was "actively not a feminist." Now, she says, she and her coworkers are adapting feminism to their community's specific needs. A number of our participants end up saying they are feminists by their own definition.

Most of the women we asked agreed to participate. Of those who declined, some cited time constraints. A few saw their stories as commodities they wished to control; one said she wanted to remain "in charge of" her public persona. Another decided that her story should wait for her memoirs. A daughter of a prominent feminist who wanted to participate was simply "not interested in talking about my mother anymore." Of the women we interviewed, in several cases a mother or daughter had second thoughts about revealing personal information and withdrew from the project.

Reasoning that participants might speak more readily with someone of similar age or experience, we planned that Tina, in her mid-fifties, would interview the mothers and thirty-year-old Christina would interview the daughters. But after conducting interviews both separately and together, we realized that our cross-generational perspectives broadened the discussion. One of us might pursue a topic that the other was blind to, often with unexpected results. Sometimes Tina would ask a question and Christina would think, "My God, how

can she ask that?" and vice versa. Endeavoring to accord each participant her own dignity, complexity, and voice, on all but two occasions
we interviewed mothers and daughters separately.

Life stories shift and evolve, especially with respect to interpersonal
relationships. A twenty- or twenty-five-year-old daughter reflects differently upon her relationship to her mother than does a thirty- or
thirty-five-year-old. Also, marriage, long-term relationships, work,
and children are key identification points between daughters and
mothers, and relationships often change when the status of one of them
changes. Several older daughters we interviewed readily admit that in
their twenties they would not have been ready to discuss their relationship with their mothers. The mother-daughter relationship is, by
its nature, unevenly balanced. Daughters generally have only one
mother, but nearly all the mothers we interviewed have more than one
child. Mothers have, at least partially, established their identities before a daughter is born, whereas a daughter, in discussing her experiences, is reflecting on a relationship with a powerful figure against
whom she has measured herself for her entire life.

At the same time, daughters have enormous power in the relationship—the power of judging. As one daughter confided, "My mother is
so fearful of what I might say about her. Nothing I end up saying can
be as terrible as what she fears." Another told us, "At first my mother
didn't want to do the project because she was afraid that I would say
things that contradicted things she said, and there we'd be in print,
publicly disagreeing, which she doesn't even like to do in private."
Whether or not they exchanged drafts of their narratives was left up to
individual mothers and daughters. One mother waited days to open
the envelope containing her daughter's story, only to experience relief
that her daughter was less critical than she had imagined.

In preparation for the interviews, we sent each participant a list of
questions intended not to limit the conversation but to serve as a guide
(see Appendix). We tried to ensure balance by pairing evaluative questions with their opposites: "What did you do right as a mother?" was
balanced with "What do you regret?" "Which of your mother's traits
would you like to replicate as a mother?" was set against "What do you
perceive as her weaknesses?" For many, the questions prompted painful
discussions. One asked, "Have other women told you how much they
cried while going through this process? My daughter and I cry every
time we begin to talk about your questions."

Some daughters, either protective of their mothers' feelings or seeing their mothers' work as so vital that they had no right to complain, were reluctant to say anything critical. One daughter explains, "We have a generation of daughters who are not only dutiful but protective of their mothers to an utmost, devastating degree." Other daughters, momentarily estranged or attempting to establish separate identities, were in no mood to identify their mothers' strengths. Most, however, were eventually willing to identify a complex range of feelings. One said, "I want to be fair about my mother. It's easy to identify what I call weaknesses, and for that reason it has been good thinking about the strengths for this interview."

Over the course of eighteen months we interviewed sixty-five women in homes and offices, hotels and restaurants, Christina's New York apartment and a Washington congressional suite. Making contact with such busy women was no small feat. Some interviews took months to arrange; a few fell into place serendipitously. "I guess you'd better come over this evening," said one busy activist on the spur of the moment when we reached her by phone. Naomi Wolf, pausing between speeches for an interview in the Albuquerque airport, talked hurriedly into the tape recorder all the way to the gate and nearly missed her plane. Our own schedules added to the complexity. Because we both teach, most interviews had to be conducted during winter and spring breaks.

In the 1994 winter chill of New York City, we began interviewing in earnest. Most days we conducted two to four interviews; occasionally we did five. On one busy day Marie Wilson met us at the Ms. Foundation and took us, amid snow flurries, to the quiet space of her nearby apartment. Held up in traffic, we rushed from the taxi to meet anchorwoman Carol Jenkins and her daughter, Elizabeth Hines, at Carol's NBC office. That evening Maryann Napoli's husband served up delicious Italian fare while we interviewed Lisa and Kara and awaited Maryann's return from work. A few days later, in Washington, D.C., Eleanor Smeal met with us at the Fund for a Feminist Majority office before rushing off to a rally, and Nkenge Toure fit in an interview between phone calls at Potter's Vessel, where she works with AIDS-afflicted babies and mothers. In her Georgetown apartment, Evelyn Torton Beck lit candles to commemorate the occasion.

Between interviews—in taxicabs, in restaurants, sprawled out in hotel rooms—we turned on the tape recorder and talked about what we had just learned, lest we forget some significant point. When the work went smoothly, we often forgot we were mother and daughter; we were just two colleagues working in sync. Faced with conflicts and anxieties, however, we sometimes reverted to our familial roles. From time to time we hit snags—business unfinished, issues unresolved, therapy required. Our styles, at best complementary, sometimes conflicted. During interviews, Tina was happy to linger over recollections of the past; Christina was usually eager to move the story along. Late one night we were interviewing Julie Olsen Edwards in her Soquel, California, home—our fifth interview of the day—when Christina suddenly said, "Mom, I hate it when you say that." As we exchanged glances, Julie turned both tape recorders around to face us. "Now, *this* is interesting!" she said with a laugh.

Once collected, hundreds of hours of taped interviews required transcription. Locating skilled transcribers took time (one work-study student persistently typed "Mel Brooks" for "bell hooks"), but eventually we found two: Clara Baker, daughter of Tina and sister of Christina, and Kim Holman, Tina's former student. Clara added a graduate student's perspective to the conversation; Kim contributed a single mother's point of view. In the margin of one transcript, we found Kim's scribbled note: "I'm a lesbian who grew up middle-class, moved into a working-class situation, tried being married to a very sexist man, became a single mother on welfare, got a college education, and now proudly call myself a feminist. I must have something to offer!"

Living at a distance made collaboration difficult, but we were fortunate during the summer of 1994 to spend five weeks together at the Virginia Center for the Creative Arts, where we began crafting eight- to ten-page narratives from twenty- to sixty-page transcripts. Shaping the stories was like chipping sculpture from rock: The material was solid and the shape was there, but revealing and refining it required slow, meticulous work. Tina created the first drafts of the mothers' stories, Christina the daughters'; then we exchanged drafts and revised to create a second version, exchanging again for a third and sometimes a fourth round of revisions. During breaks we continued our running conversation.

We constructed each narrative in the first person, omitting questions with the goal of sculpting the material into a coherent essay—a form often referred to as "first-person biography." The use of "I" as a rhetorical device is designed to capture not the writing voice but the rich flavor and unique idiom of each woman's speaking voice. The genre is not without problems. Some participants, especially writers, objected to the spoken "I" in a written essay. "That's not the way I write," they would say. From the beginning, however, we encouraged mothers' and daughters' participation in the process by allowing them to approve and amend their final narratives. Some reworked narratives within the framework we provided, adding information not included in the interview; a few rewrote extensively. But in the end, most revised very little.

As authors our goal was to balance two competing agendas—honoring our participants' wishes and remaining true to the purposes of our project. Mothers and daughters were assured from the beginning that nothing would be published without their approval. "You could have simply taken the stories as they were and ended up with a sensational book," said Barbara Seaman, "but you would have had everybody angry at you." Some women, shocked at the extent to which they had revealed themselves in interviews, wanted to censor sections of the material; a few withdrew from the project. Many narratives entailed hours of negotiation before both we and the participants were satisfied. The resulting book is not unlike a patchwork quilt: pieces stitched together with the thread of each woman's resolve to tell her story in her own way, and with our commitment, as authors, to the integrity of the book.

These narratives are collaborative. In a review of Amy Hill Hearth's *Having Our Say: The Delaney Sisters' First 100 Years,* Mary Helen Washington contends that in the oral history process the interviewer not only composes the written narrative but is "an active presence who helps to create the very story that she is trying to elicit." Washington continues, "The capacity of the interviewer to represent the other is inherently limited, problematic and not innocent." Consciously or unconsciously, in framing the questions we defined the discussion. In crafting narratives from transcripts we largely retained the participants' own words but shaped the material according to the purposes of our book. (In the only exception to this practice, we entered the process at the shaping stage after Clarissa Pinkola Estés and her daughter Tiaja had conducted their own interviews using our questions as a guide.)

In telling their stories, these mothers and daughters interweave two ways of looking at the world—the historical and the personal. Our participants, ranging in age from twenty to eighty-three, span virtually the entire century. Some issues of concern to women in the early part of the contemporary movement are different from those of concern in more recent years. Some issues are age-specific, or specific to mothers or to daughters; others are common to all. Interestingly, daughters of the older mothers we interviewed are around the same age as the mothers of the youngest daughters. We have ordered the narratives chronologically from oldest to youngest mother to give a sense of the evolution of the women's movement.

The women's movement progresses to the degree that we are willing to tell the truth about our lives, says Gloria Steinem. Yet in reality none of us knows the whole truth about our lives, nor do we choose to tell all we know. Telling one's life is an organic process, grounded in the moment when one speaks. Inevitably the information we reveal is partial. Sometimes participants have chosen to remain silent about important aspects of their lives lest their candor hurt the people they love or the work they do. Some chose not to reveal their sexual preference; others have remained silent about physical or emotional battering. Some downplayed the help of loving men lest it be misconstrued as dependence. Telling the truth about our lives opens us up to public censure—a risk most of us take with caution. The same forces that keep other women silent are operative in the lives of these mothers and daughters, and silences remain. Yet to the extent that these women have chosen to speak their difficult truths, mothers and daughters everywhere, and the women's movement, will benefit.

For most of the mothers we interviewed, feminism was the tool that enabled them to dictate their own stories, reinvent their lives, and create more equal relationships. A measure of their personal influence and the influence of the women's movement is that generally the daughters share their mothers' values. In the end, the feminist mothers in this book have raised feminist daughters. None of the daughters has rejected her mother's political beliefs. Many who do not consider themselves feminist activists are active feminists, carrying on the feminist legacy in their own ways. If not marching in the streets, they are pursuing change for women in the workplace, in interpersonal relationships, and in the courts. Feminism has become the fabric of their lives.

Part of the reason for this shift in emphasis is that, thanks to their mothers, the world the daughters live in is a world transformed. "What I had to fight for," one mother told us, "my daughters can assume." Many of these mothers marvel at how much more self-actualized their daughters are than they were at their age. "These women are not like the women of my generation," says one mother. "They have a language.

I didn't have a language until I was forty years old. They have a kind of inner knowledge and clarity, and that is different." Another says, "My daughter takes for granted the principles of feminism and is secure in her ethnic identity. She has a confidence in the way she looks at the world and at her relationships that it took me years to achieve."

As mothers and daughters in our book talk to and about each other, many conversations emerge across the pages. As they reach across their differences in age and experience, they reflect upon the nature of modern feminism, its promises and costs, its successes and failures, its personal impact as well as its public agenda. This conversation carries on across ethnic and class boundaries; it involves us as interviewers as well as the women interviewed. Ultimately, we hope that our readers, too, will join the discussion.

Christina and Tina, 1965.

Christina and Tina, 1995.

Christina Looper Baker
and
Christina Baker Kline

CHRISTINA LOOPER BAKER was born in Gastonia, North Carolina, in 1939 and now lives in Bangor, Maine. A professor of English at University College of Bangor, she chairs the Liberal Studies program. She received her BA from Furman University in 1961, her MAT from Duke University in 1962, and her PhD in American Studies and Women's Studies from The Union Institute in 1991. Recipient of the 1992 Presidential Outstanding Teacher Award at the University of Maine, she is the author of *In a Generous Spirit: A First-Person Biography of Myra Page* (Illinois, 1996). With her husband, professor and writer William J. Baker, she has raised four daughters.

CHRISTINA BAKER KLINE was born in England and grew up there, in the South, and in Maine. A graduate of Yale and Cambridge, she was a Henry Hoyns Fellow in writing at the University of Virginia, where she received her MFA degree. Her first novel, *Sweet Wa-*

ter, was published by HarperCollins in 1993. Currently she is working on a novel set in Maine, *Desire Lines,* and a nonfiction book about becoming a mother. She lives in New York City with her husband, David, and son, Hayden, and teaches creative writing at New York University.

CHRISTINA LOOPER BAKER
A Mother's Story

When my daughter Christina was born in an English maternity hospital on a misty January night in 1964, I gave her the name that had been given to my mother and that my mother had given to me. The name was part of a larger legacy I wanted to pass on—a legacy that valued books and music and art, that encouraged creative expression, that celebrated ideas, that cared about social justice, that cherished family and friends. I wanted her to have these things from my past. I did not know to want for her a feminist future.

For those of us who bore children in the early years of the current feminist movement, it has not been easy to mother our daughters. With one foot in the conservative fifties and another in the liberated seventies, we shifted back and forth between two worlds. We gave our daughters mixed messages. We told them they could climb mountains, but our own feet were unsteady. Many of us were either caught in conventional marriages or filing for divorce. At the same time that we encouraged our daughters forward into a brave new world of equality for women, we often demonstrated a lack of power in our own lives by allowing ourselves to remain in traditional roles.

The women of my generation who became feminists in the late sixties wanted to revolutionize society; we also craved equality and respect in our most intimate relationships. Having too long accepted marginal status, we determined to move ourselves to center stage. We found strength in collective struggles for goals ranging from reproductive rights to equal pay, but the effort to change our personal lives was more difficult. Despite consciousness-raising groups, we often felt isolated in our attempts to effect change on the domestic front.

As the feminist message struck home, some women left husbands and children, rejecting the nuclear family altogether. Others exchanged one partner for another. Some chose to raise their children alone. Still others, myself included, clung to the thin threads of what was good in our marriages, determined to transform them from within. Change did not come easily. Our daughters watched as we painstakingly attempted to dismantle the patriarchal family structure. Now in their late twenties to mid-thirties, they have come of age and inherited the task of creating new structures. Far from plunging blindly into marriage and homemaking, our daughters proceed cautiously, anxious to avoid the mistakes of their mothers.

As the eldest of my four daughters, Christina observed most clearly my shift from traditional Southern woman to feminist. Born into a middle-class family in Gastonia, North Carolina, I was raised to take my place in the patriarchal succession—to marry, to bear children, and to encourage my husband's success. Early on I learned that masculine needs and wishes took priority over feminine ones. The day after graduating from college, I married a college football star named Bill and went to work teaching high-school English in order to support us while he completed a theological degree. When we left for England two years later for Bill to pursue doctoral studies at Cambridge, I was pregnant with Christina. We agreed that I should take the year off from work.

Financial circumstances dictated that I return to teaching when Christina was nine months old. Reluctantly I placed her in an English nursery. Because my own mother had stayed home to nurture her children, I was ill prepared to turn my child over to the care of others. A second pregnancy prematurely ended my time in the workforce, and Cynthia was born at home in our Tudor cottage in Swaffham Bulbeck, a village outside Cambridge, when Christina was eighteen months old. By then I had read John Bowlby's *Child Care and the Growth of Love* (1953), which convinced me of the importance of the mother's presence to a child's healthy emotional development. Guilt hounded me, and I feared that I had irreparably damaged Christina by my absence during her most formative months. I determined to make up the lost time with her and to avoid the same mistake with Cynthia.

By the time rumblings of the women's movement sounded in the late sixties, we had returned to the States and were living in east Tennessee. I listened to the message urging women to free themselves from their chains and began to consider the ways my gender role bound me. I determined to devise ways for my daughters to grow up without the restrictions I had known. Everything I learned about the new possibilities for women got fed into Christina and Cynthia along with their morning granola.

Practically, my understanding of feminism was inextricably bound up with my role as mother. Theoretically, my relationship with feminism was ambivalent, however, because of its distorted view of motherhood. Feminist thinkers from Simone de Beauvoir to Shulamith Firestone identified motherhood as the root of our oppression. In their view I was truly oppressed, particularly since I had given birth to two more daughters in the early years after the family's 1970 move to Maine. Clara arrived in 1971; Catherine, an IUD baby, was born in 1972.

Among feminist groups I encountered an attitude of dismissal, sometimes overt hostility, toward the subject of motherhood. At one gathering I was sharply reprimanded for identifying myself as "a mother." Clearly I was out of step. "You're nuts!" exclaimed a reproving feminist friend upon hearing that my daughters came home each day for lunch. "Why would you let your kids come home when they can eat at school?" She had no conception of the exchanges that took place between my daughters and me over soup and sandwiches, nor could she gauge how that interaction fueled my enjoyment and growth as well as theirs.

Conversations with my daughters pulled me into their schools and into the larger community as an advocate for feminist principles. The causes I espoused usually focused on children: safer births, parents' right to accompany sick children in hospitals, and individualized instruction in schools. My husband and I drew our daughters into discussions about the Vietnam War, the civil rights movement, and social injustice in general. Near the end of the war, Christina wrote a letter to President Nixon: "I'm eight years old and I don't see why anyone would want that awful war to go on and never stop. If you would please stop the war, I wouldn't have to be a war nurse when I grow up." Although Christina did not yet know that she could be a war doctor as well as a nurse, she had begun to see the political in personal terms.

In the mid-seventies, finances required that I resume teaching full time. Of necessity, and with difficulty, I dispensed with the cultural myth that says good mothers should do everything for their children. Christina and Cynthia began to shoulder responsibilities that would normally have been mine, often volunteering more assistance than I expected. Christina took over much of the cooking; Cynthia assumed the laundry chores. Their help was essential, but what they lost in free time they seemed to gain in confidence and self-esteem. They helped care for their younger sisters to the extent that Clara and Catherine saw them as additional mothers, and the younger ones grieved their loss for years after their older sisters left home for college.

Reinventing motherhood was one thing; reinventing marriage and the family was something else. By far, my hardest task as a feminist was achieving parity with my husband. In order to teach Christina and her sisters that they had the right to claim equality with men, I had to model for them a mutually respectful relationship with their father. To this end, I determined that no injustice in our interactions—from demeaning gestures to offensive labels to unequal workloads—would pass unnoticed. Each micro-inequity, however slight, would be challenged. The turning point in our relationship came when Bill realized that it was not in his daughters' best interest, and perhaps not in his own, to continue living in a strife-filled, sexist household. Keeping faith with his four daughters demanded that he regard their mother with respect. Today, after struggling for more than a third of a century, we have achieved a balance in our marriage of which most days we can be proud.

Christina grew up and left home before I completed my metamorphosis as a feminist. Shortly after she graduated from Yale in 1986, I entered the Union Institute's PhD program in American studies and women's studies. I continued teaching full time while working toward the doctorate, with the exception of the year I spent recovering from a heart attack. (I believe that the stress-induced attack resulted less from overwork than from a heart broken by my failure to effect justice for my youngest daughter, Catherine, assaulted by a group of boys in Germany.) Five years after I began (and the day before Cynthia's wedding, in the summer of 1991), I finished my dissertation. While we women went to a bridal shower, my husband, Christina's husband, Cynthia's husband-to-be, and a male friend abandoned their bachelor party plans and instead spent the evening proofreading my dissertation. They cheered my success as their own.

I marvel at the differences between my daughters' lives today and my life at their age. They have grown up assuming they can do anything they choose. Freed for the first time in history from compulsory childbearing, they can enjoy their sexuality without the pressure to marry. They can wait to have children until they are ready, personally and professionally. My feminist daughters appear to have it all, and in many respects I envy their options. In reality, however, they face a daunting prospect. To them falls the task of reinventing motherhood so that it does not eclipse feminism, and redefining feminism so that it does not exclude motherhood. I have tried to give Christina and her sisters a foundation that honors the goals of both motherhood and feminism. Without the integration of the two, feminism will never speak for all women.

> The turning point in our relationship came when Bill realized that it was not in his daughters' best interest, and perhaps not in his own, to continue living in a strife-filled, sexist household.

For Christina and Cynthia, that process of integration has begun. While interviewing for this book, Christina and I arrived at the San Francisco airport late one night in March 1994 to an urgent message to call her sister. Fearing bad news (why else would such a message await us?), I rang Cynthia in a panic. When her familiar voice at the other end of the phone exclaimed, "I'm pregnant!" my panic turned to elation. Instantly our identities expanded to include our new roles: Cynthia would be a mother, Christina an aunt, and I a grandmother. Our mother-daughter relationships deepened in resonance with the promise of new life to come.

When Christina was sixteen, the seeds for this project were sown in an unusual mother-daughter collaboration. Often after school she helped me grade the stacks of essays that came with teaching college composition. I trusted her with that responsibility because of her keen intellect and literary skill. Today Christina marks her own students' essays and she, like her sister, has begun the work and the privilege of raising children. With part-time help, Christina is determined to continue making time for her career as well as for her family and community.

Daughters surpass mothers, and in many ways Christina has surpassed me. She has facilitated my feminism as much as I have encouraged hers. Yet I will continue to pass on my experience to her. Women today live an average of twenty years longer than they did earlier this century. Christina's generation will continue to learn from mine as we chart a feminist course through the years beyond fifty, when so many women do our best work. In addition to all the other delights of grand-mothering, I will take pleasure in watching her and her sisters hand down to their children a feminist legacy.

CHRISTINA BAKER KLINE

A Daughter's Story

Having grown up with a feminist mother is such a large part of my identity that it is an inextricable part of who I am. Of course I am a feminist—I breathe, I drink water; I am a human being. I have never understood what it was that people didn't get about feminism, why they thought it was some kind of frightening, militaristic movement of hostile, unshaven women waving bras and coat hangers and demanding male body parts. To me growing up, feminism was embodied in a slim, dark-haired woman with a soft Southern accent who wore pretty floral dresses—and also organized petition drives, marched in demonstrations, and gave lectures on gender and cultural identity.

On the shelves in my mother's study—a study created only five years ago by dividing in half the large, airy room at the back of the house my father had inhabited for fifteen years by himself—are rows and rows of books. Mostly paperbacks, broken-spined and dog-eared, these books chart the history of the women's movement. Opening any one at random, you will find pages of text highlighted in yellow, underlined in black, annotated in red. The inside back covers are filled with quotes and page references, and lined paper covered with notes (dated 1978, 1982, 1991) is stuffed between the pages.

My mother is a professor, but unlike the stereotypical scholar, she doesn't lock herself away in libraries; she doesn't hoard knowledge. In fact, her particular method of learning involves discussion—and discussion of discussion—as much as it does reading and studying. My father is just the opposite: When he is working, he closes the door to his study and allows no visitors. My mother keeps the door wide open and invites people up for tea.

In my mother's relationship with her study I find the essential aspects of her lifetime of growing and learning, and, consequently, the genesis of my own beliefs. The fact that the study is new, for example, is not insignificant. For eighteen years, while I was growing up, she did her work at the dining room table. She always said that she didn't want to be far from her four daughters—she wanted to feel "connected." I remember coming home from school and finding her surrounded by mountains of books and an avalanche of papers, with one of my sisters fingerpainting beside her on the floor. None of us asked to be near Dad; he was upstairs and didn't want to be disturbed. Mom was fair game—infinitely interruptible. It was somehow understood that she would look after the children and he would be free to disappear into his study, emerging from time to time for coffee. Implicitly, the work she did was secondary.

> None of us asked to be near Dad; he was upstairs and didn't want to be disturbed. Mom was fair game— infinitely interruptible.

My mother has always said that she prefers to be in the middle of things. She claims that her conversations with friends and family are as important to her as anything she gets from books. I have often wondered, however, how much this attitude may have been shaped by the necessity of raising and nurturing children within a somewhat traditional family framework.

For a number of years the way my mother lived her life and the feminist beliefs she espoused seemed at odds. While my sisters and I were being taught about the importance of self-reliance and self-empowerment, we were also acutely aware of how much our mother relied on our father in all kinds of conventional ways. He paid the bills and took out the trash; she fulfilled most of the expected wifely duties. Our family was a strange hybrid of two worlds, traditional and radical.

In *Madame Bovary* Flaubert writes, "Always there is a desire that impels and a convention that restrains." As I see it, my mother was, like many women who came of age in the late fifties and early sixties, restrained for years by the conventions of the society into which she was born. In fact, just before I was born, my father was finishing a PhD while my mother, a Phi Beta Kappa scholar herself, taught high school to pay his tuition. They were young and fresh-faced: In the pictures from that time my mother is wearing slim pants and buttoned-up sweaters and my father is in classic starched madras shirts. Within several years, however, the picture radically changed. My parents, impelled—again, like many of their generation—by a desire to break out of the mold, became hippies (albeit fairly restrained ones by the standards of the time). My mother wore macramé jewelry, my father grew a beard, and we lived on a farm in Tennessee and traveled around in a Volkswagen bus with Day-Glo butterfly stickers on the sides. My sister Cynthia and I were raised in boys' shirts, boys' pants, and practical shoes, with short, shaggy haircuts and faces often covered in jam. We built playhouses for ourselves using the dining room table, chairs, and blankets. These houses would remain standing for weeks. We ate around them.

My mother, Cynthia, and I began to define ourselves as feminists at the same time. Mom was thirty, I was five, Cynthia was four. Mom would tell Cynthia and me what she was reading and what she was thinking, and it all made perfect sense to us. Of course women should be paid the same as men for the same work. Of course the princess Atalanta should be free to marry whomever she chose. Of course Daddy should stop treating Mom like a second-class citizen.

But this was where it became difficult. As my mother became more involved in the women's movement, the ferment between my father and her increased. He spoke quietly and caustically, and often with an amused eye toward his small audience; she screamed and cried and smashed butter dishes against the kitchen wall. It was more fun to laugh with Daddy than to cry with Mommy, so our allegiance was divided. If we simply accepted that he was a jolly, benign presence and she was overly sensitive, then we wouldn't have to face the frightening possibility that the entire structure of our family might have to be dismantled.

At times it was scary to have a mother who was forming her identity at the same time that I was forming mine. Nothing was final, nothing was secure. Her opinions changed with her reading; as she found new role models she discarded old ones, relentlessly shedding identities and revising beliefs. We often didn't know from one week to the next what form her free-ranging political activism would take—in the family, in her friendships, in the world at large.

But overall, feminism's effect on our family was gradual—an evolution, not a revolution. My mother turned into a feminist so slowly that by the time she had completely metamorphosed, she seemed never to have been anything else. For a number of years she resembled a lot of the other moms in the neighborhood, though there were subtle differences for those inclined to notice. One of my most vivid memories of my mother is of her sitting in our kitchen in Bangor, Maine, in a sturdy rocking chair, talking on the phone. Other mothers talked on the phone, too; but most of them were talking to each other, not to the news media. At ten I watched my mother tackle the issue of historic preservation as she tried, single-handedly, to save an old mill targeted for demolition. Somehow, almost instinctively, she managed to galvanize the local television stations, community leaders, showboating activists, and women like herself who found themselves sick and tired of putting up with the status quo without doing something about it.

Of course, because our family remained structured for so long to accommodate a primary breadwinner (my father) and a helpmeet and child-rearer (my mother), we children paid a price for my mother's interest in activities outside of the home. It was no use telling my friends in sixth grade, as we stood on the corner in front of the deserted movie theater in the drizzling rain waiting to be picked up, that my mother had other things to do and couldn't always be expected to be everywhere at once. Other kids' mothers were never late; in fact, they were usually early, sitting in their cars with the engines running as we left the theater, or dance lessons, or play practice after school. A couple of times my mother forgot us altogether, and then I vowed never to be put in such a humiliating position again. I'd rather accept the pitying smiles of the other mothers than the exasperated sighs of my friends as they craned their necks looking for our rusty gold station wagon.

As the years went by, it became more and more obvious that my mother was different from most of my classmates' mothers. She wore Birkenstock sandals before the Grateful Dead made them trendy; she experimented with astrology and mythology and health food long before women's magazines discovered them. For lunch Cynthia and I ate brown whole-grain bread with natural peanut butter and a sandwich bag (recycled) of granola while the other kids ate cheese puffs and Del Monte pop-top chocolate pudding. In elementary school Cynthia was so mortified by our menu that, like a diminutive drug dealer, she arranged for a pickup every morning on the corner: Her best friend brought an extra Oscar Mayer bologna on Wonder bread, and Cynthia threw her whole-grain sandwich in the trash.

Despite her activism, my mother rarely took part in national feminist events. She joined the National Organization for Women and sent donations to various women's organizations—even when my father, saying that money was tight, asked her not to—but her focus was the community, not the nation or the world. In our hometown she fought for better schools and tackled drug abuse. She helped educate local police about battered women when few people understood what a battered woman was. And whatever the cause, she refused to back down when she was sure she was right, even when it would have been easier—and certainly more ladylike—for her to do so.

My mother's struggle with her identity as a mother and a feminist, her attempt to create a balance between the personal and the political, is, to me, one of the most important lessons she could have taught me about feminism. As she has come to grips with the contradictions in her life, my own attempts to find out who I am and what I stand for have become increasingly important to me. As I have defined my identity as a feminist I've found that I'm not radical enough for some and perhaps too radical for others. Finding my place and my voice in a movement so diverse and with so many passionately held, intelligent viewpoints could have been perilous. Instead, thanks to my mother, I know that being a feminist is a process of constantly defining and redefining who I am. There is no blueprint. The journey I undertake must be my own, and the decisions I make must reflect my needs and desires as much as they do the dominant ideology of the movement. Feminism must be large enough to accommodate all kinds of women—all kinds of choices.

In raising me as a feminist, my mother gave me the tools to shape my own destiny. I grew up believing that I could do anything I wanted, that I was entitled to happiness, that I had a responsibility to find my own way. I grew up knowing that people who loved me would trust me and support me in whatever I wanted to do. "Only connect," writes E. M. Forster at the beginning of *Howards End*. Personally, intellectually, and politically, my mother has codified this impulse into an ideal. She lives her life the way she treats the books in her study: not with cool detachment, but with passion, focus, and commitment. Her desire to connect with people—as much a part of her identity as a feminist as of her identity as a mother—has perhaps influenced me more than anything.

Witness to my mother's efforts in the community, I learned what a difference activism can make in the life of a place and the potential one person can have for effecting change. As I have seen my parents grow and change together, I've come to understand the importance of discussion, debate, and negotiation in defining and refining important relationships—and I've also learned that I deserve a mate who treats me as an equal. Now at an age when I am beginning to have children myself, I think about the legacy of feminism that my mother has given her daughters, a legacy that will be handed down, like a family heirloom, for generations to come.

Tillie and Julie, 1995.

Tillie Olsen

and

Julie Olsen Edwards

TILLIE OLSEN was born in Nebraska in 1912 and raised in Omaha. Her father, who worked with his hands all of his life, was the State Secretary of the Nebraska Socialist Party. A Dression-era high school dropout and a young mother, she early entered the world of everyday jobs and became an activist, whether in her neighborhood, her PTA, on the job, and in the labor and left movements of the 1930's, including the Communist Party. What she calls her "conscious feminism" came in that period. She wrote and was published when young, but, she says, the necessity of raising and supporting four children through "everyday jobs" silenced her for twenty years. Public libraries were her college. She is the recipient of eight honorary degrees and many other awards, including the 1994 REA Award for the Contribution to the Art of the Short Story. She has taught or been writer-in-residence at M.I.T., Amherst College, and Stanford University among others. Her books include *Silences*, about human potentiality and the circumstances that deny its flowering; *Yonnondio: From the 30's; Mother to Daughter, Daughter to Mother: The Daybook and Reader;* and *Tell Me a Riddle.* Her work is widely taught and appears in over 190 anthologies and in 13 languages. Olsen is a longtime resident of San Francisco.

JULIE OLSEN EDWARDS was born in San Francisco in 1938, the third of four daughters. She married young and, in order to earn a living and still be with her two children, "did all the traditional, at-home, woman things"—running a boardinghouse, operating a daycare home, foster parenting, ghostwriting theses at night. She and her husband put each other through college, and it took them fourteen years to complete their undergraduate and graduate degrees. In 1971 they both joined the Cabrillo College faculty in Santa Cruz, California, where she directs the Department of Early Childhood and Family Life Education. Publications include the short story "Mother Oath," about the stress and isolation of a young mother and the connection between mothering and political commitment; an article, "Class Notes From the Lecture Hall," about the impact on her teaching of having been raised by activist working-class parents; and *Embracing Diversity,* written by her sister Laurie Olsen, edited by Edwards, about teachers' responses to the issues of immigration and racism in the California public schools. She and her mother have also co-authored "Mothers and Daughters," an introduction to the Aperture Press book of the same title.

TILLIE OLSEN

A Mother's Story

This Mother/Daughter

It is not that I am distant from my motherhood. But I am eighty-four; so long a mother, grandmother (great-grandmother now too). It is sixty-four years since that December, 1932, when I was born into first mothering; near half a century (1948) since the last of the four daughters was born—a sixteen-year span between. It is long, long, since that more than thirty-year, whirled, expending—so rich in yield—mostly non-writing—time of active mothering is behind me.

Yet motherhood remains central in my life;—more than illuminator, instructor of my feminism—always (as always my mothering) touchstone for sustenance, hope, connectedness, self-knowledge; human understanding, beauty and anguish; yes, and wellspring, passionate source for all I am, do, write.

Including granddaughters, we are four generations of conscious feminists in our family—my eastern European, revolutionary immigrant mother, the first. As an illiterate girl, she broke from the centuries-long chain of illiterate women before her whose lives*— for all the creative, spiritual, art capacities they brought to it—were primarily beast-of-burden, compulsory child-bearer lives (as still remains so for most of the women in this world—as yet).

The respective times, the place, the circumstances profoundly shaped the nature and goals of each of our generation's feminist movements; as well as the boundaries of what could be—and actually was—changed, achieved. So too, for each of us, did our respective time, place and circumstances profoundly affect the nature and boundaries of the changes we each could make in our own beings and relationships, in-

*Insofar as we know, as they could leave no written or spoken record.

cluding mothering; the nature and extent of our activism; and the changes we were able to make or contribute to in our larger world.

What did *not* change for any of us was our essential vision towards what in my mother's time, my earlier life, we called Women's Emancipation; in our recent time, Feminism or Womanism. That vision has remained basically the same: true, dependent upon partial advances, but interlinked with the ages-old struggle of humanity against what limits, harms, demeans; and ever towards full flowering humanhood: Whitman's "to soar in the fullness of freedom, velocity, power." In each generation, that vision (and activism) has become ever more dimensioned, inclusive.

And, I even more joyously add, so too our movements, have each in succeeding generations become ever more multi-dimensioned; ever more multiple in numbers—AND in actual worldscope.

JULIE OLSEN EDWARDS
A Daughter's Story and
A Mother's Story

As a child, I never considered my mother a feminist. I didn't know the word or the concept. But I always knew she was an activist, a believer in justice, a world-changer. I remember coming home from school one day and repeating that old chestnut, "I complained because I had no shoes until I met a man who had no feet," and my mother snapped back, "Then I hope you complained twice as hard, because both conditions are lousy and neither should be tolerated!"

All four of my grandparents were Jewish immigrants from Russia. Although Dad was born there, he and my mom were the first generation to be raised in the U.S. I was born in the Depression years, in December of 1938. Mom had been seriously ill, and the doctors wanted her to have an abortion. I think it was an act of courage and hope that she went ahead with the pregnancy. It was the time of fascism in Europe—Hitler in Germany, Franco in Spain. Several of my folks' closest friends fought in the Lincoln Brigade in Spain, trying to stop Franco, stop fascism. I am named after their friend Julius Eggan, who died there, in the retreat across the Ebro. This naming has been important to me.

My earliest memories of my mother are from the war years. Dad was overseas. Instead of her usual on-her-feet jobs, Mom was working for the CIO War Relief and Service Man's Committee and trying to keep things covered at home with a whole series of baby-sitters who came, stayed a few months, then left for defense industry jobs. Mom would come home from work, exhausted, to three needy kids, and I remember being conscious of how much was on her shoulders, wanting to help, wanting to take care of her. I remember deciding to be funny, to be entertaining, thinking that if I was friendly to the baby-sitters, maybe they would like us, maybe they would stay.

The end of the war ushered in a rare period in our family. Dad became the publicity and educational director of the International Longshoreman's and Warehouseman's Union. Mom was pregnant with her only planned child, my baby sister, Laurie, and for a while was home full time with us kids. Through the GI Bill we actually bought a house. I remember this time with joy, and I know it shaped my deep desire to be home with my own kids when they were little.

My parents were political activists, unionists, Communists. During the McCarthy period they were under serious attack. Dad was subpoenaed by the United States House UnAmerican Activities Committee. My mother was named on the radio as a spy. We had friends who were jailed, friends who went underground. We were San Franciscans. We had seen what happened to our Japanese neighbors. We were Jews who had lived through the Second World War. The government was opening the camps up at Tule Lake again, and we presumed we could all be hauled off and incarcerated. The Teamsters union raided the ILWU, and Dad was without a job. He went back to the docks and warehouses but was red-baited out of work. Mom was doing office work again, but we were very broke.

Countering the fear, however, was my parents' vision. They put our experiences into historical context. They took me with them to rallies and meetings, and I felt surrounded by community, aware we were not alone even if the larger world was hostile and dangerous. When Emmett Till was murdered, they took me to hear his mother speak. "Look around," they said. "Look at the hundreds of people who know what has happened was wrong, who want to change the way things are."

Like most families on the Left, my folks believed in children's intelligence. They saw us as capable, believed we had rights, listened to us, took us seriously. In an era when children were raised with the back of the hand and the belt, it was an amazing gift.

As a child, I thought my parents' marriage was wonderful. They went through some tough times and serious struggles, but they deeply respected each other. They were physically demonstrative—holding hands, Mom sitting on Dad's lap, kissing, patting each other. I didn't know the word *feminist* in those years, but I knew my parents were intellectual companions, comrades in their beliefs and causes. Dad's respect for Mom's intelligence, her capacities, her ideas, was a given in my life. It never occurred to me or to any of my sisters to be with men who expected to make the decisions, run the show. Still, my mother held the family together. She did the cooking, cleaning, child care, doctor's visits, holidays, laundry. And she worked. Not at a career, but at everyday jobs that kept a roof over our heads and food on the table.

Everyone always wants to know what it was like for me to grow up the daughter of a famous woman. But I didn't. Mom came into her writing life when I was grown, when I was already struggling with figuring out where my kids and husband ended and I began. I was, am, delighted for her. I love being known as Tillie's daughter. I am in awe of her gift and feel great joy in her achievement.

I met my husband, Rob, in high school. His family were Oklahoma small farmers, sometime sharecroppers, sometime seasonal workers. For about seven years they would put in a crop in the spring, it would fail in the summer. Then they would move to Denver to work in the mines until it got too cold, then out to California to work through the winter, and back to Oklahoma in the spring to try a new crop. I grew up urban working-class. He grew up rural poor.

I got pregnant in July; we were married in August. So we were never without children. Rebekah and Tobias are two and a half years apart. I did all the things that working-class women did in order to stay home with their babies. I ran a day-care home; I ran a boarding-house; I worked as a ghostwriter and editor. The choice was never career or family, but rather what kind of work I could do that permitted me the most time at home with the kids. Rob drove a truck and worked at a dairy and in the warehouse industry.

We both went to school. Although neither Rob nor I recognized the idea as a feminist issue, we were mutually committed to each of us getting an education. It was a crazy juggling act. Rob worked swing shift, got home around midnight, and got up early to take morning classes. I packed up the babies and took the streetcar out to San Francisco State to meet him at noon. He took the kids home while I attended an afternoon class. When I got home, he went to work. Rob was home weekends while I worked as a waitress or a cashier. In 1966, ten years after high-school graduation, we both got our BA's and started the trek through graduate school.

I wanted to be home with my children for many reasons. It was the end of the fifties, and the message was that if there was any possible way, being home was the *only* thing for a woman to do. But the other part was that I was in love with those babies, passionately in love. Everything that happened to those children mattered, and it seemed I was the only one who could mediate between them and the world.

And there was my own need. I remembered my own childhood yearning for Mom to get home from work. I wanted to be with my children, wanted them to be with me. I didn't like letting my kids out of my sight. And oh, the hours of thought, care, imagination, intensity that went into those years! I loved their play, their questions, their energy, the sheer sensuality of their bodies snuggled up against mine. I took them to the library, the museums, the parks. We sang together, danced together. They came with me to classes, lectures, parties. I was enchanted by their unfolding, their blossoming.

I hated being a housewife, doing housework, laundry, cooking. No matter how hard I tried, I couldn't make our various flats and apartments look like the magazine pictures, couldn't somehow produce gracious meals, have closets full of ironed, mended clothes. I felt tremendous shame over the clutter, the mess, the chaos. I used to have nightmares about suffocating in the dirty-clothes hamper or being buried alive in dirty dishes.

I was an ignorant and naive mother. I had no friends with young children. Mom and Dad had moved East, and I was thrown onto my own resources. Rebekah was a sick infant, and I was exhausted and filled with a sense of profound incompetence because I could not make things right for her. I read every book about children I could get my hands on but neither looked for nor expected to find any books on what my life was. There was no social analysis available to help me think through motherlife, only traditional therapy, which reinforced the notion that I just couldn't get it together as wife and mother—that I was resisting, failing at womanhood.

Rob and I started out in a traditional marriage. I did everything relating to home and kids. When he occasionally helped me, I said, "Thank you." My rebellion began in 1968, when I needed to study for my master's exams and Rob said, "I can't baby-sit." It was a moment of revelation. I started screaming, "These are your kids too. Why is it *my job* when *I* do it and *baby-sitting* when *you* do it?" and stormed out of the house. We spent the next fifteen years fighting about cooking dinner, doing laundry, and getting groceries. We still argue about housework.

Rob and I struggled over all the classic issues between men and women—"You don't talk to me enough. You don't tell me your feelings enough" versus "I need more time for my work. Don't get in my way." We struggled over how to maintain intimacy when we

were utterly drained, when we lacked financial and emotional resources and the kids required more than either of us had. We were
going to school, working, raising children, and we were very very
broke.

We stayed together partly because we were committed to the kids,
partly out of sheer inertia and dogged stubbornness. In some ways feminism saved our marriage. It gave me a forum to try to sort out Rob's
and my individual issues from the conditions of our lives. We joined a
self-led couples group that grew out of my consciousness-raising
group. Feminism helped me understand the importance of having the
economic means to go it alone. Knowing I could support myself and
our kids if I had to made it clear I was in the relationship because I
chose to be, because there was enough nourishment between Rob and
me to counterbalance the struggles.

Rob and I had met in 1954, when we were fifteen. We grew up together. We organized civil rights protests, marched against the Vietnam War. We lived through assassinations and tear gas and riots. We
have packed up and moved fifteen times. We have provided comfort
and solace through the deaths of friends, parents, siblings. And we
have laughed together, traveled together, worked on the same campus,
celebrated each other's victories. With all its flaws and warts and blem-
ishes, our relationship is still profoundly important, central, and rich
for me.

Rebekah and Toby were very close. Despite the prices they paid for
our overworked lives, the two of them became a team. Of course they
argued and fought at times, but they depended upon each other and
loved each other dearly. My growing sense of feminism helped me
avoid some of the more obvious traps of isolating them from each other
due to gender. Both learned to cook, to do laundry. Both were cuddled,
snuggled, delighted in. Shocked by the recognition that I was expected
to love Rebekah but be proud of Toby, I consciously let them know I
felt both emotions for each of them.

It is heartbreaking to feel powerless to buffer the injuries in your
children's lives. Bekah taught herself to read when she was four, but at
five she entered a cruel and rigid classroom with a teacher who humiliated children. I knew something was wrong, but the teacher said Bek
was never a problem. "Why, she never even says a word or leaves her
chair!" This about my constantly active, jabbermouth child! She
stopped singing and dancing at home. She brought home the same

painting every day. "I know how to do *this* one right," she said. And she lost her ability to read.

We didn't get her out of that classroom until January, and then only by pulling her out of school entirely and taking her with me to work. She didn't read again until fourth grade. Teachers tried to tell us she was retarded or emotionally disturbed. Feminism helped me believe I had the right to fight for her despite the words of the "experts." In fourth grade she began reading again; by fifth grade she was reading high-school material, and she is now one of the most literate, well-read people I have the privilege of knowing. A natural scholar, she is now in a doctoral program in literature. Her synthesizing mind looks at literature as an anthropologist would, and she thinks about poetry in terms of architecture. She is in love with words and the worlds she can paint with them.

Rebekah has struggled to find her own life path. She has many deep friendships. She and her partner have a deeply loving, respectful relationship. She is also a very private person. Santa Cruz is a small pond in which I am a relatively large fish. Unlike me, Bekah grew up with a public mother, and it has been hard on her. I teach hundreds of students in classes where I talk about my mothering, my children, my feminism, my radical politics. I am often on the radio or in the local papers. Unlike me, Bekah did not have a community around her to buffer our family "difference," to share my activism.

I think I was a hard mother to shake loose from. We were so close, so connected. It is still so easy to hurt each other's feelings because we matter so much to each other. She has had to struggle, I think, to find out what parts of her song are her own, to recognize for herself the absolute uniqueness of her voice.

Mothering is the hardest work I have ever done. I still grieve over things I couldn't do for and with the children. Work kept me away from them far more than I wanted. But I gave it my best. I was a loving mother, an involved mother. I fostered their delight in being alive and their capacity to love. I made it possible for them to respect and care for each other. I don't believe parents raise children in a vacuum. You raise your kids in a time and a place. In many ways my kids have not been able to escape the social construction of what makes a man and what makes a woman. But both Rebekah and Tobias have retained much of who they are and they have evolved into strong, loving, creative, and intelligent people.

The first time I remember hearing the word *feminist* was at a parents' meeting at Rebekah's nursery school. Someone came in, threw *The Feminine Mystique* on the table, and said, "I have just read this junk; anyone who wants it can have it." I remember reading it and being so confused. Friedan spoke so effectively of the isolation, the narrowness—but it was such a middle-class book! It had nothing to do with our lives, in which work was a necessity, not a fulfillment. I was outraged when Germaine Greer, asked on television what was wonderful about feminism, responded that it meant she didn't have to wear underpants. Here I was struggling with economic survival, lack of school funding, nonexistent health care or child care, lousy housing—I thought she had no contact with reality at all.

> **Mothering is the hardest work I have ever done.**

From the beginning my focus on feminism had to do with mothers, conditions of child-rearing, and economics. My dream was never to make women's lives look like men's, but to transform both. Making it possible for women to exploit others is not my idea of feminism. I still do not think it is a victory to have women on the board of Dow Chemical.

I direct a community-college program in early childhood and family life education. Reeling from the mother-blame that permeates the social sciences, I encourage my students to think of their mothers as women, women who lived at a particular time and were shaped by particular pressures and possibilities.

I teach parents and child-care workers, two groups who should be allies and are often pitted against each other. Quality child care is wonderful, but it cannot be done cheaply. Child-care workers, almost all of them women, are undertrained, underpaid, overworked. They have no rights, no benefits. They are told the only way to think about professionalization is for parents (mothers) to pay more, and they know firsthand that most women do not have high-paying careers and cannot afford to pay more.

The result is that many children, at the age when they most need to establish relationships and attachments, experience a continual turnover of adults who care for them most of their waking day. The pressure on women to go back to work within weeks or months of birthing means that mothers are not even getting to be with their children through infancy. There is no time to develop the synchrony, the ability to read each other, know each other, that makes intimacy and understanding possible.

I am delighted that my kids want to become parents, but also worried. Raising children today is so difficult. In a political climate that wages war on children, families end up having to go it alone. Rarely is there extended family or neighbors or even access to friends who are discovering their children along with you. The isolation makes parentlife even more complex and more confusing, and it makes the multiple economic stresses even harder to navigate.

As in the fifties, mothers of young children today have no analysis available to them to help them think about their lives, their children's lives. They have been told that the feminist movement is over. They believe that they have free choice, that they are "liberated," and that their children are growing up free from the pruning that results from gender expectations. The economy forces them into a life that involves grueling, round-the-clock work, with their children held hostage to the mortgage. And having been told that it is the feminist movement that has made their lives so complicated, they do not look to each other or to collective solutions to ease the pressures and provide support.

If I could create a magic world, no one would work full time and everybody would be with their children at least part-time. That would be the fully human life: the joy of kids, the joy of work, and the space and time for connection to community, society, the world. Those are, of course, the things I want for both of my children.

And if my daughter, my mother's granddaughter, chooses motherlife, it will be one more reason to keep feminism alive, to create the conditions that permit the raising of children to be the enrichment of life rather than a restriction of life—and in that richness to create a motherhood that becomes not just the connection between generations but the deepest connection between all peoples of the earth.

Elizabeth ("Betita") and Tessa, 1959.

Elizabeth ("Betita") and Tessa, 1990.

Elizabeth Martínez
and
Tessa Koning-Martínez

ELIZABETH ("BETITA") MARTÍNEZ is a writer, lecturer, and activist. During the 1960s, she worked full-time in the black civil rights movement with the Student Nonviolent Coordinating Committee (SNCC), and also participated in the women's and anti-war movements. Moving to New Mexico and the Chicano movement, she worked mostly with women on such projects as the bilingual newspaper *El Grito del Norte*. An activist in the San Francisco Bay Area since 1976, she also teaches Ethnic Studies and Women's Studies part-time. She has published many articles on issues of social justice as well as five books including *500 Years of Chicano History*, which is the basis for her first video.

BORN IN NEW YORK CITY in 1954, Tessa Koning-Martínez is an actress. She earned her BA in theater from Evergreen College. Before moving to San Francisco, where she now resides, she lived in Mexico City and was actively involved both with professional theater companies and with the independent theater movement working with groups based in poor and working-class neighborhoods. She has toured nationally with El Teatro Campesino and Teatro de la Esperanza. She has performed with many San Francisco companies and is a founding mother ("comadre") of the Latina Theater Lab. Koning-Martínez also teaches and directs as an artist of the California Arts Council.

ELIZABETH MARTÍNEZ
A Mother's Story

It took a long time for me to put my daughter, Tessa, at the center of my life. It took a long time for Tessa to begin believing she was a priority, perhaps even *the* priority, in that life. There is no separating our personal tales from the times in which we lived: times of great social upheaval, threats to the planet, and stubborn hope. In that climate some of us adopted a distorted concept of commitment. We made personal concerns secondary at all times; the most important purpose was to "serve the people." With comrades beaten, jailed, and killed in waves of repression, who could worry about anything else? Between 1963 and 1983, two decades, I remember perhaps four weeks of time off. Harsh as it sounds, I embraced this life and its meaningfulness. We thought we were fighting for a better world—and in some ways we were.

My parents were loving people of great dignity. Near the end of the 1910 revolution in Mexico, my father had come to the United States and worked his way through university, eventually becoming a professor of Spanish. My mother, of Scotch-Irish heritage, became a nationally renowned high-school Spanish teacher. Inside our home, a place of Mexican music and crafts and Latino friends, my parents created a castle of security for me. I was the only child of color in our all-white suburb of Washington, D.C., and attended all-white schools through college. Prejudiced next-door neighbors would not let me play with their daughter. As a teenager, I sometimes longed to be blond and blue-eyed. My father was dark, and in Washington, where he and I were once sent to the back of the bus, that could be a serious problem then. Later, when I began writing for publication, I used the name Sutherland (an old Scottish family name) rather than Martínez, out of an internalized racist concept of what *sounds* literary in this country.

Like so many women, I harbored another kind of internalized oppression: sexism. After graduating from Swarthmore College, a Quaker school near Philadelphia, I worked in the United Nations Secretariat researching colonized territories in Africa. I knew well that it was men who would give me interesting (or boring) assignments and recommend a promotion (or not). Later, when I asked for a raise after years of hard work as an editor at Simon and Schuster, I was told, "You don't need a raise; you don't have a family to support." By then I was a single mother, but I didn't argue with their decision.

While working at the UN, I fell in love for the first time, married, and two years later became pregnant with Tessa, my daughter. I was happy because of my desire to have a child with this man I loved, rather than out of any desire for children, or starting a family, or being a mother. When Tessa was born I loved her for herself, but I still didn't define myself as a mother. In my parents' home, I myself had been an only child, and the presence of children remained rare. Yet my mother was always there for me in ways that I did not offer my own daughter at the same age.

Perhaps my contradictory attitude toward motherhood reflected internalized sexism. Though I did not admit it then, my self-esteem depended on male approval, on feeling attractive to men. When my marriage to Tessa's father seemed to lose its romance, we parked our infant daughter first with her grandmother and then at a nursery in Europe and spent several months traveling Europe together. I didn't regret this at the time; it seemed necessary to sustain what I then considered my most important relationship. Only later did I ask myself: How could you willingly leave your one-year-old child for six months, and with people she didn't know?

World events also made me see myself not as a parent but as seeking to be a revolutionary and I did not attempt to balance the two. In 1959 I visited Cuba shortly after the revolution that ended years of dictatorship. Peasants from the countryside filled the posh lobby of the Havana Hilton, now renamed the Havana Libre, and danced in the street. The whole country was alive with a new vision for the future. Deeply inspired, I joined the Fair Play for Cuba Committee and published a book, *The Youngest Revolution: A Personal Report on Cuba.* By 1961 I was calling myself a socialist. Within the next fifteen years, I would return to Cuba six times and travel to Eastern Europe, Russia, China, and North Vietnam for several weeks each.

Soon after my first Cuban trip, I began working with a defense committee for Robert Williams, head of the Monroe, North Carolina, NAACP. Too militant for the Ku Klux Klan types running the town, Williams was falsely charged by them and forced to flee Monroe for his life. The following year, 1961, the Student Nonviolent Coordinating Committee (SNCC) was born out of the sit-in movement begun by African-American college students sitting in at whites-only lunch counters across the South. SNCC's original goal was to coordinate the student protests, but soon it moved on to the more dangerous work of voter registration. In New York I joined Friends of SNCC while working as a book editor at Simon and Schuster. To support SNCC, I convinced S&S to publish *The Movement,* a book of civil rights/black liberation photographs with text by Black playwright Lorraine Hansberry, which I edited.

After five years at Simon and Schuster I became books and arts editor at *The Nation.* When a Klansman's bombing of a Birmingham Baptist church in 1963 killed four black girls, I knew I had to work full-time for the movement. In the summer of 1964 I worked for SNCC on the Mississippi Summer project when 1,000 mostly white Northern volunteers went South to bring national attention to racism. Out of that came another book, *Letters From Mississippi,* edited from letters written home by volunteers. Back in New York, I coordinated SNCC's New York office.

Tessa was ten at the time, and I spent too little time with her. Few SNCC staff members and none of my close friends had children, then or during the preceding ten years in New York. "Movement people" with children struggled on their own or turned to parents and hired baby-sitters for help. The absence of collective child care reflected the sexism of the time. In the early 1960s most women activists accepted that their priorities had to be fighting for civil rights, against the Vietnam War, in support of liberation struggles in the Americas, Africa, Asia—all the revolutionary causes of the time. On occasion I connected Tessa with my movement life. Once I arranged for her to spend several months in Cuba as a teenager; another time I set her up to interview SNCC chairman Stokely Carmichael for a school project.

The late sixties were complex. SNCC was slowly declining, and the women's movement was flowering. I became involved with New York Radical Women, a well-known group of mostly white women doing what we called "consciousness-raising." Many of the women were perceptive, thoughtful, strong. But on the evening of the day that Martin

Luther King was assassinated we met, and nobody else seemed interested in spending much time talking about this shattering event. I never went back.

Did I call myself a feminist then? I must have given that impression to some. One acquaintance insisted I was at least a spiritual member of WITCH, the Women's International Terrorist Conspiracy From Hell. But, I remained trapped inside that old-time internalized sexism. If a man walked out on me, I was devastated. Letters I wrote during that period, filled with pain and confusion, speak about the difficulty of being a woman even with a women's liberation movement going full blast.

The chaotic sixties combined gender-role liberalization with massive confusion about new gender concepts. If a woman wasn't a "chick" anymore, then exactly what was she? And what was femininity? A woman could be proud in discovering her feminism and simultaneously humiliated by male infidelity. At the time I did not see the effects on Tessa of my internalized sexism. When one of my lovers criticized her unfairly on supposedly political grounds, I didn't take Tessa's side. I placed the wishes of my close male companions first and worried more about my relationship with the man of the year than about Tessa's emotional needs. My self-centeredness had roots in sexism, but in the end I am responsible for it.

The pattern continued when we both moved to New Mexico. In 1968 I was asked to help start a bilingual newspaper there, as a voice of the Chicano struggle to win back the land. The black civil rights movement had reached a serious decline by then and its successor, the Black Power movement, remained confused and divided. The role of nonblacks like myself had become problematic. The idea of going to the Southwest to edit a movement newspaper seemed crazy at first; finally I went "just for two weeks, to check things out"—and stayed eight years. It was instant love: People spoke Spanish, and I could be Martínez again instead of Sutherland. Also, for the first time, I wasn't working under male leadership; Beverly Axelrod, the movement lawyer, and I became the first editors of *El Grito del Norte* (Cry of the North).

Tessa worked on the paper as a writer and photographer. She already spoke fluent Spanish, but the identification was more complicated for her. I was half Anglo and half Mexican in a movement dominated by pride in Chicano ethnicity. Tessa's father was European, so her identity was less clear-cut in those identity-conscious times. She saw contradictions in the early years of the Chicano movement that many of us didn't acknowledge until later: people supposedly dedicated to social justice treating each other in ways that were not respectful, men who called themselves revolutionaries treating women like dirt. While recognizing the need for structural change in society, she saw such contradictions as hypocrisy. She wrote a fine article for *El Grito* called "The Revolution Is to Be Human," about the need for men and women to respect each other.

> The chaotic sixties combined gender-role liberalization with massive confusion about new gender concepts. If a woman wasn't a "chick" anymore, then exactly what was she?

Our newspaper staff consisted mostly of young, working-class women with a collective feminist consciousness. At the time there was no women's movement as such in New Mexico, except around the University of New Mexico, and those feminists were almost all Euro-American (or Anglo). Many Chicanas saw the women's movement as middle-class and framed by another culture, which it was. But they did not recognize that some key issues raised by the women's movement, such as domestic violence and child care, cross racial lines.

In 1969 the first national Chicana Youth Conference took place in Denver, and thousands of young people attended. A women's workshop reported back to the full assembly their consensus that "we don't want to be liberated." I think they meant they did not want to be associated with the women's liberation movement for reasons already mentioned. Also they may have feared male opposition. In those years Chicano men typically made devastating accusations against any feminist-acting Chicana: one, "You're being divisive," and two, "You're acting like a gringa," or Anglo woman. For many Chicanas, nothing felt worse than those charges of betrayal.

Tessa left New Mexico in 1972 for college. We stopped publishing *El Grito* and formed the Chicano Communications Center, which utilized the written word along with political street theater, guest speakers, and bilingual historical comic books. The center published *450 Years of Chicano History in Pictures* (now in print as *500 Years of Chicano History in Pictures*) and built a coalition against racism and oppression with two other Chicano-movement groups. But the Chicano movement was floundering because of its failure to achieve clarity about goals and strategy. Some of us began searching for a larger organization, with a clear vision: a socialist party.

While I was away with my dying father, one of the party-building organizations took over the center and eventually destroyed it. I moved to San Francisco and joined a socialist organization, the Democratic Workers' Party. Unlike other left parties in the 1970s, its leaders were women who offered intelligent, sometimes brilliant analyses of events. It seemed free of the dogmatism shown by other parties. In 1976 I came roaring out of that last painful New Mexico period, in love with my new political home.

Along with everyone else, I worked eighteen hours a day; we had no private lives, a fact in which we took pride. For Tessa, who also came to live in San Francisco, it must have been the final nightmare: She had already experienced over ten years of my being a full-time political activist, there for her only in emergencies or on occasions like graduation. Here came another decade, with no end in sight. I felt terrible when canceling yet another appointment with her, but it didn't seem wrong to me; it seemed an unfortunate necessity. I tried to recruit Tessa to the party; she worked on a cultural project for a while, then pulled back. She must have seen more than I did. By 1986 members realized that our group was hopelessly undemocratic in its internal workings. With this and other painful realizations we dissolved the organization to which we had given many years. I moved on to teaching, writing on Latino issues, and working against the massive attack by right-wing forces. As in the past 30 years, my best work often focused on producing visual and written materials for youth about people's struggles for social justice.

Achieving social justice will take much longer than we thought in the 1960s and early 1970s. But the years have seen advances, especially against sexism. Women have gained space and a respect that at one time we didn't have. Many young women do not know what it used to be like for females; they take for granted simple expressions of equality. This ignorance hinders understanding the value of stubborn, organized struggle. For none of today's equalities have been given to us: women fought for each and every one.

The years since my organization dissolved opened the way for a new relationship between Tessa and me. Suddenly in charge of my own time, I tried to make up for the endless series of broken appointments. Suddenly, of course, she was busy and not available because of her work as an actress. I am so very proud of Tessa as an actress, and have been since her first performance at thirteen. I would not miss any performance, any play she directs, any production effort. Other theater people like working with her, they say, for she is unusually cooperative.

In our new relationship, all sorts of emotions and complications demand attention. What started as my wanting to make amends for the past has become more relaxed; my feelings of guilt have not been obliterated but at times transcended. We went on our first vacation together in 1993 in Mexico: not bad and sometimes good.

There is much to regret but also to celebrate. Tessa and I supported each other in a spirit of courage and love through my mother's long dying. My mother loved us both so much. When she was in her mid-80s, she had a series of strokes that left her helpless. Although she had written a living will, I let her be kept alive for two years on a feeding tube. It took a long time to decide that the tube should be taken out: sometimes it is hard to distinguish between rightful death and wrongful existence.

The night she died, Tessa and I came back late to my apartment and had a glass of wine with a toast to my mother. Then we talked until dawn. Tessa told me about things that had been difficult for her in our relationship, things she had not said before. At some point I had the sense just to listen. I didn't even feel defensive, and was glad she talked. Finally she said, "Well, I guess you're not so bad after all."

Who could ask for anything more? But perhaps there will be more—after all.

TESSA KONING-MARTÍNEZ
A Daughter's Story

As a child of mixed parentage, I always felt different. My father is Dutch and my mother is half Mexican. The kids at school assumed I was "Polynesian." When I lived in Washington State during a big struggle over fishing rights, white fishermen, certain that I was Native American, hurled "squaw" and other racist insults at me. I also felt a great confusion as a teenager in the midst of the Chicano Nationalist trends. Throughout your life people are making assumptions. It is really in the last several years that I am able to say I am glad to be multi-racial, I am glad that I understand something about racism.

When I was born, my father was a writer and my mother worked at the United Nations. As an infant I was sent to live with my father's mother in Holland for about nine months, but I have no conscious memory of that time. I also have no memories of living with my father. I was very young when my parents split up.

My mother's parents were important to me as stable parent figures. When I was young, I spent holidays and summers with them just out-side of D.C. They took me to visit my grandfather's family in Mexico City when I was six. They were good role models for me; both were highly educated and had solid careers. They remained married for over fifty years and kept alive their affection for each other. Like my parents, they were writers and readers, and were adamant about education and literacy. I was an early reader, which was mostly my grandmother's doing.

From my parents and my grandparents I inherited an interest in politics, both in the community and around the globe. They encouraged me to travel in order to gain an international perspective. When I was fourteen I spent the summer in Cuba. That experience broadened my horizons in important ways. For the first time I saw my country from the outside, and I met people from all over the world. I remember thinking, "I'm an internationalist," when I realized that people who spoke different languages were all the same, all human beings with hearts and minds. From that experience, I began to care about what happened in the world.

I did not learn good parenting from my parents. As a child with my mother, I always got my own breakfast. One day the teacher asked us what we had had for breakfast, and when she got to me, I said, "Ice cream." I didn't know anything was wrong with that until I saw the teacher's face. She said, "Your mother let you have ice cream for breakfast?" and I said, "Well, she was asleep. Breakfast isn't her thing." While my mother was doing her book, there were long periods when we ate TV dinners every night. If she cooked dinner, it was usually quick foods—hot dogs, hamburgers, corned-beef hash, creamed corn.

I want to be fair about my mother. I want to be honest about the strengths and weaknesses in our relationship. For a divorced mother and a daughter who is an only child, separating the issues, whether feminist, psychological, or emotional, can be difficult. I have wrestled with these issues for a long time. When my mother left me to go to work, it was traumatic. I thought it would be great to have a mother who was there when I got home from school. My friends, however, say, "Wow, it must have been great to have a mother who wasn't always home and bugging you about your life." Nonetheless, I would like to be there for my children and to communicate better with them emotionally than my parents did with me.

My mother wasn't very good at dealing with her difficulties, be they work or trying to quit smoking. Coming home and yelling at your loved ones is no way to cope with the situation. I wish she had known what she needed to do to straighten out things in her own life, so that her behavior would not have affected me. While I was growing up she weathered several bad relationships. As a child I heard things that I didn't need to hear and saw things I didn't need to see—things that weren't good for me. She was with one man for a long time who was really messed up. He was physically abusive. Years later, when I learned he had died, I was angry that I never had the opportunity to give him a piece of my mind.

My father wasn't around much, so I was less critical of him than I was of my mother. I cut my father a lot of slack. If someone is seldom around, you tend not to get as angry as you might because you feel insecure about their affection. My father feels remorse about not being there for me when I was growing up, and he has acknowledged some things he did that hurt me. I suppose nothing about the way he grew up prepared him to do more.

My parents were comrades, but they were not good mates. I believe my father wanted somebody around to look after him, and that's why he eventually married my stepmother, who is more traditional than my mother. These are questions I have wrestled with: Shouldn't good friends make good mates? How can people get married who don't share passionate interests? My parents were kindred spirits; they were both passionate, but obviously that didn't make a good marriage. And my mother has never remarried.

My mother does not speak of her emotional life easily. Personal insight and understanding were not something she passed on to me. For example, she never sat down and talked to me about sex; instead, she left a book out for me to read. It is ironic to think that someone as worldly as she would not be able to sit down with her pubescent daughter and discuss sex. We never discussed boys or boyfriends when I was a teenager, although my mother was having relationships, and so was I.

I became an uppity adolescent during my mid-teens. Around the age of fourteen or fifteen I began to realize that sexism is everywhere—on every billboard, every song, every television show. I was strident and said things like, "Don't you dare open that door for me; I can open it myself." At one time when we were living in New Mexico, I thought my mother was not feminist enough. The political groups she was working with tolerated a lot of sexism. In some ways I was more radical than my mother. On the other hand, she could be very liberal. She never tried to keep me on a tight rein. Whenever I had run-ins with the law, she was absolutely on my side. She never said, "What do you mean, you got in trouble at a demonstration?" She never identified with authority figures just because they were authorities; she sided with me. She was an advocate mom.

When I left home at the age of seventeen, I remember thinking, "This state is not big enough for me and my mother." Even though I loved New Mexico, I had to choose between staying there and getting involved with my mother's work or going off and establishing my own identity. I realized it was time for me to get out of the house.

When I entered college in 1972, I began to study acting again for the first time in four years. Around the age of eleven, I had decided that I wanted to be a stage actress, and I did some work at the New York 92nd Street Y. We left New York, and acting, when I was fourteen. I can say now that acting has been a constant in my life. What I like about it is that you can be anything: Whatever the role is, that's what you are. Sadly, interesting and rewarding roles for women are limited. When you start looking at parts and counting how many there are for women, you say, "Can we have a little parity here, please?"

For four years in the mid-seventies I lived in a collective household in Washington State. Although we were mostly students, we were a consistent group. We bought our house as part of a land trust, and we held regular household meetings. That experience introduced me to the environmental movement. Rent was fifty dollars a month, and we bought our food through a co-op. Nobody had kids yet. Our household was influenced by a new concept called Reevaluation Counseling. One purpose of RC was to train people in effective ways to talk to each other. You didn't go to a therapist and talk about your childhood behind closed doors; instead, you talked to the people around you.

In the collective we were very conscious of sexism. Feminism was a regular topic at our meetings. We had endless discussions and arguments about men not doing their share and about how they needed to change their attitudes and expectations regarding women. When we divided the household chores, we tried to be egalitarian. If a woman did the dishes one time, a man did them the next; if a man changed a tire, a woman changed the next one. Belonging to the collective household was an important experience. Men and women both expanded their preconceived roles. The women got stronger, and the men learned they could cry. That had a lot of meaning, and it still does.

My mother did not approve of the collective. She considered it a hippie experiment. At the time she had a very strict Marxist-Leninist analysis. The collective had a shared bank account and a compost heap and belonged to a co-op, but because we weren't organizing people in factories, she saw us as narcissistic. My mother was interested in class struggle, not in refashioning an individual lifestyle. She was very dogmatic. At the time I saw this conflict between us as an attempt to impose her political and individual will on me. I was angry that she didn't respect my choices. Interestingly enough, some of the things I was learning about then she has come around to herself, such as looking closely at personal relationships and trying to understand family dynamics.

Personally, I feel an internal tug-of-war about being an activist. The last time I was really involved in a political organization was in 1983. Since then I have worked in short-term coalitions, but I have not been an activist of my mother's scope. Every time I read the newspaper, I feel a pull because there are serious problems in our society and in the world. In handing down her feminism with its aggressive, progressive political consciousness, my mother bequeathed me an important legacy. As a woman and as a minority, I know that if you think about people from different backgrounds and races and countries, you can't help but be moved or feel angry about the injustices they face.

I am definitely a feminist, with a particular political outlook. Men and women must be quite different. I don't know how else to explain human history. I have become more feminist in valuing the environment, the earth, and nature. In a modern, technology-based society, men and women begin to look alike in many ways. Yet in the history of the world, men have been out making war and women have not. It doesn't matter what part of the world you're in, what time in history, the men were making war.

Some people still think feminism means you have to be hairy and burn your bra. Some think it's not nice to be confrontational with men or other women. Some think feminism is a middle-class phenomenon and see feminists as women who put on three-piece suits, walk into a boardroom, and kick around their secretaries in the process. Some women have trouble with the concept of sisterhood because they have grievances with other women. But I cannot imagine not calling myself a feminist. We need feminists because we have a long way to go. We need affirmative action, and we need a feminist perspective in the media and in the arts. There's still a lack of equality in many areas.

When I was younger, I was ambivalent about making a commitment to one person. Now I would like to be in a long-term relationship. I wish I had more maturity in that area. I want someone who can appreciate me and care for me, who understands my interests, background, and experience. I need somebody who understands what the acting life is all about and who values and appreciates its ups and downs. Recently I have decided that I want to have a child—a realization that I have come to later than most of my friends. It is a difficult area for me personally, because I was an only child and grew up with a single mother, a scenario I don't want to repeat.

A recent trip with my mother to Mexico reminded me that we are nearing the stage in our lives where a role reversal often occurs and the child becomes a caregiver for the parent. On the trip, my mother had unexpected trouble with her hip and needed me to look after her. Having to care for my mother in this way brought up some deep-seated feelings of resentment. I realized the importance of working through my feelings about my own childhood before she gets much older. Today I am able to say to her, "This is what I need and what I can do—how is it? Do you have what you need?" My mother has thought about this, too, and is trying to be aware as well.

One of the biggest sacrifices my mother made to live her activist life is financial security. That's no small thing. On the other hand, she has a network of people who care about her. Activism has certainly created a family for her that she doesn't have through marriage.

> One of the biggest sacrifices my mother made to live her activist life is financial security. That's no small thing.

Today I live in San Francisco, several blocks from my mother's apartment. Sometimes I'd be more comfortable if I felt more independent. But I like my mother a lot now that she has mellowed. We enjoy working together and discussing many topics. We joke around and have fun together. She is also a real fan of my acting, which is wonderful for me.

Patsy and Wendy, 1953.

Wendy and Patsy, 1992.

Patsy Mink

and

Wendy Mink

CONGRESSWOMAN PATSY MINK was born in Maui, Hawaii, in 1927 and is of Japanese descent. She attended the University of Hawaii, where she earned a BA in 1948 in zoology and chemistry. Because little work was available for women in her field, she made a transition to the study of law at the University of Chicago Law School, where she earned her JD in 1951. Representative Mink has devoted her entire adult life to public service. Currently she serves as a member of the U.S. House of Representatives from the Second District of Hawaii. High on her list of concerns are gaining economic equity and gender equality for women. She resides with her husband in Honolulu, Hawaii, and Washington, D.C.

LIKE HER MOTHER, Wendy Mink has devoted her adult years to the study of politics and is actively concerned with women's issues. Mink was born in Chicago in 1952 and grew up in Hawaii. She says she has been a feminist all her life, and she has worked for the Equal Rights Amendment, welfare rights, reproductive rights, pay equity, and sexual safety for women. She earned her PhD in political science at Cornell University in 1982 and is now Professor of Politics at the University of California–Santa Cruz.

A Mother's Story

While I was pregnant with my daughter, Wendy, in 1951 and '52, I was administered a drug that dramatically affected both our lives. My doctor was participating in a University of Chicago experiment to test whether diethylstilbestrol (DES), a form of estrogen, prevents miscarriages. Years later, dust-covered records in a Chicago basement revealed that the blind study had created tremendous health hazards for a thousand women involved in the experiment and their offspring. For years Wendy had puzzling physical symptoms, the cause of which remained a mystery. In 1976, on her twenty-fourth birthday, I received a letter saying, "You were in this test, and our records show that you were given DES. Are you alive? Are you sick? What happened to your child?" They even requested we participate in a follow-up experiment to track the effects of the drug on offspring.

In 1978, I and two others won a significant settlement from the University of Chicago and DES manufacturer Eli Lilly because they had not informed us that we were part of an experiment. Our daughters have been less successful in court. Wendy sued, but since she didn't have cancer at the time, she was awarded nothing. A two-year statute of limitations prevented her from recovering for any DES-related medical problems that developed since 1976.

There was no women's movement in the mid-1950s, when the DES experiment took place, nor when I first entered politics. In my youth I didn't understand that there was such a thing as discrimination against women. I lived my life as I felt inclined, never considering myself a lesser being because I was female. I attribute this to the influence of my parents, who treated me and my brother with absolute equality.

My maternal and paternal grandparents came from Japan to Honolulu in the late 1800s to work in the sugar plantation fields. They came on two-year contracts, but they liked Hawaii and violated their contracts in order to stay. My maternal grandparents fled to Maui, where, undiscovered, they lived in the hills and raised eleven children. My grandparents spoke only Japanese, but my American-born parents spoke English. After graduating from the University of Hawaii, my father became a civil engineer; my mother completed eighth grade at a Christian boarding school on Maui, married, and had two children.

I was born on December 6, 1927, on the island of Maui. My early years were wonderful. I grew up in the free and easy atmosphere of the country, playing cowboys and Indians and climbing trees. My parents pretty much let us wander, the entire countryside at our command. I attended school across the street from our house until fourth grade, when my parents wanted me to become competitive with white children and got me into the all-white public school established for children of business and plantation owners. The switch was terrible. The white children were standoffish, and I was an intruder. But while I never felt comfortable or made friends, being at the school opened up many opportunities.

I was fourteen when Pearl Harbor was bombed. My family quickly became aware of the enormity of the incident when first-generation Japanese who had traveled to Japan for business or other reasons were rounded up and put behind bars. Nine thousand people from Hawaii were moved to concentration camps in California and Arizona. As Japanese-Americans, we were ostracized and relegated to the category of potential traitors and enemies of America. My schoolmates, mimicking prevalent themes and slogans, teased us and called us "Japs." As Americans, we felt terrible at being treated this way.

The year before the war ended, I entered the University of Hawaii. During my junior year on the mainland, I was shocked to discover that the University of Nebraska had placed me in the International House rather than a dormitory because of my color. When I protested, I was told that dormitories were for white kids. In response, I whipped up a huge storm on campus with articles in the school paper about discrimination. Everybody, including parents and trustees, got all riled up, and within months the policy changed. Unfortunately, my plans to return to enjoy the newly integrated environment were interrupted by illness.

From childhood I had been preoccupied with the idea of becoming a doctor. All my studies were directed toward that end, and in 1948 I graduated from the University of Hawaii with a major in zoology and chemistry and a minor in physics. At the appropriate time I applied to twenty-five medical schools—my parents willingly paying the application fees. But my dream never materialized. Had I been male I would have been accepted because of good grades, but medical schools across the country simply were not accepting women. The reasons may have been ethnic as well. In any case, I was shattered, and I was left with nothing to do. The jobs I qualified for were unrelated to my goal.

One day my boss said, "Don't be so depressed; life doesn't end just because you didn't go to medical school. Surely there are other ways to express your individuality and your desire to serve people." I asked, "What can I do?" and she enumerated possible careers. "Why don't you go to law school?" she said. "You like to talk." I had no idea what the study of law entailed, but I took her up on it, and in 1950 the University of Chicago accepted me as a "foreign student." I didn't bother to say they were wrong to think me foreign.

In my third year of law school, I met my husband, a master's student in geology, across the bridge table at the International House. Four months later, in 1951, we were married. John's grandparents came from Lithuania and Czechoslovakia. Upon hearing the news, his mother said, "Oh, how nice." But when we called to get my parents' blessing, my mother hung up on us because John was white. I understood her reservations, but I was disappointed. Skin color was never relevant to me.

Wendy was born a year later, in 1952. By then I had completed my law degree, but no one would hire me, not even as a law clerk. I continued to work evenings at a low-wage job in the university library, but I didn't want to shelve books the rest of my life. When Wendy was five months old, John and I headed back to Hawaii. When the plane landed in Honolulu, we called my parents and said, "We're here." They came to the airport and met John and Wendy for the first time, and that was it. They loved them.

Moving to Hawaii with no promise of a job was difficult for John. He considered the move necessary to get my family back together, but he didn't get the job he felt entitled to and the small island made him claustrophobic. Accustomed to driving for days on the mainland, he said, "In Hawaii I drive this way and I hit the ocean, I drive that way and I hit the ocean." I knew John was having a hard time, but we seldom talked about it.

The hiring situation was no better for me in Hawaii than in Chicago, so I decided to set up a private law practice. My father had invested heavily in my education and was more than willing to help me establish my practice. In the beginning, my clients were nonpaying and I wasn't that busy. A sitter cared for Wendy when I was at work, and in the evenings my parents took care of her if I was occupied. John and I did things with Wendy whenever we could. We took her campaigning and leafleting, and we never left her if we could take her. She began attending a child-care center when she was three.

Because I spent so much of my time organizing and attending meetings, John played a large role in raising Wendy. He was happy and supportive, and I felt comfortable leaving her while I went off to meetings. She never said, "Mom, I want you to be at home." One of us was there all the time, so I don't believe I shortchanged her. We lived in the country, and the commute to school took an hour and a half each way. Though I may not have been with her many evenings, for six or seven years Wendy and I shared three hours together in the car, doing her homework and talking.

Getting John to help was not a struggle, because he believed that women are equal. We never sat down and said, "That's your job; this is my job." It just happened that the things I like to do around the house he doesn't, and what I don't like to do he doesn't mind. I don't particularly like housework, but John doesn't mind it. He cleans, does the laundry, and anything else needed indoors. I like yard work—cutting grass, trimming hedges, and watering and fertilizing plants. Before becoming so politically active, I also enjoyed cooking.

I became interested in Democratic politics through friends who pulled me into party workshops and seminars. One thing led to another, and soon I was elected to the state legislature. Campaigning took a lot of time, and much of my political activity in those early years I did alone. Equal pay for equal work was one of my early achievements. Male legislators got up on the floor and ridiculed the legislation ("Equal pay?"), but in 1957 they voted for it. We took pleasure in the fact that Hawaii adopted the bill six years sooner than the nation. As a representative, I helped open up state government after noticing that it was always the same people who served on important commissions. "A lot of talented people want to serve," I said. "Give them an opportunity." In all, I served three terms in the Hawaii legislature.

When I first ran for national office in 1959, I lost by 8 percent. Losing felt awful. It's terrible enough to be rejected by just one person, but to be rejected by thousands you thought were in love with you is devastating. That's why most people don't run for office. You can run again only if you believe strongly that you have something to contribute. After losing I said, "Never again," but soon I reentered local politics and was elected to the Hawaii state senate in 1962.

In 1964 a seat opened in the U.S. House of Representatives, and I decided to seek national office. This time I campaigned for federal aid to education, which became law my first year in Congress. As a representative, I pushed for equity in education. We held hearings to determine how textbooks were demeaning to black people and looked at gender discrimination in the handling of federal funding. When we wrote Title IX, out of a belief that federally funded institutions should treat girls and boys equally, I had no idea how far-reaching it would be and how it would withstand all the court tests. Though just twenty words long, Title IX has produced stunning results in prohibiting sex discrimination.

Wendy, in sixth grade when we moved to Washington, D.C., expressed little opinion about my politics during her teenage years. While attending the National Cathedral School, she went through a rebellious period—the usual stubbornness and resistance against the school's authoritarian discipline. She didn't dare miss classes, but when special events were scheduled, she'd slip off to Georgetown instead. The school would call and say, "Your daughter missed such and such, and we don't know where she is. You'd better look for her." We'd find her, looking self-conscious and conspicuous, hanging on the corner with a group of kids watching the crowd. She was also politically active—mainly against the war in Vietnam. Once she got to college, she began to appreciate more of what I had done and the changes I had advocated.

Wendy is far ahead of me now and much more radical in her politics. I consider her an activist, but I don't know what did it—perhaps osmosis and my constant lecturing on the fundamental principles of equity. I've probably been tempered over the years, so she's going to have to take my place as a rabble-rouser. Wendy has continued my work in the different but equally important arena of academics. She has certainly, at great risk to her future, become a champion of those principles on the campus. She was involved in a successful Title IX discrimination complaint regarding a campus rape because she felt that the victims were not accorded proper protection, nor the rapist adequate punishment. She is an uncompromising firebrand. I have to admire her.

I think Wendy has found satisfaction in her life. She has found her niche and is growing with it spectacularly. The University of California has given her many responsibilities, which she carries out with great relish. Recently head of the systemwide affirmative-action committee, she served as conscience for her coworkers regarding issues of equity, justice, and fairness. As a parent, I am proud of her academic achievements and proud that she is not just an academic.

Wendy is my only child. I did not make a conscious decision not to have more children; I just didn't have them. I like that she is doting on her parents. We don't have to constantly say, "Wendy, when are you going to come and see us?" She is always able to visit, either in Washington or Hawaii, so we don't feel the distance. I worry about her health, which is fragile because of the DES exposure. Also, she was nearly killed in a car accident in 1975 when, as a passenger in the front seat, she was thrown through the windshield.

I am a feminist—one who cares about the role of women in society—but I do not believe the women's movement is broadly enough based. In limiting itself to a certain segment of society, it leaves out the rest. Millions of women, such as those on welfare, are not connected to it, but I don't see the feminist movement getting involved in welfare reform; women of color are the only ones who care about this issue. I would like to see preschool childcare become part of the official educational program so that childcare workers' pay is comparable to that of teachers. Childcare workers are currently paid less than animal-shelter employees. Why aren't feminists campaigning for better salaries for childcare workers? Is an animal more precious than a child?

The women's movement still focuses on middle-class white women, which I don't see changing. The "glass ceiling" is an upper-class ceiling for those aspiring to be bank presidents and executives, not those who can never rise above the minimum wage. The majority of people working at minimum-wage jobs in the United States are women. That's the glass ceiling I am committed to doing something about. American women must stand up and be counted. The new women in Congress have absolutely made a difference—forty-nine is better than twenty-nine—but to get more women into office, it must be easier for women to run. If we could just persuade women to support more women candidates, more would win.

Politics has kept me on my toes. To continue in it, one has to look to the future. I hope to stay in Washington as long as I can, but the moment I can't compete physically, I'll quit. I don't think I paid any price for my dual role as career woman and mother, but a supportive husband made it easier for me to do what I had to do. After forty-three years, John and I are still married. He has served as my manager for seventeen campaigns and is still at it. Ultimately he accepted the island, and today he regularly flies back and forth between Hawaii and Washington as a highly sought-after geology consultant.

I have no regrets. My greatest achievement has been balancing my family and my career—taking care of my parents when they needed me and being available for my

> Childcare workers are currently paid less than animal-shelter employees.

daughter. You do your share and others will be willing to do theirs. You can't be a casual observer of your life; you have to be prepared to commit a whole lot to make it work.

A Daughter's Story

At the time I was born, in March 1952, my mother had graduated from law school and was looking for work. Finding no opportunities to practice her vocation in Chicago, she decided to go back to Hawaii, where she was from. My father, a geologist, was amenable to the idea, so when I was six months old we moved to Honolulu. But law firms in Hawaii were no more open to the idea of a woman practicing law than elsewhere in the United States, so my mother eventually decided to hang out a shingle and go into solo practice.

Until I was three, my grandparents and baby-sitters took care of me while my parents were at work. My mother's family is close and interdependent, and my grandparents were important people in my life. In the Japanese tradition, we were all connected in a collective identity as a family, so there was, and is, lots of interaction and mutual assistance. I knew that my relatives were people I could count on; everybody was available for everybody else. My immediate extended family was fairly small—my mother's only sibling had two children—but my grandmother had ten brothers and sisters, many with three or four children each, and many of them were closer in age to me than to my mother.

We lived in various neighborhoods within the city of Honolulu until I was five or six, and then we moved to an old sugar plantation town called Waipahu, twelve miles outside the city. It was tract housing; every house had a yard, but they all looked the same and were fairly close together. I was quite aware that we lived modestly, but so did the rest of the family and everyone else we knew.

I grew up inside Japanese-American culture. My mother's maternal grandparents had emigrated from Japan to Hawaii in the late 1800s on a sugar contract. As soon as my great-grandfather figured out a way to do it, he got out of his contract and became a shopkeeper and a postman. Their eleven children, born in Hawaii, were native-born American citizens. My father is Lithuanian and Slovakian. His family was working-class—coal miners and factory workers.

Growing up, I never felt alone, but I did feel different—both from people I went to school with and from people in my own family. This stems, in part, from the fact that I am mixed-race. My father is the only white person in my mother's extended family. Also, my mother is a professional, which was very unusual when I was growing up. Many of my classmates assumed that I was different, and lonely, because I didn't have a "real" mother. They assumed that my mother was unavailable to me because she worked outside the home.

In truth, much of the time she was gone from home, I was with her. We went shopping, to political rallies, to coffee hours. When I was in elementary school, I would often go to her law office after school. She shared a suite with my grandfather. My grandmother worked for him, so I would hang out with them. My mother was always active in politics, even when she was practicing law. I wasn't lonely when she wasn't around, though; I was usually with my cousins or with friends. It wasn't as if my parents made a choice to pursue a public life at the expense of a private one; they took me as many places as a four-year-old could reasonably go. I was completely integrated in their lives.

My mother was elected to Congress when I was twelve. I was proud of her, but I had always felt proud of her. Her fame was just a part of who she was, so it seemed natural to me. But moving to suburban Washington, D.C., was a culture shock. The fact that my mother was Japanese, against the Vietnam War, and a feminist in a culturally conservative town didn't win me many friends. Discrimination in Hawaii had shown itself in silly things, such as other Japanese-American kids assuming I didn't know how to cook rice because that wasn't part of my complete genetic profile. They were not unfriendly; I just had the sense that they saw me as different. Not until we moved to Washington did I experience out-and-out racism and learn what it was to be "other" for white people.

At first we lived in Arlington, Virginia, and I went to a public school there. Under Virginia law at that point, miscegenation was illegal; Loving v. Virginia, a landmark case, had not yet been decided. This was 1964 and 1965. The white kids called me a "Chink" and told me to ride in the back of the bus and made fun of me for not dressing like them. (I wore knee socks instead of nylons.) Once, in high school, I agreed to accompany a friend on a blind double date, and when the guy showed up he threw a tantrum, saying, "I am not going out with any damn Filipino." Other people treated me as an exotic, asking me when I learned to speak English or if I wore a grass skirt all the time in Hawaii. To some I was a Jap; to others, a Chink. As Vietnam heated up, the word *gook* was added to the arsenal.

I spoke out against the prejudice. I answered it. But that is what you live with if you're not part of the dominant culture. You find ways of coping by learning to direct your anger in creative ways like politics or the arts, or you repress it, or you explode. I chose the political path, attending my share of civil rights marches and antiwar marches not only to express my feelings but also to participate in some process of public political education.

Sometimes I reported instances of prejudice to my parents, and they would get angry and want to intervene on my behalf. Other times I wouldn't tell them, because I didn't want to spread the anger any further. They taught me to try to put things in perspective by insisting that racism is an unfortunate pathology in our society, which we might work to get rid of, but it wasn't about me; it was about other people's myopia. Talking with them about my experiences with slurs and discrimination helped me to get rid of the immediate aftertaste and to decide how to cope with my feelings. Early on, I decided that fighting inequality would be a central part of what I ultimately chose to do with my life.

I was different from my friends in a political sense. Most of them had come to their politics through rebellion; I didn't have to work toward my politics that way. For my friends, going to a march was a defiant act, whereas my parents would say, "Can we come along?" Sometimes I rebelled against parental discipline (once or twice I didn't call home and missed curfew on purpose). But my parents were not very strict, and I didn't present many challenges to them on those fronts.

From the age of twelve I was politically active on my own terms. My first antiwar march was in April of 1965, on the Mall in Washington. I went with my father and was converted to the cause from that moment forward. As a high-school student at the National Cathedral School, I helped organize mobilizations against the war and marches against hunger in Africa. With friends, I put out an underground newspaper, I wrote a lot, and I debated these issues in debate club. The administration of the school and the majority of students were utterly hostile, but there were fifteen or twenty of us who could be very persuasive.

As a student at the University of Chicago, I became involved in anti-war activity; we marched up and down the streets, waiting for Mayor Daley to send out the clubs. I directed a voter-registration drive and was an organizer in the community where I lived. In 1972 I transferred to Berkeley, where I knew I'd find a more culturally and socially diverse student body. I also imagined that there would still be some political vitality there. But although there was some third-world organizing, the anti-war activity had basically stopped. The Me Generation and a lot of drugs had taken over.

Joining the women's movement was a natural move, and as soon as things started happening with the younger branch of feminism, I knew I was allied with it. How I wanted to connect directly, I wasn't really sure, but I always thought of myself as a feminist. Fairly early on, I was involved in the choice issue. In 1970 I interned in Senator Kennedy's office, where I worked on the issue of abortion statutes in different states and how women's rights were balanced against the medical-necessity arguments. I have sustained an interest in reproductive rights ever since.

One of my most difficult experiences was as a graduate student in political science at Cornell, where I filed a complaint against a professor who had harassed me and two other women. When it first happened to me, during my first year in the program, I reported the incident to two faculty members, who advised me to develop a thick skin: "That's just the way he is," they said. I was furious, but there were no grievance procedures, and sexual harassment had not yet been fully recognized as sex discrimination. Two or three years later, on the eve of a comprehensive exam he would evaluate, the professor reminded me that I had turned him down and let me know he knew I had reported him to his colleagues. He claimed he wouldn't hold the earlier incident against me on the exam, but it was a chilling and intimidating interaction that renewed my sense of vulnerability. I reported this incident, too, but to no avail. A year later he harassed a friend of mine in an even cruder manner, and she and I filed a complaint. We spent much of the Spring of 1980 fighting the university and the department over it, which was frustrating and painful—and professionally very risky, especially since some faculty warned us we would be branded as troublemakers. But my mentor fought hard to get the department to take us seriously, and in the end we received a letter of apology from the department chair and convinced the department to adopt a sexual harassment code. My graduate years were poisoned by all of this, but at least we raised people's consciousness.

In 1975 I was severely injured in a head-on collision. The accident altered my perspective. I decided to do my best because I might not have another chance, and I resolved not to be wedded to fixed patterns. Realizing that uncertainty exists helped me deal better with life.

> For my friends, going to a march was a defiant act, whereas my parents would say, "Can we come along?"

As I worked toward my doctorate I became more and more convinced that I wanted to teach in a public university. Partly as a reaction to the elitism of private education, I wanted to participate in a democratic educational project, not a market educational project where one comes in contact only with students who have the money to pay for what they're getting or the luck to find financial assistance. Luckily, I received an offer from the University of California–Santa Cruz, where I have been teaching since 1981.

As a professor I have continued to be politically engaged. I chaired the Status of Women Committee for six or seven years; I do a lot of work on sexual harassment; and though I teach in Politics, I make it a point to teach courses that count for Women's Studies credit. I teach a course on women and the law, or feminist jurisprudence, and another on U.S. social politics, which is a race, class, and gender course.

I think that everybody who considers herself a feminist is at least fundamentally contesting the sex-gender system and the power and domination under which we live. But there are many different feminisms and many different feminist agendas, not all of which are happily reconciled with one another. Being a woman of color in a largely white movement means that there have been plenty of moments when I felt exoticized or regarded as marginal to the conversation, or even the exception that proves the rule. Not wanting to separate myself from feminism has meant struggling to find ways to build bridges—bridges that can bear the weight of differences among women. I am not yet satisfied with what we have achieved.

My hope for feminism is that the movement can reorder its priorities. Regardless of whether or not people feel welcomed in the movement as a whole, we can continue to rally around such issues as choice and sexual assault because of women's common experience of vulnerability. But we must also move beyond our individual standpoints to join in fighting other women's oppression. On issues of race and class in particular—welfare, for example—I would like to see far broader feminist commitment. I'd like to see an expanded politics of reproductive choice, one that includes the right to choose motherhood. Reproductive politics has been about abortion and fertility control, not about a woman's right to have healthy babies and social support if she chooses to have children. This has been a serious mistake.

My mother is a highly regarded and effective legislator. I hope that the kinds of policies she cares about actually come to pass. Serving as a member of Congress is shockingly exhausting work. I'm always concerned about her working too hard. She gets lots of pleasure out of her work, and that is not what I object to. I worry about the long-distance travel, the relentless schedule, and her long hours.

I am proud of her early opposition to the war in Vietnam. She was consistent and strong on that issue, despite the fact that she was called "Madame Binh" and other nasty names and has had to bear that as a consequence throughout her political career. I am proud of the women's legislation she helped to craft: Title IX, the Women's Educational Equity Act, the day-care bill that Nixon ended up vetoing. I am proud of her for always having good instincts.

My mother was a good mother in that she always let me know that she cared and that in a fundamental way I came first. Many things claimed her attention, but I knew that I was her first priority. If I needed her, she would be there. We were not particularly close when I was in high school; I wanted distance to create my own independent way. I wasn't rejecting her, I was just finding myself. I think it is important for a daughter to carve out her own path. Not that my mother wanted me to be like her; she always made it perfectly clear that I should do what I want to do. She conveyed a sense that I needed to make my own choices. A good feminist model, she taught me that while it may not be easy, living your life to your own expectations is perfectly possible and terribly rewarding.

Jo Ellen and Helen, 1952.

Helen and Laura, 1951.

Jo Ellen, Helen, and Laura, 1995.

Helen Rodriguez-Trias
and
Jo Ellen Brainin-Rodriguez
and
Laura Brainin-Rodriguez

HELEN RODRIGUEZ-TRIAS is an international leader of the women's health movement and the mother of four grown children. Born in 1929 in New York City, she grew up in Puerto Rico and New York. She received her MD from the University of Puerto Rico School of Medicine in San Juan in 1960, where she graduated first in her class. As well as teaching at numerous institutions, including the University of Puerto Rico, Yeshiva University, Fordham, and Columbia, she has been active in the Committee to End Sterilization and in the Coalition for Abortion Rights and Against Sterilization Abuse (CARASA). She serves on the board of the National Women's Health Network, and in 1977 received its Distinguished Physician's Award. She currently works as a consultant in health programming, with particular focus on primary-care and HIV prevention programs for women, and the development of effective programs to serve persons with limited access to health care. Rodriguez-Trias and her husband reside in Brookdale, California.

Jo ELLEN BRAININ-RODRIGUEZ, was born in New York City in 1949. She earned her MD from the University of California School of Medicine and completed her psychiatric residency at St. Mary's Hospital and Medical Center, both in San Francisco. Brainin-Rodriguez now works at San Francisco General Hospital as chief psychiatrist of a unit that houses the Women's Focus Team and the Latina Focus Team, and is a clinical instructor at the School of Medicine. She both teaches residents and provides direct care. She lives with her husband and two daughters in San Francisco.

LAURA BRAININ-RODRIGUEZ, a public health nutritionist, works at the San Francisco Department of Public Health. She was born in Ohio in 1951 and was educated at the University of California—Berkeley, where she received her MS and MPH in nutrition in 1982. As a community nutritionist with the Health Promotion Program at Stanford University, Brainin-Rodriguez was responsible for the development and implementation of an athletic-nutrition program and campuswide nutrition education. She designs and delivers classes on such topics as healthy eating, eating disorders, and vegetarianism. She resides in San Francisco.

A Mother's Story

Shortly after I joined the women's movement in 1970, my daughter Jo Ellen told me that she and her younger sister had been sexually abused by their stepfather, whom I had divorced four months earlier. Her revelation made the women's movement a personal matter of survival for me. I first dared to speak publicly about the sexual abuse of my girls in a consciousness-raising group of fifteen women. When I finished, there was total silence. No one could deal with what I had said. Then my daughter Laura, sitting next to me, said, "I want to talk about it, too. This is my mother; I am her daughter." Tears came to my eyes. Speaking before other women was the beginning of our healing.

In the 1970s women were not prepared to speak about incest. It was becoming clear, however, that women's rights were about better lives for women in the intimacy of our homes as well as in society—that the personal was political. As a pediatrician, I began to address the problem of sexual abuse. I taught women and children to speak up and doctors to listen. But Laura and I both had therapists who minimized and invalidated our experiences. Even today it is difficult for us to trust. Sometimes I am still inappropriately mistrustful, or I misread signs and become too trusting, as I was of the man I married when my children were small.

When I was born in 1929 in New York City, my parents' marriage was already going downhill. My father, a prosperous businessman, squandered his gains on alcohol. When he drank, his urbanity disappeared and he threatened violence in a booming, rough voice. My mother returned with us to Puerto Rico before I was a year old and finally divorced him in 1939, when I was ten. She brought me with her to New York, seeking a better life, like many Puerto Ricans before her, and left my fourteen-year-old sister with Aunt Estela, my childhood nurturer. When we left Puerto Rico, I did not cry. My mother denied her feelings of loss, too. I did not see Aunt Estela again until I returned to study at the university.

The year of my return to Puerto Rico, 1947, was highly charged politically. University authorities refused to allow Nationalist Party leader Pedro Albizu Campos, just released from federal prison, to speak on campus. Students struck and the university shut down. I was peripheral to the student movement but began to identify with the political struggles of the island. After a year I quit school and joined a leftist youth organization. I returned to New York, where I met my first husband in the office of a left-wing Columbia University student publication. David, twenty-three, was an editor; I was nineteen, author of an article on Puerto Rican student activists.

As suited two young leftists, we were married in 1949 in a nontraditional ceremony. Ten months later Jo Ellen was born. I followed David to Lorain, Ohio, when Jo was three months old. In Lorain we were asked to vacate our furnished room after a black couple who were our friends visited us. Finding no place that allowed children, we sent six-month-old Jo back with my mother to New York while we bought and restored a house. When my mother brought her back to Lorain five months later, Jo acted fearful, as if we were strangers. I felt guilty and pained. It was a month before her first birthday, seven weeks before her first Christmas, and I was seven months pregnant.

Laura, born in January, thrived during the bitter Ohio winter. Eighteen months later David arrived. Having three children in two and a half years was horrendous. I felt inadequate and frightened. Dave tried to help, but he worked three rotation shifts as a machinist's apprentice and was president of his local union. When he was home, he got impatient with the babies. I feel compassion now toward the naive neophytes we once were, but back then I was dying of loneliness and isolation.

My mother stayed with us on and off for two years. In Lorain she discovered a lump in her breast and had a radical mastectomy. When she left for Puerto Rico, I said, "I am not going to be alone here anymore," and went with her. Jo Ellen was three, Laura not quite two, and David only five months old. My decision arose out of sheer desperation and pain. At twenty-five I was embarrassed to need my mother so desperately. I did not want to admit it to Dave or myself, but I think I knew then that I would not be back.

Dave came to Puerto Rico in an attempt at reconciliation, but I already had a lover, whom I later married. My lover was divorced, with two sons. My mother urged me to stay with Dave. "He may not be the ideal person," she said. "He has a bad temper, but he's sober and decent and the father of these three children. That counts for a great deal." I felt guilty, but X was seductive and passion got in the way of reason. Furthermore, he seemed devoted to me. When I told him I wanted to study medicine, he suggested I stop working after we got married and start school right away. I trusted him because he seemed unconditionally supportive. He helped us financially during the divorce from Dave and became my lifeline. I grew more dependent on him each day.

My mother vehemently opposed my marrying X. We quarreled bitterly, and she left for New York. X and I married in the summer of 1954. In September I enrolled in the university's premedical course. I loved school and discovered my capacity to concentrate and do well. A year later my mother died of breast cancer in New York City. We made peace in her bare hospital room and I told her that I loved her, always had. She expressed her happiness that I had gone back to school. Sadly, considering what X turned out to be, she apologized for her opposition to him, saying, "I was mistaken."

In 1956 I entered medical school. I was twenty-seven and on top of the world. In all honesty, I was not a great mom when I was in training. During the premedical years I had more time with the kids, but with the pressures of medical school I had no time or energy to spare. Jo, Laura, and David attended a nursery school run by a Canadian missionary, and I had irregular hired help. But my husband was the present parent. He came from a large and apparently close family, with a mother considered by everyone a saint. Ashamed of the broken family I grew up in, I trusted his ways with children more than my own.

I suspected him of sexual abuse only once. During my third year of medical school, I arrived home one evening to find seven-year-old Laura in our bed. Irritated with her, which I deeply regret, I said sharply, "To your bed. You know I don't like children in adult beds." At the time X feigned deep sleep. The next day he said, "Last night you pulled a fast one on me, accusing me of something improper with Laura. She was just sleeping here and so was I." He attacked me as disturbed and evil-minded, and I cried and apologized, convinced that my view of men was distorted. I never suspected again. I wish I had been able to say to Laura, "Come here, baby. I won't be angry at you, and I will always love you, no matter what you tell me is happening." She might have told me then and spared the girls years of abuse and me years of being deceived.

As it was, the deceptions continued through the years I imagined myself happy and the children safe. I finished medical school with highest honors, six months pregnant with Daniel. Being on call every other night was a nightmare, but we had household help, and my husband seemed devoted to our new son, the two girls, and David.

Daniel, at three years of age, began to prefer his sisters' clothes. In those days whatever was wrong with a child was always the mother's fault. Women's magazines counseled mothers to avoid raising sons to be "sissies." Daniel's father wanted me to punish him, but instinctively I felt it was the wrong approach. When Daniel was five, a child psychiatrist shattered me with his conclusion: "In my experience, when a boy wants to dress like a girl, he is being encouraged, and I rather suspect that you, Helen, are the one who is encouraging him." No stranger to mother's guilt, I suspected I had poisoned my children. I had three rebellious teenagers and a severely disturbed child, or so I thought. The next day we took the children to a favorite, secluded beach. I swam out, crying, and considered going under—the only time I have considered suicide. I only refrained because I thought that if I had harmed our son, I had a responsibility to heal the harm.

Professionally I kept advancing. After medical school and pediatric training, I began teaching. I received increasing acknowledgment from my peers, but my husband's resentment grew. "You can't get a raise," he would say. "I don't want a wife who earns more than I do"; or, "You doctors are such bores at parties. I have never met people like you, always talking about your work." He told friends that I had fooled him into believing that once training was completed I would be more of a homebody.

Ironically, the more active I became as a parent, voicing opinions about his harsh discipline of the kids, the angrier he became. I was "the other rebellious adolescent," he moaned, "as if three weren't enough!" Interspersed with his complaints were romantic interludes of intense wooing, now recognizable as the cycle of abuse. At the time our problems seemed mainly my fault—for wanting a career, for choosing one so demanding and rewarding, for succeeding, for speaking out, for laughing too much, for weeping when hurt, for having three difficult adolescents from a first marriage, for having a little boy not masculine enough, for not being a good mother.

During the late sixties we turned to various "experts": a psychologist for the two of us; a psychiatrist for eleven-year-old David for bedwetting; one for Daniel at nine because of his girlish behavior; a psychiatrist for Laura, at sixteen involved with a delinquent boy; a psychiatrist for me for general unhappiness and failure as a wife and mother. These male professionals happily confirmed what Daniel's child psychiatrist had implied: I was an unnatural woman, a threat to my husband and my children.

By 1970 Jo, Laura, and David had left home, and I felt the enormous void in my marriage. Sessions with a woman psychiatrist marked the beginning of my understanding of my situation. Toward the end of the first year of therapy, I confronted my husband, telling him, "I think you need to get into treatment yourself. Find out why we are having problems with the kids. Why has everyone else in this family needed therapy except you? I can't believe that everyone else is sick and that you're totally okay." He resisted, and I said, "It is not negotiable. Get into therapy, or we get a divorce." He insisted on visiting my psychiatrist first to tell his side of the story. Returning home, he wept and expressed sorrow for his "maltreatment" of the children. I drew close to comfort him for what I thought he meant by maltreatment—the harsh punishments, the beatings, the mocking sarcasm. Then he said, "I have considered suicide." The comment struck me as insincere and manipulative, and I distanced myself.

The next day he was his old self again. "To think that at my age I would be falling into the hands of a psychiatrist, and all because of you!" he said, leaving the house and our marriage without even saying good-bye to Daniel. My ultimatum had provoked the end, but I didn't know why. Within three months we were divorced. In early September Daniel and I moved to New York with Maria, our housekeeper of seven years and our security and support. Before me lay the challenging job of chief of pediatrics at Lincoln Hospital in the South Bronx.

When X announced his forthcoming marriage a few months later, I refused to send Daniel, still pained over the divorce, back to Puerto Rico. I doubted my decision, however, and consulted with Jo Ellen, in New York for Thanksgiving. She gazed at me steadily for a long moment and said, "Mami, he is very bad for children."

"Why do you say that?"

"Because he molested us regularly when we were little."

I questioned her perceptions. "Children often fantasize. Is it possible?"

"This is no fantasy, there is no misinterpreting what happened; it went on for years," Jo Ellen said. "I intended never to tell you, but I have to protect Daniel."

I was shattered. For weeks I hardly stopped crying. I had known and loved X for eighteen years, been his wife for sixteen, borne his son, praised him as a good, if strict, father. Even after the divorce, I felt guilty that I was taking his son to New York. If I had been so wrong about this man, how could I ever trust my senses again?

In January 1971 I used the occasion of a trip to Puerto Rico to recruit house officers for Lincoln Hospital as an opportunity to meet with all three kids and Anita, who would later become David's wife. During our days at the remote country house of a friend, we spoke of things long hidden, many of them painful and frightening. We wept and shouted, understood and misunderstood one another, but for the first time we spoke about our feelings without pretense.

On Monday I called to arrange an appointment with X at his office after work, ostensibly to speak about Daniel's visit. As we one by one entered his office, X's expression changed from surprise to fear. "I am not here to talk about your visitation rights with Daniel," I said quickly. "I came to talk about your abuse of the girls."

He rose and began to push past us, but Jo Ellen and David pushed him back down, saying, "Sit down. You are going to hear what we have to say."

"Who said so?" he said defiantly.

"We said so," we responded in unison.

Screaming, "Police, police, help!" he attempted to flee. Jo and David thrust him back into his chair, but the moment they relaxed their hold, he turned, kicked in the window, and jumped out, screaming, "Police! I am being attacked!" I last saw him cowed and shaken, sitting on a grassy knoll ten feet below the window, a small crowd gathering. The man who had terrorized my children had become a nothing. Throughout the melee, Laura had stood in front of the desk, her hands in her skirt pockets. Later she said, "I could only see cut-glass ashtrays to hit him with; I feared I might do him great injury." He may have harmed her the most, shy little girl that she was when he started molesting her. Her anger must have frightened her greatly that afternoon of our confrontation.

The following day a news article billed X as a prominent business-man and former governor's aide, attacked by unknown assailants. A second news article identified the assailants as family members and cited X's former wife as having seriously wounded him with high-heel shoes. Three days later, Jo Ellen, Laura, and I were arrested at the airport. Our arrest made headlines, and we were charged with assault, battery, and attempted murder. Meanwhile the "intended victim" stayed home, virtually unharmed.

A friend posted bail, and Jo and I returned to New York; Laura and David remained in Puerto Rico. After putting us through a lawyer's expense and several trips to Puerto Rico for hearings never held, X dropped all charges. True to type and guarding appearances above all, he stated that in the interest of restoring the proper father-son relationship, he would forgive our actions. Of the family, only Daniel has a relationship with him now, and it is superficial.

In 1981 I met Eddie, a nurturing man, who has helped me heal and brought peaceful joy. Eddie taught labor studies at Cornell. Our marriage works because he lets me be me, as I let him be himself. I am in a new phase of my life—much more creative and secure. Being older gives me great freedom, and I am less self-conscious than I ever was. I say what I think or feel without getting terribly upset about the way I am perceived.

> She gazed at me steadily for a long moment and said, "Mami, he is very bad for children."
> "Why do you say that?"
> "Because he molested us regularly when we were little."

I regret marrying so young. If I had had a college education and seen more of the world before becoming a mother, I might have done better. I regret my dependence in my second marriage and the eagerness for a stable, happy home, which blinded me to reality. I regret not being more attentive, not taking more time with the kids. Above all, I regret not having learned more from my mother, a wise woman, before I lost her. But my life is not one of regrets. Right now it is full of rejoicing.

Being a mother has shaped my idea of feminism. I believe that the essence of feminism is nurturing strength in ourselves in order to defend our children. Protecting our children and allowing them to grow up with a sense of empowerment is an essential part of feminism. For me, mothering and feminism have been intertwined. I am optimistic about feminism's future as I see it in my daughters. They are more sophisticated politically than we were twenty-five years ago. They understand how to deal with power and how to work inside the power structures of society.

I want to leave my children and grandchildren with a sense of life-long growth and survivorship, a sense of joy in life and joy in struggle. The women's movement is about survival, about finding our strength and using it to help other women. We reach out to each other to build a different kind of society—one where women are equal in power to men and where children are truly prized.

A Daughter's Story

Watching my mother become a doctor was a deterrent to my becoming a physician. I once asked her, "Why did you have to graduate first in your medical school?" My mother didn't graduate first by a slim margin; she graduated first with eight medals. It was in all the papers. She had three kids and was six months pregnant at the time, and was one of only four women in her medical-school class. What she told me was that she was so terrified she would come out last that she had to blast through. I think a lot of it has to do with her own feelings of inferiority and the fact that she had been put into slow classes when she first went to New York from Puerto Rico by people who didn't recognize her talent.

I never wanted to do anything that was as engrossing as my mother's work, but I became interested in medicine when I was doing health education in Boston, specifically work around abortion and birth control. Though I love what I do, I am less driven than my mother to achieve professionally. I believe there are certain people in a given historical period whose actions make a huge difference in people's lives over the long term. Perhaps my mother is one of those people. I am making different choices.

I was born in New York City in December 1949. My parents had been married a little over a year. My dad was a union organizer, and shortly after I was born we moved to Lorain, Ohio, where he had work. My mother was also an organizer, but after I was born she was mostly a housewife. Within two and a half years, she had three children. The only memory I have of Lorain is of my parents arguing. When I was three and a half my mother left my father, moved with her three children back to her native Puerto Rico, and became a medical student. Her mind and her time became occupied with school, and I have memories of her studying for hours. Late at night we picked her up at the library in my stepfather's car.

As the oldest child, I became the primary baby-sitter and parent substitute. My mother married my stepfather when I was four, and my youngest brother, Daniel, was born when I was eleven. Before we had a maid, I came home from school, washed all the breakfast dishes, and then ran around making all the beds so that when my stepfather came home and started dinner, the house was tidy. I resented being held responsible for the behavior of the other kids, particularly in my teens, when my sister, only a year younger than me, had fewer responsibilities. We had a traditional division of labor in the house, despite the fact that my mother was atypical both as a student and later as a physician. My brother David never washed dishes; he mowed the lawn and washed the car—macho chores that had to be done only once a week, unlike the relentless cycle of dishwashing I was assigned.

My stepfather came from a strict, fundamentalist religious background. His father was a Methodist preacher in a little Puerto Rican town, his mother a passive matriarch adored by the family. My stepfather molested me and my sister sexually from the time I was seven until I was fourteen. Laura and I began to talk about it when we were eleven or twelve. We decided to lock the room, but my stepfather picked the lock. Finally I found the courage to stand up to him and say, "Get the hell out of this bedroom, and don't ever come here again." To my surprise, he stopped. I developed the split mind-set that a lot of abused kids have: I knew what was going on, but for many years I had a dissociative response. I saw my mother as frail and I was afraid that if we told her the truth, she would be devastated.

During my childhood I existed as if in a dreamlike state. All kinds of fears and anxieties and ambivalences arose as I began to awaken sexually. I felt conflicted and guilty. Like many, I struggled with my anger, dulling it with alcohol during my teens. For a brief time when I was thirteen I had a boyfriend, and another when I was fifteen, but I did not become sexually active until I was eighteen. In my last year of high school, I often cut class. I was secretive about what I was doing and where I was going; I frequented discos and smoked cigarettes in a sneaky kind of rebellion.

I attended the University of Puerto Rico for a year before dropping out. My mother and my stepfather were getting a divorce, and he was starting to freak out. As we became more rebellious and refused to go by the rules, I think he feared we would disclose the sexual abuse.

When he offered me a ticket to New York, I took it. I had a feeling about my own power; I realized that I could make my own decisions, and as long as I didn't need my parents to provide for my food, clothing, and shelter, I could set out on my own.

Acknowledging my anger toward my mother was one of the hardest things I have ever done. The first time I said anything about how she might have protected us was in 1983, when I was pregnant with my second daughter, Tania. It took months for me just to say, in a low and gentle tone, "I really wish you had been there." In some ways I was still protecting her. It was easier for me to focus my anger on my stepfather than to confront my anger toward her. But my mother is not a fragile person. She handles conflict directly and well. Years earlier, when I finally told her what had happened, we could not have asked for a better reaction. For months she had agonized over whether Daniel should go to Puerto Rico and spend time with his father ("A boy needs his father"), and I finally snapped, "Bullshit. Let me tell you what kind of father he was." Her jaw dropped, and she burst out crying. She felt angry and betrayed. Together we pondered what the next step would be. My mother has a wonderful sense of drama, and she imagined that we might confront him like the chorus in a Greek play, singing, "I accuse you, I accuse you." Then, one by one, we'd dump buckets of paint on his head: "Brown is for the lives you've covered in shit, yellow is for your coward's eyes, green is for envy, red is for the blood on your hands." I said, "Mom, I don't think that is really practical. But it's a great image."

> Finally I found the courage to stand up to him and say, "Get the hell out of this bedroom, and don't ever come here again."

Finally we agreed on a plan: We would fly to Puerto Rico, join my sister and brother, and go to my stepfather's office and confront him. My mother called my stepfather and said that she wanted to meet with him one evening after work to talk about Daniel's visiting rights. The evening came, and my mother walked in first, followed by my sister, my brother, and me. My stepfather sat at his desk, and as we faced him my mother screamed, "I know what you have been doing all these years! All of Puerto Rico is going to know the filth you are!" He became fearful and grabbed her by the hair, and my brother and I grabbed him. He turned ashen. We made my stepfather sit down and try to explain himself. "Those were just fatherly caresses," he protested, but my mother said, "You don't pick locks to engage in fatherly caresses." Suddenly he wrenched himself away from us and jumped out the second-floor window. He jumped up from where he had fallen and screamed for the police. The next day we were arrested at the airport. In the end we got off, but it was expensive. My stepfather finally dropped the charges when he realized the publicity would be bad for him.

My mother is an incredible person who has left her mark on many agencies and people over the years. To me, that is all well and good, but it was her reaction to my stepfather's abuse that gave me the sense that the advocacy work she had done for children everywhere, she was willing to do for us. Going to bat for us was the most healing thing she could have done. The experience of the confrontation was very liberating for me.

On a professional level, the direction I have taken is in part a result of my experience with abuse. I am the chief psychiatrist of a unit at San Francisco General Hospital that treats general psychiatric patients. My unit specializes in the care of women and Latino patients, over eighty percent of whom have histories of abuse. I devote most of my energy in teaching to talking about abuse as an issue for patients we see. I think I am good at what I do. I have gotten to the place now where I call things the way I see them. I am polite and all that, but my style is to be direct. My mother is that way, too.

I met my husband, Stan, in a community clinic when I was a premed student. He had just finished his residency. We started living together right before I started medical school, and our daughter Amanda was born three months into my fourth year of medical school. Stan and I have been together for eighteen years.

When Amanda was young, I had a hard time disciplining her. Day in and day out I found myself in a battle with a four-year-old. In order to understand why I was so ambivalent about setting limits, I entered therapy. By my second visit to the therapist, I had discovered that I was pregnant with my second child. I knew I needed to understand this issue before I had two children. Pregnancy totally motivated me. What emerged in therapy was that in part I had trouble setting limits on my child because on an unconscious level I was afraid that if she was a good girl, bad things would happen to her. Gradually I realized that she didn't have to protect herself; she had a mother who protects her. She had me. After that, the task of providing my child with necessary limits that made it possible for her to sleep through the night and act politely toward others was easier. With my second daughter, Tania, I have had those conflicts much less.

As a mother I feel I pay a lot more attention to my children than my mother did to me. I am more present; I talk to them constantly and give them my thoughts on a multitude of issues. If it were necessary to choose between my job and my kids, they would come first. I believe strongly that you can talk all you want to about politics and wax philosophical about women's rights, but if you can't give love and time and attention to your own children, it doesn't matter. Women should be able to take as much time as they want to raise children. Time off should also be available for men. However, in this country, if you don't have a lot of money, then the economic realities of raising a family often make that difficult.

My identity as a Puerto Rican and Latina is bound up with my identity as a woman. Both my identities, as a Latina and a woman, are intrinsic to the work that I do as a psychiatrist. A lot of the issues that American feminism struggles with are specific to American feminism and are not issues in the rest of the world. For that reason, I think that a lot of the female population in this country, women of color in particular, feel isolated from American feminism, with its ethnocentric, nationalistic focus. We need to make the analysis more global in perspective. For example, a big issue in American feminism is equality in the workplace. That issue is very different for women of color because they share that aspect of discrimination with their men. To me, being a feminist means being politically aware of power dynamics as they relate to gender.

I hope to continue to maintain a balance between personal satisfactions, family satisfactions, and work satisfactions. Playing the guitar and dancing recharge me for the work I do on a day-to-day basis. My work can be draining. I deal with a lot of extreme personalities in a tense environment. When I come home from work, I try to put it behind me and turn into my kids' mom, or pick up my guitar, or take a dance class. There are a lot of things I would love to do with leisure time, but I don't have as much of that now as I would like.

I am a public figure in some respects. When I go to Nicaragua, I am the representative for an organization at the academic level. But being a public figure like my mother does not interest me. I am proud of her, and I think she has contributed significantly to society, but I have missed having her present for me. She has a hard time saying no. This business of having important roles is very seductive. When she and Eddie, her current husband, were looking for a place to retire, I urged them to move to California. They debated it for a long time but finally agreed to come, since most of their grandchildren are here. But she's so busy that she rarely sees them. I told her, "I didn't invite you to California to be traipsing all over the world. I want you to be a grandmother to your grandchildren."

My mom is caring and kind-hearted, with strong morals and strong opinions. She has handed her social consciousness and her sense of justice down to us and her grandchildren. She has the ability to reflect on a thing and admit a mistake, which makes all the difference in our relationship as adults. I feel very close to her now. Standing up for us in the situation with my stepfather was an incredibly powerful model of what you can do as a human being to confront injustice for your family and the people you love. Right now my mother is as happy as she has ever been; she has found a real balance in her life. I just wish she were more present for me, which is evidence of how enduring childhood longings are.

LAURA BRAININ-RODRIGUEZ

A Daughter's Story

I am constantly approached by people, especially in public settings, who say, "Your mother is so wonderful. You're so lucky she's your mother." And she was a good mother in terms of the values she passed on, the intelligence and the passion. But I didn't feel particularly mothered. She was never present in the traditional sense that moms are supposed to be present. On the positive side, I learned that women study or go to school and do things with their lives. It never occurred to me to be a housewife; it didn't even seem like an option. But at the same time I felt resentful that she was gone so much. I always felt she wanted to be the mother of the world but not my mother.

My mother has been very active in the area of reproductive rights and the prevention of child abuse, as well as in the public-health field, shaping health policy around AIDS. She has been there for innumerable young women. But with her own children she was often emotionally absent and at times irritable. My siblings and I had a joke when we were growing up about how you'd be telling her a story and she'd be going, "Uh-huh," and then you'd get to a point where you'd ask her a question and she'd answer, "Uh-huh," and you'd realize that she hadn't heard anything, not a single word. It could be very frustrating. She had a wonderful bedside manner for all these other children, but by the time she got home she was often depleted. She rarely helped with homework or asked if it was done; it was just assumed that we would do it. It would have been nice to have felt more deliberately nurtured into science or into an intellectual interest.

My relationship with my mother is now usually good. It has been forged in struggle. We have been able to be more real with each other, and we fight to explain our points of view. As a woman, my mother was asked to make choices that most men do not have to, between engaging in a livelihood you enjoy and for which you feel a calling, and parenting. She has done so much, and she has worked very hard. It had to be difficult.

I was born in Lorain, Ohio, in January 1951. My parents divorced and my mother took my brother, my sister, and me to Puerto Rico when I was two. Soon after the divorce, my mother remarried. In some ways my stepfather was unusual for a man in the 1950s: He took care of the kids while my mother went to medical school, and he cooked and cleaned and shopped. But he was also profoundly cold and certainly sadistic. He used to beat us with a belt, but when we told our mother, she was so busy trying to get through school that she would only say, "We'll talk about it later." We had the sense that our mother didn't want to undermine our stepfather's authority, since he was the parent overseeing us most of the time. But we were dismayed. My mother says now that she was unaware of the extent of the physical punishment, which is conceivable, since she was out doing clinics and studying, and he had long periods of unsupervised time with us. But the physical abuse eventually turned to sexual abuse.

> She had a wonderful bedside manner for all these other children, but by the time she got home she was often depleted.

When I was about nine, or possibly younger, my stepfather began coming into our room at night. I would wake up to find him fondling me. At first it felt nightmarish, not real. I remember the room being completely dark and not being able to see anything, and then falling back to sleep. My sister, now a psychiatrist, says that that is a symptom of dissociation; that it probably happened more than either of us can remember, but you learn to leave your body. I didn't even notice that it was happening to her. In hindsight, I realize that the sexual abuse started when my mother began her internship and ended when she finished her residency. It probably occurred when she was out on call.

The abuse continued until I was about thirteen. At different points all of us were in therapy with different psychologists and therapists, except for my stepfather. Though only my sister and I knew of the abuse, we were all in distress. It permeated the house. My mother was tremendously depressed but had no idea why. My youngest brother, Daniel, was acting out, and my brother David was a juvenile delinquent. I became a compulsive overeater. From age seventeen to age twenty-nine I was thirty-five pounds too heavy. As a trained nutritionist, I work with a lot of people with eating disorders. I know that there is a high association between eating disorders and sexual abuse.

When I was twelve I nearly told my mother what was happening, but my sister talked me out of it. We needed to protect Mom. On some level I think we felt responsible for the demise of her first marriage, as kids are wont to, so it was years before the truth came out. Since then, my mother has expressed many times that she wishes she had had the capacity to choose better male role models for us. I have never given her grief about it or made her feel guilty. I've worked through my anger. I've been fairly sympathetic with the quandary she found herself in. The bottom line for me is that she was not the perpetrator and when she did find out about the abuse, she did not protect my stepfather.

Coming through that experience was hard work. I was not able to resolve the weight issue until halfway through graduate school. My major tasks were to learn to love myself and to gain self-esteem. Balancing those led to a resolution of my food issues.

During high school in Puerto Rico I became a hippie; I had long hair, went barefoot, smoked dope, and rejected traditional values. Since we weren't really Puerto Rican, I always felt like an outsider. I was part Jewish and the product of a divorced family, both of which, in a Catholic country, were considered bad things. Also, our family did not practice any religion. My mother was raised in Catholic schools, but, hating their hypocrisy, she put us in Protestant schools, where they took roll call on Monday to see if you had gone to church. It didn't matter what church you went to, as long as you went. We didn't go, and it was very embarrassing. All I wanted was to be a Catholic. You could do whatever you pleased and then confess, and it was all over. Besides, the Catholics could dance, and enjoy music, and paint their faces. As an adult, I am profoundly cynical about organized religion because of its misogyny and hypocrisy. I would rather go for a walk in the woods.

Early on in my college career I realized I had no direction and no purpose being in school, so I dropped out of Barnard and returned to Puerto Rico, where I did arts and crafts for a few years. Eventually I went to Hunter College in New York and then got my degrees at UC–Berkeley. I was good at sciences and enjoyed school, but the expectation that because I was my mother's daughter I would become a physician killed it for me. Also, I do not believe in the way that Western science views health, breaking the body into little systems that are discrete and unrelated to one another. I didn't have the forbearance to fake it and play the game long enough to get through school; I am too anti-authoritarian for that. So I decided to become a nutritionist.

When I was twenty-three another event altered my life: I was assaulted by five strangers in a national forest in Puerto Rico. I was skinny-dipping with a friend when a gang suddenly appeared and began taunting us. I reached down to get some rocks to throw at them, and then they got very angry and grabbed me by the hair and slapped me and threw me against the rocks. My friend just froze. I tried talking the gang out of it, and then I tried getting away from them, but it was useless. They threatened me with a gun and beat me up, and one of them raped me.

Because I had no faith in the system, I did not go to the authorities. Puerto Rico is a violent place, and there is a lot of violence against women: domestic violence, sexual abuse, and assaults from strangers. As a result of what happened to me, I was no longer naive and trusting. I became an expert in self-defense. Now I carry tear gas, I own a stun gun, and I would not hesitate to kill or maim anyone who tries to hurt me. Because I am a small woman, almost child-sized, I have to compensate with body language and mental energy; otherwise, I fear, I'll be taken advantage of. Feeling afraid detracts from one's focus and one's ability to get on in life. In a feminist future, I want to feel safe.

My mother taught me to think of women as equals, at least theoretically, but I don't think my mother started calling herself a feminist until the seventies. Most certainly I call myself a feminist. I define feminism as the belief that women are entitled to all the rights of being human—respect, equal pay for equal work, appreciation, the right to walk the streets in safety, the right to be as fully developed and accomplished as is humanly possible within one's circumstances. It is entitlement to a full life.

I have had moments of activism. I was active with the American Friends Service Committee in the eighties; I was on a producer-consumer project that promoted inner-city food access and linking farmers to people, and before that I was part of the Puerto Rican Socialist Party for a few years. There were periods of my life when I would be out of the house four nights a week because I had a meeting, and I finally looked at my life and said, "This is not working." My problem is that I hate meetings: Give me a task, and I'll do it. I think I have a little streak of hyperactivity, so it is hard for me to sit for long periods of time talking out policies but not doing anything.

I just started a full-time job with the San Francisco Department of

Public Health. The work is interesting and seems quite worthwhile. We'll see how I do with the set schedule. For nine years I kept a part-time job at Stanford University, which gave me some stability and benefits, and then I consulted. This arrangement gave me the option of having three- and four-day weeks if I wished. That is how I wanted to live my life. I hate to be monitored.

In some ways I have surpassed my mother. I have no trouble asking for what I deserve from people seeking my knowledge and expertise. My mother has great difficulty in that area. I remember one conversation with her where she had spoken at a conference at a hospital in Chicago and I asked, "So, how much did they pay you?" She said, "Oh, no, I should be paying them." I told her I was sure that the hospital had a fund for honoraria for their speakers. She asked, and was appalled to learn that they did, but that if you don't ask, they don't offer. She also found out that if you don't mention your fee, they usually suggest a fee that is higher than you would have thought to ask for. I had to teach her that you get only what you ask for. You have to be profoundly specific. That is what men have always done.

It is important to me to make things work at a personal as well as a professional level. They have to be integrated, not separate. I have never married, nor have I children. I would not be interested in being married unless I was married to a soulmate—someone who is really there for me. I don't particularly want to have children. By now I am at peace with not ever being a biological parent. If I were partnered to a man who very much wanted children, I might consider adoption, though I wouldn't do it on my own.

I haven't felt the need for long vacations because I have tried to maintain an ongoing balance between work and play in my life. I don't know how full-time work will change this for me. I am not as concerned with pleasing people as my mother is; I refuse to let myself get coerced into unrealistic deadlines. I won't make myself crazy trying to meet someone else's schedule. I don't know if my mother perceives herself as being stressed, but she tends to put up with more than I do. I would like her to slow down. She is just beginning to enjoy life. I constantly urge her to block out time for vacations. She went on a ski trip recently and really liked it.

I think my mother is a little driven at times. If I want to move at a slower pace, there is not much room to do that in her presence. If she has an agenda and she wants to get something done, she will push to get it done. If you happen to be in the way, or if you want to do things differently, it is a struggle: You have to stand your ground or bail out. Sometimes I find myself going along and then feeling depleted.

My mother is a very principled person and has a strong inner core. I think that certain of my values, a world vision and perspective, have come from her. She has an enormous capacity and willingness to go after what she wants, as long as it's for someone else's benefit. I have learned persistence from her. She is intense; I think of myself as a pretty energetic person, and she leaves me in the dust. She also has a wonderful childlike quality, an enthusiasm and joyfulness, that enables her to see things in a way that seems new and fresh. She is very determined— in a good way. I have learned from her that there is nothing to be gained by being a passive spectator in life.

Alix and Polly, 1972.

Polly and Alix, 1995.

Alix Kates Shulman
and
Polly Shulman

Alix KATES SHULMAN, a writer and lecturer and the mother of two grown children, was born in Cleveland, Ohio, in 1932. She earned her MA in humanities from New York University. In 1969 she wrote a widely publicized article, "A Marriage Agreement," which was based on the proposition that women and men should play equal roles in taking care of their children and household. Her first novel, *Memoirs of an Ex-Prom Queen,* was published in 1972 and became a best-seller. Shulman has written ten books, lectures regularly on aspects of contemporary literature, feminism, anarchism, and various social issues, and teaches writing and literature. Her latest book, *Drinking the Rain: A Memoir,* was published in 1995. She lives part of the year in Manhattan with her partner, Scott York, and part of the year on an island off the coast of Maine.

POLLY SHULMAN, an editor and journalist, was born in Manhattan in 1963. After attending Hunter College High School, she studied math at Yale University, from which she received her BA in 1984. She worked at the *Village Voice* for ten years, as an editor at the "Voice Literary Supplement," before recently taking a position as senior editor at *Discover* magazine. A resident of Park Slope, Brooklyn, Shulman also writes freelance reviews and articles.

ALIX KATES SHULMAN

A Mother's Story

It wasn't until I became a mother that I felt the defeat and humiliation of being female. Before my first child was born, in 1961, long before the women's movement, I'd been defiant and ambitious; from puberty on I'd planned never to have children. Because of my androgynous name, secretly I considered myself a boy, but one who enjoyed using feminine wiles as a tactic in the war between the sexes. Then, as I approached thirty (in those days, the cutoff age for having children), I called a truce in the war, and the day I gave birth I surrendered, abandoning my independence, fearing that to fight on would endanger the children. To have done otherwise seemed selfish—and useless, too, since I believed motherhood to be my destiny. Acceptance seemed the only dignified stance toward what felt like an inevitable defeat.

I had been married a total of fifteen years when the women's movement erupted into my life. My children were four and six. Feminism reversed the submission and compromise that were part of the surrender of marriage. I no longer felt I had to sacrifice either myself or my children; I could carry my children with me into the future we were creating. Feminism gave me back my defiant voice, enabling me again to stand up and be active in the world instead of passively accepting the marginality I had felt condemned to once I had children. Feminism gave me a way to understand, perhaps escape, my predicament and be a mother with pride and honor. It unified the conflicting parts of me, restoring and legitimating my rebelliousness. Feminism was the tool with which I could mend my life and rejoin the world.

I was born on August 17, 1932, in Cleveland. My father was a lawyer, my mother a housewife who'd been forced by the then-current laws to quit her teaching job when she married. I had a conventional white middle-class suburban childhood, except that my father and I had wonderful ongoing intellectual rapport. He was a family man; he set up a card table in the living room to write his briefs, and I learned to write by watching him. He encouraged me, gave me books we could discuss. My mother was also a reader, and my father used to say, "Your mother is really the smart one." But since my parents followed traditional gender roles, it didn't seem to matter that she was smart and in college. (At six, I watched her walk down the aisle in cap and gown to receive her BA.) She became a project designer for the WPA—a job she loved but gave up when World War II started, because otherwise, with two breadwinners in the family, my father would have been drafted. After the war she bought into the back-to-the-kitchen propaganda and became an unpaid community organizer, sometimes contemptuously referred to as a "clubwoman." Because I loved them both, in my teens I felt divided by my parents' values: the social strivings of my mother versus the self-contained independence of my father.

In college I had a long affair with a married professor who instilled in me a desire to live the life of the mind. I fell in love with books and learning. It was very sexy, exciting; my professor-lover sent me off to get a diaphragm, and it became my symbol of freedom and rebellion. My rebellion and power were sexual, and I was determined never to yield my power to any man. I thought sex was the main power a woman had. I didn't believe in marrying "for love," which seemed far too ephemeral. Better to choose someone who would respect you and lead the kind of life you wanted to lead.

In 1953, at twenty, I went off to Columbia as a graduate student. I wanted to be a philosopher, but women were not philosophers then. Seeing all three women in my department treated like freaks, I soon married a fellow graduate student, dropped out of school, and became an editor to support us. My marriage was empty and lasted only five years. Then in 1959, feeling the press of time, I married the father of my children, who looked to me like a family man. That marriage lasted twenty-five years. At first it was exciting, romantic, close. But after we had children, it became embattled.

With the birth of my children (a boy and a girl, the fifties' ideal family) my whole life changed. Now it belonged to others. In my first marriage I had earned money and maintained my independence and spunk; in my second marriage I gave up freedom for family. Having chosen to become a mother, I gave it my all; soon being a good mother became my new purpose in life, which I pursued with pleasure and verve. Still, some part of me mourned my lost independence, and some instinct kept me from withdrawing from the world entirely. Terrified of not being able to support myself if my husband ran out on us (and from the moment I had children it was clear the honeymoon was over), I tried always to have some freelance job to do at home—for emergency money and to keep a toe in the world, especially after my husband began having affairs. No matter how vulnerable and humiliated I felt over the loss of my independent self, at least I still lived in Greenwich Village; I hadn't given up utterly and moved to the suburbs, where I would have been totally dependent.

I loved raising my children in the city, where I could participate in the civil rights and antiwar movements (albeit as a woman) and take my children to play in Washington Square Park. I delighted in watching them grow and acquire language. I taught them to read and draw, sew and cook, do new math. I took them often to the library and read them books. The first books I wrote were for them, for children—that's how I became a writer.

One day in 1967 a friend who had heard young feminists talking on the radio called me excitedly and said, "These women sound like us! We have to go to a meeting." Suddenly the world opened up and everything felt possible again. Soon I joined Redstockings, WITCH, New York Radical Feminists. I couldn't get enough.

I never felt any conflict between the movement and motherhood. Feminism healed my conflicts. Once I joined the movement I never again felt I had to sacrifice anything or choose between being a mom and having my own independent life. To me, all the sacrifice and compromise preceded feminism, and feminism reversed them. In fact, it was as a mother that I most deeply engaged with feminism. I spoke up for mothers, defended mothers. To the young women in my group I was that rarity, a genuine mother-housewife, who could speak of motherhood not from theory but from experience.

Not that being a mother in the women's movement was easy; motherhood was always one of the great explosive divides. Women without children often felt stereotyped by society as incomplete women, failures; those with children felt confined and marginalized. Each side thought the other privileged. Single women without children said, "You have the respect of society"; mothers said, "You have freedom." There wasn't much mutual understanding. But in my own life, motherhood and feminism were integrated from the start. One of the first projects I organized, Feminists on Children's Media, the pioneer group investigating sexism in children's literature, I embraced as both mother and feminist. (In 1969 the American Library Association offered us a big slot at their convention, and we met every month for a year in my apartment, preparing a talk, a slide show, and a bibliography, "Little Miss Muffet Fights Back." Few librarians had heard the word *sexism* before we presented our program.)

By then I was writing—short stories and children's books. But I always felt I had to fit writing into the interstices between domestic and maternal duties. I would drop the children at nursery school, run home, take the phone off the hook, and write for three hours until I had to pick them up, which was the end of my writing day. I wrote *Memoirs of an Ex-Prom Queen* that way—the most efficient writing I ever did.

I thought I was lucky to have work I loved that I could do at home, because it enabled me to be a full-time, hands-on mother. I considered that a great gift to both me and my children, ensuring them both my maternal presence and the model of my passionate engagement. But it turns out what they saw was something else: a disciplined, invulnerable person, with standards hard for them to live up to, who was always working.

I took over the study for my office—a beautiful little room overlooking Washington Square Park. I worked there every day. My husband was in some ways supportive, but in other ways he subverted my work. Even after I began publishing, he acted as if I had no right to that room (he had two offices!) or to my own time. No longer the submissive, compliant wife we had both expected me to be when we married and had children, I fought back, even though my ideal had been the gentle family I'd been raised in. My husband was a fierce fighter, and in fighting him I became fierce myself—something I now regret. When he was away (which was much of the time), the children and I were harmonious and close, but when he was home there was contention. Back then I thought the children could only benefit from those principles I struggled so hard for. But what they experienced was conflict between their parents, not my principles. Our constant conflict was hard on them, as was our divorce, years later.

In 1969 I wrote "A Marriage Agreement," published in the underground feminist journal *Up From Under.* By proposing that men and women play equal roles in taking care of their children and their households, it was a defiant manifesto proclaiming the status quo no longer acceptable. As the subject of a 1972 six-page spread in *Life* magazine, it caused a furor. When *Redbook* reprinted it, thousands of women wrote in. Some asked, "How did you get your husband to agree?" The answer is, either he agrees or the marriage is over; but I never said so outright, and I began to feel there was something inauthentic about my not making clear how much struggle was involved.

Despite our best efforts, our agreement didn't work very well. My husband tried to pass as a feminist, but in fact he was very angry. It was as if he had been deprived of his birthright—a helpmate who would have dinner on the table and the children ready for bed when he came home. I think my husband was humiliated by feminism. He was no longer the king, the center. I wanted him to take responsibility; he wanted to escape. Once he left for a year and then returned "for the children's sake," but the marriage was essentially over. By then we lived separate lives, separate sex lives, everything.

I was very open about sex with my children. I talked freely about birth control, about orgasms, about women's sexuality. They had all the information, but since their parents weren't sexual together, they didn't have a loving sexual relationship in their lives as a model. The important sexual relationships of their parents were secret affairs with others—several of mine lasted years—but the children never observed them.

In some ways, the true erotic center of my life was the women's movement. That was where my passions lay—I was energized, stimulated, excited by our meetings, conversations, my women's group. The new ideas were erotically charged for me. With feminism I became self-confident, and I dumped my self-hatred and the feeling that I was this yucky, creepy female. Suddenly, being female was honorable; it was great. Dropping my body shame, I was finally able to have orgasms and to ask for what I wanted physically. I felt respected as I hadn't before. So feminism and sexuality and sexiness and erotic energy and power were all connected for me.

A movement so charged and challenging for me, I thought, must have a similar effect (through osmosis?) on my children. I assumed that my daughter, a female, would be as invested as I in feminism's success, that my son would be the "new man" for the "new woman." I never realized that my children could feel displaced by or jealous of my work. It didn't occur to me that they might experience the movement as a barrier between them and their mother.

I may have been fuzzy about love when it came to men, but I knew what it meant when it came to children. My children were the center of my world, the transforming experience of my life. All my novels are about the centrality of the mother-child relationship.

Polly was four when I became a feminist. I felt saved by feminism and believed Polly was saved along with me. My in-laws treated my son and daughter quite differently: They wanted my son to shine and Polly to be a sweet, passive girly-girl in pink dresses. I felt my feminism rescued her from that fate. From the beginning I took Polly seriously. I think feminism enabled me to nurture her best qualities: her startling perceptiveness, her wit, her depth, her wide-ranging talents. We were very close. Despite our differences, from the temperamental to the metabolic, we always had a conversation that was real and deep and never stopped, and I loved her as I loved myself.

> In some ways, the true erotic center of my life was the women's movement. That was where my passions lay.

As a child, Polly had a certain feminist consciousness. In junior high she founded a math club to train younger students for the math team and a literary magazine to be run collectively, without an editor—a feminist ideal. In elementary school she befriended a pariah and made people change their behavior toward her. Thinking back, I'm struck by how brave, independent-minded, and principled she's always been, though she's not an activist in the conventional sense. What you breathe as air isn't what challenges you, and she grew up breathing the air of feminism. The problems of her generation are different from those of mine, and in some ways I can't comprehend them. The world she inhabits is a hard world because, although more is permitted women now, so much more is expected of them. Which means increased pressure and anxiety. The idea that I could save her along with me was a utopian delusion—the idea, which some of us held for a brief moment, that by making feminist changes we'd somehow make things easy for our children. The big problems—sexism, racism, violence, poverty—are probably as great as before, though different.

I tried to teach my children to take nothing on faith: Decide for yourself, question authority. But, of course, that instruction came from me, the big authority. Only now am I beginning to learn that my children could not easily oppose me, in part because I hold my views so passionately.

Exposing my children to the publicity that came with making my feminism public opened them to the ridicule and envy of other children. As Polly has made me see, she didn't get to choose how she was represented, by either the media or me. My being a public person was always double-edged. As she herself has written, the children of feminists or of any revolutionaries are Exhibit A of the revolution. They feel as if how they grow up and perform will elicit a judgment from the world on the revolution itself (isn't that how this book will be read?), so they're never free.

I'm not sure there is such a thing as "feminist child-rearing." First, there are so many different feminisms. But beyond that, how you parent involves not just your political commitment or ideology but your whole sociological and psychic makeup. I happily took all sorts of risks when I alone had to face the consequences, but I was reluctant to take risks for my children. (In this sense, I suspect parenting may be inherently conservative.) Giving up security and challenging the status quo always bring on anxiety, and my anxieties focused on my children, whom I tried to protect and support, leaving them perhaps too little room to make their own instructive mistakes. Ironically, I so wanted them to be strong and independent that the force of my desire may actually have hampered them. Another ironic consequence of being a feminist mother is that we often find it difficult to speak candidly about the liabilities of motherhood in our society for fear our children will take our complaints personally. Instead we may mute our criticism, causing our children the confusion of double messages.

I don't think feminism necessarily determines how you live or how you mother. It's just one part of life. Mothering is so unsupported in our society that every attempt to raise a child is a complex juggling act, and where you decide to stand on principle is quite subjective. In the end, I think all you can do, feminist or not, is try to raise your children lovingly as best you can, pass on what you know, and keep your fingers crossed.

POLLY SHULMAN

A Daughter's Story

I consider myself a feminist, though the ways in which I act as a feminist are not as public as my mother's. My mother pushed me through any number of protest marches in my stroller, enough to last me a lifetime. Don't ever ask me to go to another march! The same goes for the kind of activism where people sit in a room together and argue about whose turn it is to use the microphone. I spent a lot of my childhood listening to those arguments, and that isn't how I want to spend my time. You might say that's my luxury, that if my mother and her cohorts hadn't carried their signs up and down and wrangled over their schisms, I'd be locked up in a kitchen somewhere. (Mom taught my brother how to cook, but she didn't teach me.) Fair enough. I have the luxury of assuming feminist ideas and writing from those assumptions. I believe that feminism is about making sure that as many choices as possible are open to women and men about how to live their lives, and that we aren't restricted to rules that somebody else thinks we ought to obey. Ironically, though, Mom and her political sisters could be pretty restrictive in their rules.

I was born on February 2, 1963, in Manhattan. My mother was a "housewife," as they called them then, and my father worked in his father's textile business. Though they didn't get divorced until I was in my twenties, I can hardly remember a time when my parents didn't seem to hate each other. It's hard to say why, exactly. At the time, my mother used the terms of feminism to explain their war, calling my father a "sexist tyrant" and other politically charged names, which seemed to fit him fairly well. Almost as if to please her, he responded by acting like one. This put her in the right, where she liked to be, but it must have been an infuriating way to run a relationship.

In feminism, my mother found a framework and a structure for her moral righteousness. My father didn't have anything parallel to fall back on. But my mother wasn't a feminist when they got married—that came when I was six or so, a decade into their marriage. He had signed up for marriage to a beautiful, charming, kittenish wife who stayed home and took care of the kids and gave dinner parties for his business associates. She changed the rules on him and then was outraged that he didn't like it. I remember his bitter resentment at the housekeeping tasks she assigned him, not because of the tasks but because he was required to do them. In fact, he was always the one who vacuumed and mopped and scrubbed. My mother never did those things.

My mother says that they tried not to fight when we were around, but I heard them whispering and saw them trying to kill each other with glances. We lived in a big, rambling apartment on Washington Square, and I slept in what had once been the maid's room, a tiny room at the end of the kitchen, at the back of the apartment. I spent a lot of time hiding in that room or in some sort of metaphorical equivalent. I was afraid, but I didn't know what I was afraid of; I had no vocabulary for what awful things might happen.

Around the time I started school, my mother started writing and became successful fairly quickly; *Memoirs of an Ex-Prom Queen* was a best-seller. She also became an active feminist. People were always coming up to me and saying, "I saw your mother's picture in the paper," which I hated. I felt they were busting my cover, and there was no room for me. They were hauling me out of the tiny room I had made for myself to hide in. At the same time, my father, who had taken over his father's business, went bankrupt. Tensions were already high, but her success and his failure pushed their marriage over the edge.

As time went on, my father was around less and less, and my mother closed the family ranks to keep him out. When he left for a year—like a cliché from a chauvinist-pig joke, he ran off with the twenty-year-old receptionist—my mother, brother, and I became a unit. It was hard to bridge the gap when my parents decided to reconcile. My father either didn't try very hard or didn't know how. After a while I felt he didn't know me anymore. He had jobs out of town and gradually began spending more and more time away.

It never occurred to me that I had picked sides, because my mother never explicitly asked me to. In subtle ways, though, she ensured my loyalty to her. She made it seem as if she and my brother and I were a wonderful little community and my father didn't deserve to be a part of our club. I knew it wasn't my fault that my parents hated each other, but I was miserably depressed and hated myself. I spent a lot of time being sad privately. I thought I was sad because the girls in my class were mean, or because I was bored at school, or because I hadn't done my history paper. I never considered that I might be unhappy because my mother and father were fighting. That would have been a betrayal.

At the Friends' Seminary in Manhattan I was in a class with the same twenty-five kids from kindergarten through sixth grade. The teachers tried to teach Quaker values, such as social responsibility, but the kids weren't particularly Quaker. They were ordinary New York City private-school kids, interested in what each other was wearing and who had a better Barbie. My mother's ideology didn't help. Partly in reaction to her traditional girlhood, she was puritanical in her dress code. Anything that seemed like dressing up she considered sexist. When a friend told my mother about the androgynous jumpsuits in the boys' department of the Sears catalog, she was delighted. After that, Teddy and I went to school in these horrible blue denim jumpsuits that zipped up the front, and the other kids made fun of us.

Mom, of course, looked great in those jumpsuits. Somehow, in a radical and careless way, she always managed to look great. She is wiry and delicate-boned and energetic. I was a chubby little kid and a gawky adolescent, and I thought of myself as horribly ugly. I wasn't one of the class goats, but I was quiet and studious and considered myself a weirdo, a big, enormously awkward Martian. I felt helpless, imprisoned by fate in a Martian body. I must have taken my mother's strictures against using one's looks to get power seriously—much more seriously than she did herself. Or maybe I was just trying not to compete with her.

I tried to please my mother by fighting her fights in my own life. In grade school the boys took over the schoolyard for their ball games and the girls were relegated to the corner. I never wanted to play a ball game in my life, but I knew that what was happening was sexist, so I organized the girls to protest to the teacher. The boys were furious; they knew I didn't want to play ball, so why was I ruining their game?

Finally, at Hunter College High School, I found a niche for myself. Hunter drew students from the five New York boroughs. You had to pass an entrance exam to get in. Imagine—a whole school made up of the kids who'd been the class nerd in their grade school. I entered Hunter with the first coed class; the upper classes were all girls. Growing up with my mother had prepared me for the experience of being at a feminist place, and I loved it. My friends were the ill-groomed rebels: lesbians, red-diaper babies, computer geeks.

I didn't rebel against my mom in high school. People were amazed at how well we got along and often told us how lucky we were. She gave me all the freedom anyone could have wanted, and I never used any of it. I never even stayed out late. I thought of us as very close. Except for a few lapses (I kept my room a mess, and I never changed the cat litter), I was a perfect daughter. Because she didn't take disagreement easily, I kept my mouth shut. I didn't even oppose her in my thoughts. Consequently, much of what might have been competition with my mother became cooperation instead. She said we always discussed everything, which basically meant that we discussed everything until I agreed with her or she agreed with me.

> **My friends were the ill-groomed rebels: lesbians, red-diaper babies, computer geeks.**

As part of her ideology, my mother tried to be open about sex. Our family was fairly nude. We went around in our underwear and left the bathroom door open. Mom explained about menstruation by showing me a tampon, how you put it in, where it goes, demonstrating on herself. She also had a speculum lying around that we were supposed to play with. We didn't actually want to play with it—would you?—but she thought it was a great idea.

Despite all this openness, Mom was secretive about her lovers. It was always either a secret between us or a secret I pretended not to know. Her relationships seemed to be more about intrigue and power than affection and warmth. I rarely saw her contented in a relationship when I was growing up (though she's married to a wonderful man now, and they seem comfortable and happy together). She talked about sex as if it were an incredibly difficult project, fraught with all sorts of horrors: The man might not be sensitive to your needs or give you enough pleasure to come. I never got the sense that it was fun.

I didn't want to know as much as my mother wanted to tell me. I heard so much about her sexual experiences that I thought her sex life was *the* sex life. She told me how to have orgasms, but it turned out not to be how I have them at all. For years I couldn't figure it out; I didn't realize that my mother and I might just be different. Despite her encouraging me to have sex, taking me to the doctor to get a diaphragm, and suggesting that I might want my male friends to stay over, I didn't become sexually active until I was in college. I found the idea frightening and repulsive.

Mom was a small, feisty, flirtatious ideologue, rigidly committed to whichever ideology had happened to catch her fancy, until she moved on to the next one. Whatever she believed in, she insisted her family had to believe in, too. I often get mad when she changes her mind about something that used to be absolutely sacred. Meat used to be wicked, but now she and her husband eat a lot of it. We never had Kleenex in the house because it was evil; we used toilet paper to blow our noses. Now facial tissues abound in her home. Growing up, I had no idea there were choices. Isn't that ironic? Isn't that what feminism is supposedly all about? It was as if my mother said, "You are so lucky. You can choose the things I like."

Growing up, it seemed like wherever I went, Mom had already been there. There was no point in doing anything. Mom had already done it, and done it better than I could with my resources, so why bother? She was even better at being a child than I was—she was always more playful, imaginative, and adorable than I could ever hope to be. What was left for me?

Writing is the thing I do best and most intently, but of course it already belongs to my mother. I've always been afraid that I would be a better writer than she is, and she frequently tells me she thinks I am. I'm sure that's one reason I haven't managed to write much of anything. I have a hard time figuring out how to write—not so much which words go where, but how to arrange my attitude toward my life and my responsibilities. More than that, I have trouble believing in my authority. I hem myself in with qualms, maybe to keep myself from turning into a tyrant like Mom.

My mother always wanted power, and she could never get enough of it. That sounds like a nasty criticism, doesn't it? It shouldn't. If our society weren't still so sexist, it would sound like a simple description of an ambitious person stuck in an oppressive situation. Power was a rare and hazardous commodity for women in Mom's generation, and it was hard for them to come by. In her prefeminist days, Mom had a battery of wiles she used to get people, mostly men, to let her do what she liked; when she discovered the women's movement, she reviled her wiles. I think she thought of them as a slave's ways. Still, she never really gave them up. Though it was hard to be the daughter of such an embattled person, the alternative—being the daughter of someone cowed, someone defeated—would have been far worse.

What I admire about my mother is what she did because she was brave; what I don't like about her comes from what she did because she was afraid. She worried about raising us, worried that we would fall down and kill ourselves, worried that our father would leave her with no money, worried that somebody would decide she was a lesbian and take us away from her. She was always anxious. People would say, "Aren't you afraid to raise a family in New York?" but if we hadn't grown up in New York, it would have been worse—then she would have worried that we might bump into a tree. If I have children, I want to worry about them less than my mother worried about me.

I hate that she passed on her fears, but she also passed on her courage. She's enough of a rebel to decide what she wants her life to be like and then go and make it that way. She pretends to be strong in order to convince herself that she is strong, even when she thinks she isn't. But she's stronger than she thinks. Whatever she decides her identity is, she proclaims it from the rooftop, and she fights tooth and nail anyone who tries to attack her for it. She stands up without ambivalence for what she believes in, and she's not afraid to change her mind.

Nina and Evi, 1957.

Evi and Nina, 1989.

Evelyn Torton Beck

and

Nina Rachel Beck

EVELYN TORTON BECK, born in Vienna, Austria, in 1933, is a child survivor of the Holocaust. In 1939 her family narrowly escaped from Austria through Italy, arriving in New York City in 1940. Beck earned her PhD in 1969 at the University of Wisconsin and is now a professor of women's studies and Jewish studies at the University of Maryland at College Park. She is also in training as a clinical psychologist at the Fielding Institute. Author of the much-acclaimed *Nice Jewish Girls: A Lesbian Anthology,* Beck resides in Washington, D.C., with her partner, Columbia University professor Lee Knefelkamp.

NINA RACHEL BECK was born in 1955 in Pittsfield, Massachusetts. Like her mother, she identifies herself as a Jewish lesbian woman. She earned her BS in physical therapy in 1978 at the University of Wisconsin. She has practiced martial arts for twelve years and is a black belt in Aikido and in Kajukenbo Kung Fu. She now resides in Asheville, North Carolina, where she teaches martial arts and works as a physical therapist, primarily with young children who have difficulties with motor function. With her partner, Stacy Jolles, she is the proud mother of Noah Shaya Beck Jolles.

A Mother's Story

Oddly, each time I tell my story, I find myself speaking as a daughter rather than as a mother. This peculiar imbalance reflects both the disproportionate influence of my mother (and the traumatic loss of her mother) and the uneasiness with which I still approach being a mother. But my anxiety seems less strange when I reflect on my history and the trauma of the Holocaust, which early in life marked me for annihilation as a Jew. This knowledge attached itself to my very being and infused every developmental moment in my life. To a survivor, motherhood, the act of reproducing oneself, may feel like an act of hubris, a transgressive affirmation of one's worthiness. And what happens if such a survivor doesn't yet know the baggage she is carrying at the moment of birth?

Though I encouraged my daughter, Nina, to be assertive and to think for herself, I don't think she got her feminism from me. The second wave of feminism was taking hold when I was in my late thirties and she in her teens, and we developed parallel feminist ways of thinking. I was a "prefeminist" feminist; my life choices were feminist choices, though I did not make them in the context of a theory or a movement. I did what I needed to do to survive as a wife and mother.

Survival skills are part of my history as a child survivor of the Holocaust. I was born in Vienna, Austria, the year Hitler came to power. Our small family consisted of my parents and younger brother, and my mother's mother. My mother, a talented writer and avid reader with passionate curiosity and an inventive mind, was never encouraged to use her creativity. Middle-class custom prevented her working outside the home once she married. Childbearing was expected, but my mother, herself an only child, had no interest in being a traditional housewife or mother. As a result, my grandmother, a gentle and kind woman, was my primary caretaker.

Born into the virulently anti-Semitic atmosphere of turn-of-the-century Vienna, my mother internalized a good deal of negative feelings about being Jewish and consciously gave her children British names, Evelyn and Edgar, perhaps as a protection. On the night of November 9, 1938, on what became known as *Kristallnacht,* "the night of broken glass," the Nazis entered our home, arrested my father, confiscated his small business, and shipped him, together with thirty thousand other Jews, to a concentration camp, where he remained imprisoned. On the streets anti-Jewish signs were visible everywhere: NO JEWS ALLOWED; JEWS CANNOT BUY HERE; JEWS GET OUT! We were forced out of our home; I was forced to leave school.

Because I was a pretty little girl with blond curls, my mother often took me on her frequent missions to the Gestapo, where she tried desperately to get my father released. Miraculously, she succeeded, but on condition that he leave the country immediately. When we finally obtained the coveted exit visas we were able to get only four; as a result, my grandmother remained behind. We never saw her again, and only years after the war ended did we hear that she had perished on a train to Auschwitz. Because I could have been sent away to London earlier, I felt responsible for my grandmother's death, as if my mother had had to choose between us.

After leaving Vienna in 1939 we lived in Italy for a year, escaping just before the borders were permanently closed. We arrived in the United States on June 10, 1940, on the last boat out of Italy. To this day one of my most vivid memories is pulling into New York Harbor and everyone running up on deck to see the Statue of Liberty, an image that remains a comfort. I spoke no English when I arrived and had to make sense out of the blur of sounds around me. The first word I remember learning to sound out was M-O-T-H-E-R. I liked school and quickly got up to grade level, but I felt like a perpetual outsider. At the age of eleven, before the war was over and Israel established, I joined a Marxist-Zionist youth group, which gave me a sense of purpose, a place to go, and a chance to belong. There I was introduced to notions of cooperative living and a division of labor that defied traditional gender roles, concepts that feminism later supported.

I grew up with contradictory messages from my free-spirited mother about what it was to be a woman. On the one hand, she pushed me to conform; on the other hand, she let me know how contemptible she thought conformists were. When I reached puberty and began to assert my independence, things got rough between us and I rebelled in earnest. Although my mother complained about my disobedience, I think I actually carried out her unfulfilled dreams, especially the refusal to conform.

I knew about idyllic college life from movies, yet going away to school remained a fairy tale, totally unthinkable both financially and psychologically, so I remained at home and attended Brooklyn College. In those years my parents and I had huge fights about my friends, my "bohemian" dress and hairstyle, my activities. Their constant worrying about my safety haunted me even as I deliberately defied their curfews. My mother became increasingly critical of me, but at the same time she supported my growth and encouraged me to do things my conservative father considered out of bounds, such as traveling alone through Europe when I was eighteen.

My mother was afraid of sex, however, and constantly warned me about "what men want" and how they will leave a girl after they get it. As a result, I married right out of my parents' house in my last year of college, having met my husband in my sophomore year. Although neither of us was ready, there was no other way I could have moved away from home (much less have lived with him) in those days. In that first year of marriage, when I was also in graduate school, we shared household tasks, but things changed when I got pregnant. Abortion was illegal and out of the question. It never occurred to either of us that I could work *and* have a child. Fortunately, my husband found a teaching job at Williams College. We were living in Pittsfield, Massachusetts, when Nina was born.

Having come to motherhood foolishly, unthinkingly, accidentally, I found being home with a baby depressing. I was a distracted mother, anxious to find some way to keep myself intact when the baby's demands felt like threats to my selfhood. Thinking back almost forty years, I have great compassion for that new mother, isolated and alone in that tiny New England town (fiercely Christian, openly racist and anti-Semitic)—certainly not the right place for a Holocaust survivor, a New York City Jew, to give birth.

The next year my husband received a postdoctoral fellowship in New Orleans, and when Nina was almost two we spent the year on a travel grant in Europe. Nina slept in a portable crib in our VW bus. The year was both wonderful and depressing, since I still had no direction or sense of purpose. Nonetheless, we decided to have another child; in those years it was unthinkable to have only one. Upon our return, my husband got a job in Madison, Wisconsin, a move that was traumatic for me. I still thought of New York as home, and despite its beauty Madison seemed an empty place, without vitality. Faculty housing seemed to imprison me. When my son, Micah, was born I became even more depressed. I desperately needed something to occupy my intellect.

As a survivor, I had to figure some way out. Against my husband's wishes, I returned to school and soon got a teaching assistantship that paid for baby-sitters. Few women had careers in the late 1950s, but once I actually enrolled in a PhD program, my husband was quite supportive, encouraging me when I had doubts about my abilities. Returning to school gave me a sense of purpose, which allowed me to enjoy motherhood more. I was so preoccupied with discovering my own capabilities, however, that I wasn't fully present for my children. As a result, they did not have the childhood I would have wished. Often I shut myself into my study to work. Nina resented the process of my PhD and has said that she will never get one. She refuses to place success in the professional world at the center of her life, preferring not to work full-time, perhaps in reaction to what she experienced as my "overfocusing."

I sometimes wonder if daughters have a particular way of getting lost when their mothers are trying to find themselves, especially if the daughter is the firstborn. Nina and I were close for only a few years, around the time I was nursing her (one of the tasks of motherhood I enjoyed the most). Even as a baby, and continuing into childhood, she turned inward when she was upset and rarely told me what was bothering her. Perhaps she felt rejected. Perhaps I did not hear what she said.

During Nina's early adolescent years we fought about her refusal to take on responsibilities within the family. She joined an activist youth group, and to my shock I discovered that she was smoking marijuana there and, even worse, was in love with one of the women leaders. Like a good liberal, I was proud when Nina told me she supported lesbian visibility at feminist events, but it never occurred to me that she might "be one too." I was so freaked out at this discovery, and had so little understanding of what it might mean to be lesbian or gay in a deeply homophobic world, I actually threatened to call the police. My negative response gave her the message that being lesbian was horrible and would ruin her life. This was the low point in our relationship.

An upward turn occurred during a family therapy session when the psychologist assured us that Nina was fine, but what about my husband and me? This refocused my attention from Nina's lesbianism to the contradictions in my marriage, though it took several years before I separated, and several more before I came out as a lesbian myself. I am proud to have been able to let Nina go when she needed to leave home. I convinced my husband that it was better for her to drop out of high school and live on her own than to continue fighting with us. She supported herself by waitressing while earning a high-school equivalency certificate and eventually gaining entry to the University of Wisconsin's physical therapy department. She never moved back in with us again.

> I sometimes wonder if daughters have a particular way of getting lost when their mothers are trying to find themselves, especially if the daughter is the firstborn.

Soon thereafter I completed my PhD and published my first book. Eventually I fought my way into the academy, first by commuting weekly between the East Coast and Madison, and later as a result of a sex-discrimination suit, which I won. Ironically, by the time I got my tenure-track job at the University of Wisconsin–Madison, my marriage was dissolving, and in 1973 I left it. Finally I was free to live outside the pressures of anyone else's script.

In response to feminist theorizing, which made the possibility of loving a woman seem less abnormal, I began to rethink my responses to Nina's coming out and had to acknowledge my own deeply felt life-long emotional ties and some physical attraction to women. Strange as it may seem, my daughter was my role model for my coming out as a lesbian. Freed from patriarchal perspectives, I could more easily see Nina as sturdy, wholesome, and psychologically sound. The notion that I was not necessarily limited to one-half the human race had great appeal, and soon thereafter I fell in love with a woman. Nina was not at all surprised when I came out, since she and her friends had always believed I must be a closet case for being so freaked out about her. Though I didn't officially come out to Nina for an entire year, she, and everyone else in the community, had already figured it out. When my husband left to go to England in 1973, by mutual agreement taking my son with him, Nina and I got to know each other better.

I was over forty when I finally came out as a lesbian. The irony was that by the time I came out, only a few years after Nina, there was a

supportive lesbian-feminist community around me. As a feminist professor I was well known in town, and my coming out was greeted with
enthusiasm, a fact not lost on Nina, for she had come out in a hostile
environment with support only from her circle of friends. Slowly and
steadily we have grown closer over the years, but very gingerly. I am
acutely aware that sharing a lesbian identity creates a common bond,
but it does not create trust or resolve all the tensions inherent in the
mother-daughter relationship.

Over the years, considerable healing has taken place. We still do
not talk much about the past, but its negative effect is clearly erod-
ing. Now that we are both in stable, wonderfully loving, and life-
sustaining relationships, the boundaries between us have softened. Her
Jewish lesbian wedding was a glorious event, which my partner and I
participated in with enthusiasm. It is strangely affirming that Nina
and I are both married to Jewish women. This year I was pleased that
Nina called to ask my advice about a projected move to a closer city,
and she even asked me to meet her there. I was particularly moved
when she called with the good news just as soon as her pregnancy tests
were positive.

In recent years I have experienced Nina as a delightful person with
her own integrity, one whose company I enjoy. But I do have some regrets about the past. I wish I had known how deeply the Holocaust affected me and my mother; I wish I had known what I wanted to do
with my life before I became a mother; I wish I had given Nina the formal Jewish education she asked for as a child; I wish I had not been so
homophobic; I wish I had let her develop within the family; I wish I
had supported her choices; I wish I had understood more about indi-
viduation.

But in spite of my own conflicts about mothering, I feel deeply satisfied that I have raised two wonderful human beings who share many
of my values. I can see in them the same zest for life I feel and that I
remember in my parents—the same optimism that sustained us all. I
am delighted that Nina is a voracious reader. We share a dedication to
Jewish culture and a love of music, especially folk and women's music,
as well as a love of the outdoors and hiking, which we often did as a
family. I am pleased that both my children are open-minded and appreciate cultural differences. We share a love of travel. I would like
more intimacy with Nina, but in truth I might well be overwhelmed
if she shared more of her feelings, especially if she was in pain.

I respect Nina a great deal, both personally and professionally. She is bright, sensitive, and has a good sense of humor. I find her extraordinarily beautiful, not just physically but as if her psyche were written on her face. I am pleased that Nina has had a baby and that she could do so without having to go through a heterosexual marriage. I wish I had had support from my family to work through the traumatic experiences of the Holocaust, which marked my family and probably resonate in my children in ways I have not yet discovered.

Nina has influenced me in a number of ways. I look to her for advice, especially about the body and nontraditional medicine, and for alternative, non-Western ways of seeing the world. She is far more laid-back than I am, and she practices the martial arts of Aikido and Kung Fu seriously. I respect her perspective on the world, though I worry that I have passed on the anxieties that my mother passed on to me, and which I have spent years trying to work through. The things I want for Nina are those I now believe she has achieved for herself: to be healthy and happy, to feel fulfilled, and to use to the fullest the considerable powers and skills she has. Most of all, I want her to feel good in the world, to love, and to feel loved and appreciated, as I now believe she is by her partner, as I feel fortunate to be by mine.

A Daughter's Story

My mother and I became active feminists at about the same time. In many ways I am like her. We both have a strong presence in the world and are involved in educating people and creating change. My parents had high expectations for me and taught me that I was capable, that I could do anything I wanted to do. I never thought that I could do only certain things because I was female. I was told that if I wanted to be a rocket scientist, nothing would stand in my way. In fact, I think I was expected to be a rocket scientist.

When I was born in Pittsfield, Massachusetts, in 1955, my mother had been a graduate student and my father was finishing his PhD. We moved to Madison, Wisconsin, when I was two. I have been told that when my brother, Micah, and I were very little, my mother stayed home and took care of us, but I don't remember those years. When I was five and my brother two, my mother returned to school to work on her PhD, which I resented openly. Neither of my parents was particularly available, and in my memory we were often left alone, at the neighbors', or with a caretaker named Hilda.

My parents became lefties in the sixties. My father was a bigwig in the antiwar movement on campus. When he spoke at rallies and marches, I was proud to tell people that he was my father. My parents' involvement in the antiwar and civil rights movements provided my introduction to politics and the feminist movement.

During this period, I now know, my father wanted to leave the family but stayed "on account of the kids." I remember a lot of yelling and screaming from both my parents. My most vivid memory is of standing between them and pushing them apart, screaming, *"Stop!"* They didn't stop. Both of them are incredibly strong-willed. It doesn't surprise me that there was conflict.

When I was a kid, either my mother was present and very attentive or she was absent. She went back and forth between the extremes. As a shy, introspective kid, too much attention felt invasive; at the same time, I didn't like to feel neglected by her. Her absences took two forms: one was when she was working, and often it felt like work was her priority; the other was a kind of emotional leaving—you could be talking to her and she would seem to be somewhere else. I think that this may be related to being a survivor of the Holocaust. This kind of leaving was and is unpredictable, so I learned to rely on myself. My mother says that early on I stopped wanting her nurture and comfort. I remember pushing her away and thinking, "Just leave me alone. I have my thumb and my blanket and I'll be fine."

My mother has told me that when I was born, western Massachusetts was a very anti-Semitic place. She says that she would look at me and think, "How can I, who was not supposed to survive, bring a daughter into the world? How will she be safe?" I think that she tried not to neglect me in the way her mother had neglected her, but I don't think she knew how to be with me.

I now see my mother trying to make up for the years when she wasn't there. This is sometimes difficult for me to accept. When she wanted to be physically close to me as a kid, I felt overwhelmed. The way she and my father gave attention felt smothering to me, as though some expectation came with it. There were not clear boundaries, and I did not feel that I had the power to choose. Today I try to be very clear in my relationships with children. I always ask, "Can I hug you?" or "Would you like a kiss good night?" I cringe when I hear people saying to a child, "Come here, give me a kiss." I am so aware of what it feels like to be a kid receiving attention that is not comfortable.

From the time I was eight until I left home at sixteen, we moved around a lot. I attended a different school every year. It was exciting but sometimes difficult. I learned that people can come and go in one's life, and I learned to keep people with me in spirit. Seventh grade was torturous; I did not have even one friend. In my conservative Wisconsin neighborhood school, I was teased and ostracized for being Jewish. "Hairy-legged, big-nosed kike" was one of their favorite taunts. In addition, I felt compelled to wear my McCarthy button to school along with my wool plaid skirt, woolen knee socks, and brown oxford shoes. I looked and felt different from the other kids. It was terrible, but I wasn't willing to stop being who I was. Most of my defiance was taught to me at home. The family motto was, "You think we're different? You want to see different? I'll show you different."

I did reasonably well in school but never "lived up to my potential"; I was bored. When I was in the eighth grade we lived in England for a year, and my intellect was finally challenged. For the first time in my life I worked hard. When we returned to Madison, I was sent to another school, where I got in with a group of hip kids who smoked cigarettes, drank alcohol, and took drugs; it became my life, too. By the end of that year my grades had fallen from A's to C's and I no longer cared. For the next two years I went to a variety of alternative schools, and continued to drink and do drugs in college and beyond. It wasn't until I was twenty-seven that I began to identify myself as an addict/alcoholic and started getting clean and sober.

Establishing my identity as a sexual person was not easy, and neither of my parents approved of my choice. In my ninth-grade year I began to attend a Congregational Church youth group, where I got involved with one of the leaders. Cathy was twenty-one and I was fourteen. I can see how some people might think it was inappropriate, but I have a hard time seeing it as an abusive relationship. My mother found out about us when she discovered a letter I had written to Cathy inside a paperback I left on the dining room table when I came home from school. I went off to see a friend, and on the way home it dawned on me that my mother was going to find that letter and read it. I ran home, took one look at my mother, and knew she had read the letter. She stood at the kitchen stove, cooking in a furious motion. I ran upstairs and called Cathy, who came over and tried to straighten it out. Cathy had become friendly with my parents during the course of our relationship. They were incredibly angry at me, but more so at Cathy, whom they saw as having seduced me.

My parents insisted that they didn't believe it was wrong to be homosexual; the issue was that I was a minor and Cathy was an adult. But I think that was an excuse. It would have been unhip to make a big issue about the lesbianism. At the time, my friends said that my mother had to be a "closet case" because she cared so much and because her reaction was so out of character with her political beliefs. My parents tried, without success, to have Cathy ousted from her position as a leader of the church youth group and from her staff position at the alternative school, but the other parents stood up for her. My parents refused to listen to reason; they were sure they were doing the right thing.

My mother's reaction and action then is still in many ways an important factor in shaping my relationship with her. What I came away with was a feeling that this thing that was hugely important to me was not okay. I became separated from my family, even though I was living at home. When I was fourteen or fifteen, I told my mother I was running away, and she drove me to my friend's apartment. When my money ran out I returned home, but I divorced myself from the family and refused to participate in their lives. Tensions grew, and I finally moved out when I was sixteen. I supported myself by waitressing at a drugstore and at Woolworth's lunch counter.

I was around sixteen when my parents got divorced. My mother chose to leave my father when she got a full-time job as a professor. My father took it very hard. He had stayed in the marriage when it was hard for him, and he felt betrayed that my mother wasn't staying when it was hard for her. My mother, on the other hand, felt fulfilled and free. With her newfound economic independence, she seemed happy to be free of a relationship that had not been what she wanted it to be for quite a while.

My public-school education ended after the ninth grade, but I obtained my GED, and in 1972 I decided to go to college at the University of Wisconsin. It took six years for me to get through. During that period I was minimally in touch with my family. I worked part-time and took money from my parents for tuition and books. In college I became active in the gay rights scene and took classes with a feminist orientation. I ended up getting a degree in physical therapy, but my work is now based more on Eastern healing practice than Western medical models.

When my mother came out as a lesbian in 1974, I wasn't so much shocked as angry. I felt a sense of betrayal. What was difficult for me was the highly political way she came out. She is a much more public person than I am, and in a small town like Madison, with a small, closely knit lesbian community, it felt uncomfortable. I had worked long and arduously to build my own community, and my mother burst onto that scene in a public way by virtue of who she was—a person already in the forefront of women's studies and the women's movement. It made it worse for her to come out and have it be a wonderful thing. It felt like she had taken over something that had taken me a long time to come to. I still feel angry for some of the ways she handled things. Once she ran into me at a demonstration and said how nice it was to see me becoming more political and going to demonstrations. I was enraged. She thought her way of being political was more valid than mine.

I never became academically involved in feminism the way my mother did. She is much more of a vocal activist than I am. I try to change things by living my life decently and by changing the lives of people around me. As a lesbian feminist, I have attempted to surround myself socially and personally with people—and get involved in organizations—that support my choices and beliefs. I teach feminist ideals in my work. My political involvement supports me to continue to take risks, to raise consciousness around feminist and lesbian issues.

> When my mother came out as a lesbian in 1974, I wasn't so much shocked as angry. I had worked long and arduously to build my own community, and she burst onto that scene.

Two years ago my partner, Stacy, and I got married. I never thought that I would do such a thing, even if I were heterosexual. But over a period of time, I realized that we have the power to create our own meanings. For us, marriage means a public proclamation of a commitment to a relationship, to a life together, and to a family together. It validates a belief that relationships can last.

In February of 1995 Stacy and I had a baby boy, Noah Shaya. I hope that I can integrate work and motherhood better than my mother did, but I might not. My main fear in raising a child is that I will not be present enough. I have a circle of chosen family, and I hope those people will be actively involved with raising him. I hope we can make the world a better place by giving the next generation a good direction.

Just as there are patterns in my relationship with my mother that I don't want to repeat, there are also things my mother gave me that I would like to pass along. My mother taught me a love of books. She took my brother and me to the library and spent time with us reading and choosing books. I was a fast and avid reader, reading many levels above my age group at an early age. I share my mother's ability to acquire books, and I love to keep them even after reading them two or more times.

My mother raised my brother and me to be strong individuals, to be self-reliant and self-accepting. She also taught me a love of music, especially folk music, Jewish music, and folk dancing. She was always singing and dancing. As a kid I was often embarrassed by this behavior, but I realize now that it was a great gift. Much of my sense of spirituality is tied to music, and it is certainly a force that moves my emotions more than any other.

As a kid, I wanted to be more religious than either of my parents. When I started turning my life around in my late twenties, I realized that Jewish culture had always been a part of my life but Jewish religion itself had not. Over the past ten years, I have tried to bring Judaism into my life in a way that works. Stacy and I have a ritual that is based in Jewish tradition, but it's also very alternative, politically progressive, and feminist.

I felt very proud of my mother's work as a feminist when *Nice Jewish Girls* was published. At various points throughout my adulthood, I have felt proud of her contributions. When I hear her lecture, there is a way in which I can connect to what she is saying, and I feel a closeness that is more difficult to feel in everyday interactions. Despite the difficulties I have had with my mother, I do feel close to her and very proud of the work she has done in the world. Today I am happy to be the daughter of a strong woman who taught me both by example and through adversity to pursue the things that make me happy.

Elana, Ann P. Wilson, Noah, Barbara,
and Shira, 1967.

Shira, Barbara, and Elana, 1993.

Barbara Seaman
and
Elana Seaman
and
Shira Seaman

THE FOUNDING MOTHER of the women's health movement, Barbara Seaman "triggered a revolution, fostering a willingness among women to take issues of health into their own hands" (*New York Times,* 1994). The movement opened in 1969, with publication of *The Doctors' Case Against the Pill*—an exposé charging that the oral contraceptives then in use were at once a massive overdose and a mass experiment. Senate hearings based on Seaman's report drew feminist demonstrators, led by Alice Wolfson, with whom Seaman later cofounded the National Women's Health Network. Seaman's later works include *Free and Female* (the "first feminist sex advice book"); *Women and the Crisis in Sex Hormones;* and *Lovely Me: The Life of Jacqueline Susann.*

Born in New York City in 1935, educated at Oberlin and the Columbia School of Journalism, Seaman lives in New York where she is a contributing editor of *Ms.* Magazine. *The Doctor's Case Against the Pill,* updated and reissued in both a 10th and 25th Anniversary Edition, received an "alternative Pulitzer" in 1996 from Project Censored.

ELANA SEAMAN was born in 1960 in Huntington, New York. She works as a therapist in private practice and as a social worker/therapist at the Hudson Guild, a settlement house in New York City. There she does short- and long-term bilingual counseling with children, adolescents, adults, and senior citizens, in individual, group, and family therapy. She studied sociology and women's studies at Bard College, where she earned her BA in 1983. She received her MSW in 1989 from the Hunter College School of Social Work. She holds postgraduate certificates in Spanish and early childhood therapy. Seaman and her husband live in New York City.

SHIRA SEAMAN, a teacher and mother of two girls, was born in Smithtown, New York, in 1962. She earned her BA in English literature from Oberlin College in 1983 and her MA in Teaching English to Speakers of Other Languages (TESOL) in 1989. She lived in Madrid, Spain, where she was enrolled in an intensive Spanish-language course, and in Zurich, Switzerland, where she took intensive German. Currently she teaches English as a second language at the City University of New York, Baruch College, and the International English Language Institute at Hunter College. She lives with her husband and young daughters in New York City.

BARBARA SEAMAN
A Mother's Story

I've always felt a tremendous polarity between motherhood, on the one hand, and writing and advocating as a political organizer on the other. I regret that I couldn't be a full-time mother during my children's preschool years. I thought I had the best of both worlds. During the sixties and early seventies there was a rash of magazine articles about working mothers. I was interviewed quite a few times because I had three young children and a busy writing career, and I always said it was wonderful that I could do both working at home. Now I'm not so sure. It was very confusing to the kids. If I had to do it over, I would rent a room in somebody else's apartment and leave to work, and then come back and be all there for them. What I regret is that I was there and not there. I think it led to a lack of confidence in knowing that they came first and were the most important thing in their mother's life—which, indeed, they are.

But at the same time I think that my children, each in his or her own way, benefited from the exposure to social idealism with which they grew up. They are all of excellent character and are extremely kind. Undoubtedly it was good for them to be present at various feminist events while growing up. They marched and demonstrated, made posters, answered telephones, stuffed envelopes, granted interviews to the press, and provided on-site child care for infants and toddlers. Elana and Shira were an integral part of the early women's movement, which gave them confidence that each individual, great or small, *can* make a difference. In 1975, Shira glowingly described our National Women's Health Network demonstration at FDA to her school chum, Sandy Katz, and many years later, when Sandy became a leader in ACT UP, he came to me for guidance on planning his own FDA demonstrations.

My only real complaint about my father, Hank Rosner, is that he didn't prepare me for the real world; I thought other men would be like him. When his twin sister, Sally, went to work at sixteen to help put him through college, it broke his heart. He always said that with her brains she should have been president of the Eagle Pencil Corporation, not just the president's secretary. And he fully believed his own three daughters were perfection.

As a social worker and lawyer, Hank helped to create such programs as Aid to Dependent Children (ADC) and food stamps during the Depression. Fifty years later, when my older daughter, Elana, applied to social-work school, she recalled that when she was three she had asked her grandfather what kind of work he did, and he explained that he got food for people who were hungry and places to stay for people who had no homes. She said, "Grandpa, I want to be like you!" She was, and she is. In her teens she volunteered in a soup kitchen, run by nuns, for what we used to call "bag ladies." It was in a scary neighborhood, but that never stopped her.

My mother, née Sophia Kimels, was an exotically beautiful high-school English teacher, portrait painter, and real estate trader, who left me a box of unpublished manuscripts including an autobiographical novel. Her youth was exceedingly harsh. Her father ran away to join a religious sect when she was five, and later her uncle sexually molested her. She was raised in the home of an aunt, where she was very much the poor relation in a relatively affluent and educated Jewish family. When she married my father and had children of her own, she was gifted at handling babies; she could turn an infant's tears to laughter quicker than a hiccough. The trouble was that once we got older, she kind of lost interest—except in our intellectual development. The summer I was three she sent me to sleep-away camp at Manumet, New York, and took herself off to Santa Fe, New Mexico, to write and paint. Camp closed, but she forgot to come back for me. I stayed there alone with a skeleton work crew until just before my birthday, when her teaching job at New York's High School of Music and Art demanded her presence. Later she developed an unfortunate habit of temporarily dumping my sister Jeri and me in foster homes. Homeless or not, we always looked like foster children because Sophie didn't believe in buying children's clothes when hand-me-downs from the daughters of her many friends were available.

Sophie didn't stint on culture. I may have been the only girl in my class wearing a teddy bear coat (with sleeves ending just below my elbows) years after the rest of the kids had switched to pea jackets, but I was also the only girl who had piano lessons, art lessons, drama lessons, ballet lessons, modern-dance lessons (with Martha Graham), horseback-riding lessons, speed-writing lessons, book club memberships, magazine subscriptions, theater tickets, opera tickets, dance tickets, and subscriptions to the poetry reading series at the 92nd Street YMHA. I wasn't allowed to select my own college, however. At fifteen I took a test, scored fairly well on it, and the following year was packed off to Oberlin as a Ford Foundation early admission scholar.

Except for the most extreme cases, it hardly seems that any mother deserves to be described as either "good" or "bad." These value-judgment terms are inventions of self-styled experts in the often-unconscious service of patriarchy. As feminists we should be asking, "Good for what, and bad for whom?" For many women—and I am among them—the way you spell *mother* is G-U-I-L-T. I once began writing a book called "The American Mother: Whatever You Do, It's Wrong." I never finished it. I was too "guilty"; my adolescent kids were having too many problems; I didn't want to call down the "evil eye." Nonetheless, I learned a lot, abstractly, even as I remained unable to put it into practice. In the 1980s, instead of finishing my own treatise on the American mother, forever guilty until proven innocent, I spent seven years writing *Lovely Me: The Life of Jacqueline Susann,* author of *Valley of the Dolls,* and mother of an autistic only son, born in 1946 when psychiatric mother-blaming raged out of control.

I don't own the book any longer, can't recall the author, but the title still haunts me: *Most of Us Are Mainly Mothers.* From the moment they first brought my oldest child, Noah, to me, in 1957, I was captivated and enthralled. He was so bright-eyed, curious, responsive, and trusting. But Noah became very sick, and when I asked what was in the pills they were feeding me, the doctors and nurses dismissed my questions. I eventually discovered that the pills—offered in the blithe assumption that no modern mother would choose breast-feeding over formula—were laxatives passing through my breast milk straight to Noah. With the knowledge that Noah's illness was iatrogenic (caused by doctors or medical treatment), I descended into a state of rage and anguish from which I never fully recovered, and which has fueled my writing and advocacy work. (Dear Noah! It can't have been easy to grow up as the only son in a feminist household, much less to have his baby indigestion, his case of chemical poisoning at birth, enshrined in the folklore of medical reform.) As Naomi Bliven once wrote in *The*

New Yorker, "Behind every woman you ever heard of, there stands a man who let her down." In my own case, that man was my obstetrician.

Soon after G. D. Searle began marketing Enovid, the first oral contraceptive, I was writing my own columns for magazines such as *Brides* and *Ladies' Home Journal.* When readers deluged me with questions about birth control pills, I started an investigation that culminated in *The Doctors' Case Against the Pill* in 1969. My mother clung to her presentation copy of my book like a crucifix through the next three months, which were the last months of her life. The book became a cause célèbre when Senator Gaylord Nelson based hearings on it, shortly before my mother died. His opponent on the committee, determined to defeat my dream of a warning to patients, was a cagey first-term Kansan named Robert Dole. I was terrified that we'd lose the warning if I wasn't there in Washington. Sophie urged me to go, indicating firmly that she didn't expect me to hang around for her. Suddenly, at age thirty-four, I was a staple of the TV news and talk shows, feeling horribly guilty at spending time in Washington with my two daughters, Elana and Shira, so little, my mother so ill, and Noah's seventh-grade teacher calling to remonstrate that my topic was unsuitable for a pubescent boy's mother to take up so publicly, especially in light of (hmmm) our surname.

My daughters, and my son too, are splendid human beings, reflective, generous, and wise. But, like me, they do not sufficiently protect themselves. Elana was such a wise, compassionate child that I made her my confidante and pushed her to grow up too fast. Shira was our "easy" child—easy birth, easy disposition, near-perfect health, brains, and charm. She felt neglected because I didn't fret over her as I did with Elana and Noah.

Oddly enough, I think the things that most strengthened and weakened my children were the terrible things I went through with both of my marriages. The divorces (and, at times, the marriages as well) were tough. The separation from my children's father, Gideon, in 1978, came at a great financial sacrifice. When I discovered that he was having an affair with his present wife, then a patient (his psychiatry office was in our apartment), my only thought was, "Let's get out of here." It was a terrible decision to make—to uproot Elana and Shira, who were still living at home. I still vacillate and think that financially I made a big mistake in not staying and telling Gideon he couldn't come back. A different woman could have done it, but I wasn't confrontational in that way.

I remarried too quickly—to a former teenage sweetheart turned batterer who eventually broke my ankle, and whom I divorced in 1990. It was Elana who saved my life when I was in thrall to him. If nothing else, my personal traumas allowed me to continue demonstrating to my children how, if one understands that the personal is political, one can always "make lemonade" out of lemons. I now work with the Coalition for Family Justice, seeking better treatment for women in the process of divorcing; with FAST (Families Against Sexually Abusive Therapists and Other Professionals); and with the National Council on Women's Health, where I chair the Committee on the Medical Response to Domestic Violence.

During the early years of my marriage to Gideon, he criticized my cooking and housekeeping. He examined the glasses for soap rings, and if he found any, he made me do them over. I finally made a deal with him that if I earned enough money to afford a housekeeper, he would get off my back. He agreed, and I began to write for women's magazines, using the money to hire someone to cook and clean. I always thought that if I made more money, if I brought more social status to the family, Gideon would have to recognize that I was okay even if I was not a good cook. But it was never enough.

Ann P. Wilson, a nineteen-year-old black single mother from Plains, Georgia, became my right arm, and maybe my right brain, too. The Goddess really protected me and my kids by sending her to us. Ann was strong, sensible, intelligent, and good. Some of my friends were critical and asked how I could have a housekeeper, but I never felt guilty. I did not think there was anything wrong with having a housekeeper as long as I didn't exploit her. I paid her a good salary, more than some housekeepers may earn today, with paid vacations and Social Security. I treated it like any other job and her like a valued employee. I also hired a man who came once or twice a week to do the heavy work.

I encouraged Ann to finish high school and to take civil-service exams. Around the time that Shira left for college, Ann made the list to get a job as a courthouse custodian. She's now the chief at the famous *Bonfire of the Vanities* courthouse in the Bronx, commands a good salary, and will get a pension. She may actually have more security in her old age than I, because she didn't squander her savings on divorce lawyers.

When I gave a talk recently at Oberlin, a student reviewer named Joanna Silver was disturbed by my true confession of all I owe to Ann

P. Wilson: "Barbara Seaman basically talked herself into the perfect prototype of the White, Middle-Class Feminist that we constantly refer to in my Women's Studies classes. My friends and I literally cringed while she discussed how well she treated her housekeeper, the woman who had liberated her from her husband's fetish for clean glasses. . . . [Her] brand of feminism was, and continues to be extremely exclusive, and inherently racist and classist. However, women's health care might not be where it is today if it were not for this woman who dared to defy the entire medical establishment. So, what does one do with this example of social activism?"

> Some of my friends were critical and asked how I could have a housekeeper, but I never felt guilty. I treated it like any other job and her like a valued employee.

What are the options? Most mothers can't choose not to work, but day care remains scarce. Many housekeepers and nannies are disrespected and exploited, but others are not. If we don't do more to provide affordable child care and other assistance to mothers, the slow ascent of women toward equality will stall, and our children (both grown and growing) will be in major trouble. When people ask me what I consider the gravest health crisis facing women today, I usually tell them, "Exhaustion." Women's total workload, paid and unpaid, is greater than men's; stretched-to-the-limit young mommies will just snap—or keel over. Behind every mother you ever heard of, there usually stands another woman who propped her up.

When Shira gave birth to my first grandchild, Sophia, in 1991, Elana and I were equally ecstatic. Elana called me up in the middle of the night: "I'm just lying here thinking about Sophia—aren't you?" Later we all watched a TV documentary about monkeys in which the grandmother and aunt kept snatching the baby from the mother to cuddle and kitchy-koo her—just like us. There's no free lunch, but there *is* free dessert—grandchildren.

After much thought I volunteered to be Sophia's nanny twice a week, while Shira was out teaching English as a second language. My friends in my consciousness-raising group said I was reckless. I was struggling to make a comeback from my second terrible divorce. I needed to make my deadlines and hustle my career, not to mention keep up with my advocacy work. But I have never been happier than when I am hanging out with my granddaughters, and it's given me the chance to partly compensate Shira for, as she puts it, getting the "fuzzy end of the lollipop."

When Sophia was three, I introduced her to the story of Little Red Riding Hood.

"Grandma," she interrupted when the big bad wolf entered the narrative, "that wolf, he's a bad guy, isn't he?"

"Yes, Sophia, he is."

We finished the story. Sophia sighed a contented sigh. "Grandma, you know something? That wolf, he's a bad guy. I *like* him!" And there was the key. My grandfather was a bad guy. My father was good. My husbands were bad guys, at least to me; my son and sons-in-law are terrific. There must be a gene in our family, the attraction-to-bad-guys gene, that alternates generations, passing from grandmother to granddaughter. My challenge now is to help Sophia, and her sister, Idalia, rise above it.

A Daughter's Story

My mother and I have had a very close, symbiotic relationship. Because I was the older daughter, I was her confidante. Since I was five or six, she has felt that she could talk to me about personal and private things, including problems with my father. She was always telling me how sensitive and intuitive I was; she'd say things like "I just forget that you're not an adult." When I was a little girl I felt very mature and important to be the one chosen to hear all these things. It makes sense that I became a social worker, which is a caretaking role.

It was not until I was older that I got angry about my role in the family. Now I feel that it was a mixed blessing, which on the one hand gave me a lot of confidence and a sense of responsibility, but on the other robbed me of my childhood and my innocence. I started to feel the burden of this around the age of eighteen, when my parents separated and had a horrible divorce. To this day I shy away from hearing what my mother wants to tell me, when she talks about my father.

I was born in Huntington, Long Island, on July 18, 1960. My father was working as a senior resident in psychiatry and my mother was just beginning her career as a writer. The year I was born, she wrote her first feminist article. Later when we moved back to New York City, both my parents had offices at home, but my father was less available than my mother. He managed to use up about four rooms. My mother worked in the bedroom. There was a sense that we could come in where my mother was working, but we couldn't where my father was working. I think it was a real compromise for my mother, but oddly enough she says that she got her best work done during the years when there were children interrupting her. For us, however, the boundaries were not clear enough.

My father was only half present during much of our lives. Although he was there for me when I needed intellectual support, he separated himself emotionally from the family. My mother was not an equal partner with my father—no woman was in those days. Although she had co-signed the mortgage notes, her name wasn't on the apartment title. But basically the two of them lived such separate lives that she could be more independent than most women. She was a strong, opinionated woman. Her ideas flourished; she was creative. She did a lot more parenting than my father did, but she didn't do much of the traditional work, like cooking and cleaning. Our housekeeper, Ann, did that.

My mother was always on the phone doing her activist feminist work, and different characters from the women's movement were in and out all the time. In our house there were practically no rules. I had a huge circle of friends that hung out at our house, and they thought my mother was great. She made everybody feel as though they were extremely talented and had something to offer. She was flamboyant; she came home with a different hair color and different hairstyle every month. She'd wear everything from bright colors and bell-bottoms to business suits and elegant gowns. She did not fit into one trend. I don't think I feel competitive with my mother, but she certainly has been a hard and complicated act to follow. I tried to rebel by doing all kinds of outrageous things in high school, but my mother just allowed me to do what I wanted.

Although it was hard because my mother wasn't always there when I was growing up, she was also, paradoxically, too much there. Because we were so intertwined, we had a hard time separating from each other's emotions. When I got depressed, for example, she would get depressed with me or anxious for me. Having her emotions too closely tied to me, not being able to separate, was a real problem. It was so intense, so fraught. It wasn't until I was in my twenties that I really attempted to separate. As adults, we are still trying to form a new relationship, a new balance, which has been painful and difficult for both of us.

My mother wrote an important book about the birth control pill in 1969, when I was nine. By the age of thirteen I thought I was very mature, that I was the one who knew everything and could tell my friends at school, but I realize now that it was too much to know at that age. My friends became very jealous and threatened by my connection with my mother and my knowledge and freedom. Most of them turned against me and stopped talking to me. It was extremely painful. There is something about that age that seems to promote the idea of bonding against somebody. I don't know why thirteen-year-olds do this, but they do. My mother tried to be supportive and tried to explain that they were just jealous, but it didn't help. I think I was very angry at her (although I didn't know it) because her revolutionary ideas, which I was attempting to live out, had backfired and caused me a great deal of pain.

A week before I left for college, my parents separated. My mother and Shira and I moved out of the house. Shira lived alone with my mother that year; I went to a place called Friends World College and ended up living in San Francisco. I was very depressed. I felt like I had nothing to return home to. I felt that both my mother and I had been betrayed by my father—I overidentified with her. The divorce affected me terribly. It's still not resolved for me, and I don't know if it will ever be.

I stayed at Friends World College for a year, until 1979, and then I moved back home to be with my mother. She got involved with the man who became my stepfather a couple of months later. This man was not good for my mother. He was a very angry person, and I could feel her submission to him. She was still writing and had all these feminist beliefs, but all of a sudden we began to get messages about how our stepfather was providing for us, supporting us, and we should all be grateful. But he was a batterer, and my mother became a battered woman.

The most upsetting part about having a feminist mother was trying to reconcile what her beliefs were with how she was living. There were multiple incidents and a lot of fear, and eventually he broke her ankle and she had to go to the hospital. He had been paying my rent while I was in graduate school, and I sent the postdated checks back to him. I told my mother I was never taking another penny from him and that she could live without him, too. Finally I said, "I am not ever going to come to your house as long as you are with him." I told her that she was welcome to stay at my house. She says now that that's what actually made her leave him. It was very hard at the time, because my brother called me and said, "How can you do this? Her ankle is broken and you're not going to see her? That's so mean of you."

The most painful time for me in my relationship with my mother was when she was split between those two worlds: advocating feminism but not living it in her relationship with my stepfather. For a long time I was afraid to get married, thinking that I would not be able to live my life as a feminist if I did, either, so why try? It is a question I am still wrestling with. I am trying to accept that we are all human and we try to live up to our ideals, but that we are not going to be able to do that at every moment. You don't just create an ideal and then live it—nobody can. It is an ongoing struggle. In my marriage I feel I have done a better job than my mother did of creating an equal situation, but I also have thirty years of history telling me how to do it, and my mother had none.

I was more active in feminism than my sister was for many years, but for the past five or six years I have not been politically active. I feel strongly identified as a feminist; I have no doubts about it. But maybe I am shying away from activism because my mother's footsteps are too hard to follow, or maybe it's just not where my interest lies. I am much more interested in the psyche and interpersonal relationships. As a therapist, along with working with many different people, I do a lot of work with women who have been battered, raped, harassed, or molested, or who have simply grown up in a patriarchal world. Feminism has seeped into everything I do.

I think that many daughters of feminists may not be activists because they are afraid of following the same path as their mothers. They may feel that they would lose their own identities. When I went to meetings with my mother, I was always seen as her daughter, not as a woman in my own right. When I was in college I wrote a thesis about the differences in how men and women use physical space, and because of my mother I had access to a number of famous women, whom I interviewed and quoted in the piece. My professor, as it turned out, was jealous and competitive, and was angry that I had used these women, and gave me a difficult time because of it. So it was a hard position for me to be in.

My husband, Tim, and I got involved when we were both thirty. He is a lawyer. We have been together for four years. We grew up very differently—he is Catholic and I am Jewish. His mother does not consider herself a feminist, and she will tell you she does not believe in feminism, but she taught science and math, "male" subjects, and her husband does a lot of the cooking and the gardening. Tim and I did not have a traditional wedding; we were married by a female judge who is Irish, like Tim's family, and feminist, like mine. Our immediate families were the only ones present. We had four different wedding parties: one with my mother, one with my father, one with Tim's family, and one with our friends.

Tim and I keep separate bank accounts. I feel strongly about that. It was a very specific choice; we try to go halves on the rent and the bills. After watching some of the struggles my parents went through over money, it is important for me to have control of my own.

> When I went to meetings with my mother, I was always seen as her daughter, not as a woman in my own right.

Tim and I are thinking about having children. My sister, Shira, got married first, had her baby first, and has had a second baby. I have always wanted to have children, so it has been difficult for me. I have gone through a lot of feelings about it. We are still involved in a process of trying to figure out how a woman can have children and a career, if she chooses, without being a superwoman and driving herself crazy. We all have to make decisions about how to balance these things, how to work them out. Many of the women I know are dealing with this right now, because very few women these days can choose not to have careers and just stay home. Whether or not they label themselves as feminists, they are still having to deal with these struggles. If they're not mothers, some of them are wrestling with how to live their own lives, because women in our society are not considered whole if they don't have children. It is often difficult to feel like your life is completely meaningful without children. The women's movement was not about saying that you should not have children, but that you should have options. I would like to be a mother. But I think it is a choice.

My mother will do anything for her children. While being a feminist, she still believed that her children were the most important things in her life. She was often on the phone, and we were always trying to capture her attention, and were sometimes angry at her because she seemed to be half there, with her mind somewhere else. Nevertheless, I knew that if I needed something, she'd drop everything and come running to me. My mother's apartment is open for us to go to whenever we want.

My mother has the kind of personality that when she walks into a room filled with people my age and she's the only one from an older generation, people will gravitate toward her, buzzing around her. She draws people in. She's also very eccentric. She never fit into patterns.

She has always been sloppy, leaving things all over the place. She used to walk around the house with a cigarette hanging out of her mouth and the phone ringing off the hook and big piles of books and papers on her bed. She didn't even bother to take the books off the bed when she went to sleep. She will talk to anybody about anything. One time when we were in Salt Lake City she got into a conversation about God with a Mormon woman in a store, and my mother meant to say that God is genderless, but instead she said that God is bisexual, and that caused quite a fuss. My brother saved the moment by wondering aloud what Mrs. God felt about this.

I feel grateful to have been brought up by a feminist mother. My mother is a fascinating person. She's brilliant, and the work she's done is amazing. She's always connecting things and networking, figuring out how things work together. This, it seems to me, is a particularly feminist process.

SHIRA SEAMAN
A Daughter's Story

I was born in Smithtown, New York, on October 17, 1962. My brother, Noah, was five and my sister, Elana, was two. We were living on the grounds of a mental institution in Kings Park, where my father was finishing his residency. My mother was a ghostwriter for a well-known popular psychologist. We moved to Manhattan when I was eleven months old, and when I was six we moved into a huge apartment on the Upper West Side.

My parents both worked at home; my father had his psychiatry practice there. When he was seeing patients we could not use the living room or the dining room. My father's office was locked, and we didn't dare go into it. He was seeing patients; everything was secretive. My mother, on the other hand, was fully available to us. Her office was in my parents' bedroom. She did a lot of work on the phone, which sounded to us like socializing, so we felt that we could disturb her at any time. I feel very strongly now that I don't want to work at home because I think that both situations were bad for us—my father being so close and yet so far, and my mother being half available. She never really got the privacy she needed, and we never got the attention we needed. She was always partially there.

It benefits children to have working mothers. Mothers who have no other interests besides their children can become overbearing and too involved. But to have your mother at home working when you are young and don't understand it can also be a problem. When I was growing up, there was never the sense that specific time was put aside for us. The boundaries between work and family were blurred. My mother included us in a lot of things; she brought us to meetings, and that was good for us in some ways. But I often felt that I had to compete with her work. I felt that other people got her attention and I didn't. She was preoccupied, and I sometimes felt abandoned.

Between the ages of six and fifteen I spent a lot of time with my mother, going to meetings and attending rallies. One of the more important ones was when she cofounded the Women's Health Network. Elana and I went with her to Washington. I also went on a number of prochoice marches with her, and at Passover we went to a feminist Seder. In the summer of 1975 we attended an institute called Sagaris in Vermont. The majority of the students and teachers were lesbians, and my mother was trying to teach a course on motherhood. Very few of them were interested. There was a lot of debate about whether you could be a mother and still be a feminist. A lot of people didn't think so. My mother felt very strongly that she had combined her feminism and her motherhood, but this idea was not received as openly as it might have been. When my father came to take us away one weekend, just the fact that he drove onto campus infuriated a lot of the women.

In spite of all the troubles that my parents had with each other, I always got the sense from my father that women were equal. He did not treat Elana and me any differently than he treated Noah. My mother would say that he treated her as a second-class citizen in terms of her work, but he was also very proud of the work she did. One way in which he was not much of a feminist was that he expected my mother to do the cooking and cleaning, and she never wanted to do it. When she started writing and earning money, their agreement was that she would pay for a housekeeper. And that is what happened.

Ann, a black Southern woman, started working for us when I was three. She provided a lot of the nurturing for us. She worked every day from ten in the morning until seven-thirty at night, for seventeen years. I learned a lot from Ann; I was close to her and still am. I really liked her, so I wasn't too resentful when I wasn't with my mother. But my feeling now, as a mother, is that I enjoy my children so much that I would not want to be away from them that much of the time, having someone else take care of them.

In 1978, when I was sixteen, my parents separated. I think that their marriage was essentially over long before that. I had been aware of the tension between them for a long time. We never really had a normal family life. There was a lot of stress, and my parents were not happy together. On an intellectual level they got along and shared a lot of things, but on a personal level they were such opposites that they could never resolve their problems.

My father may not have been respectful of my mother as a wife, but he was, I think, respectful of her as a woman. His own mother, Sylvia

Seaman, was an extraordinary person. She was a suffragette, and marched in the big 1920 parade, and wrote a number of books. Her most important feminist work was a book called *Always a Woman*, which was about the radical mastectomy she had in the 1950s. It was one of the first books in which a woman was open and honest about her breast cancer. My mother encouraged my grandmother a great deal with her writing and helped her find agents and publishers. In fact, it was my grandmother who first met my mother at a party and went home and told my father she had met the woman he was going to marry!

My parents' breakup came at a really bad time for me. It was the end of the summer, and Elana was about to start college, so I was alone with my mother in a little apartment. It was a difficult year. Each of my parents accused me of taking the other's side. My mother was really upset; it was a hard time for her, and because I was the only one there, she took it out on me. By January I was going so crazy that I went to a guidance counselor at school, who suggested that I leave for college early. So that's what I did. I immediately took the SAT and applied to Oberlin College because my mother had gone there and loved it, and because my brother was there.

I met my husband, Urs, when both of us were twenty-one, in Spain. He is Swiss. I was living with Elana, studying Spanish. Urs was studying architecture in Switzerland and had come to Spain over his six-week break to perfect his Spanish. We spent that time together and then I went back to Switzerland with him. Eventually he came to New York to do an internship, and then I went back to Switzerland with him and studied German and Swiss German. That was how I became interested in learning new languages and teaching English as a second language.

Urs and I lived together for five years before we decided to get married. My mother's marriages had made me very cautious about commitment; I didn't want to do it until I was sure that this was the right man and that things would work out. Urs grew up in an extremely traditional Catholic family. His father is a businessman, and his mother was a housewife until her children grew up, when she became a librarian. But somehow Urs didn't get stuck in that traditional stereotype. I would say that he is a feminist, though he might not define himself that way.

There's been so much divorce in our parents' generation that a lot of people of my generation take marriage lightly. I didn't feel that way at all. I don't disapprove of divorce, but I don't want one and I hope I never will. I went into my marriage thinking very clearly that it would be for life. Monogamy is very important to me. If my husband were to have an affair, I don't know what I would do.

Urs and I have had some struggles, but in general we have a very good marriage. When I was growing up, I imagined that when I got married and had children, my husband and I would both work part-time and raise the children part-time. I thought we would share all the responsibilities. But there's no way my husband and I can live off one salary, and Urs is not in a position as an architect where he can work flexible hours. I work part-time teaching English as a second language, and there is not much potential for making money. I always assumed that I would be able to afford household help for the cleaning; I know that would make our lives easier. If we could afford a housekeeper just to clean, we would have more leisure time together.

I hope to have a more fulfilling career in the future than I have at the moment. I am not disappointed; I planned my life so that I could have children and work part-time. I didn't want to go into a high-powered career and then have to choose between the two. But I would like to accomplish more than I have. Women still have to sacrifice something to have a good career. Men sacrifice things, too; when Urs works overtime, he doesn't have time to spend with Sophia and Idalia, and he feels terrible, because he would like to be home with them more. The difference, though, is that the woman is made to feel guilty if she is not there.

From the moment I got pregnant I knew that I didn't want some-one to watch my children all the time. I really enjoy being with them. It is good for me to teach, to have time away from Sophia and Idalia, when I think about things other than children and communicating with a three-year-old and a baby, but I am always anxious to get home to them. I know plenty of families where the mother is gone from eight in the morning until six or seven at night, and the child is with a care-taker all the time, and I think that is very sad, not just for the child, but for the mother.

My children are intelligent, outgoing, and interested in the world—I think I have done a pretty good job. But I don't think that I could be a good mother if my mother had not shown me how. My mother always gave me a chance to express myself. She made me feel like a person. Some parents make their children feel like children, in a separate category. My mother always respected my intellect and was interested in what we were saying and doing as children.

I want to raise my children with as much a sense of themselves as my mother did. I don't think she ever questioned my abilities; in fact, sometimes I think she had too much confidence. When I had problems in school, I would come home to complain to her, and she'd say, "Don't worry about it, you'll be fine. You'll never mess up; you never fail at anything." She didn't take my worries seriously; she assumed that things would go smoothly, and that was frustrating because sometimes I wanted her to acknowledge my fears. But I never had a sense of myself as inferior or the feeling that I couldn't accomplish the things I wanted to do.

> I don't think that I could be a good mother if my mother had not shown me how.

Many women feel that feminism and motherhood can't go together. I think they absolutely do. Nothing has been more important in my life than having my own children, yet I don't feel that conflicts with my ideas of myself as a woman at all. For me, being a mother is an essential part of being a woman.

I am not an activist, and I don't participate in any feminist organizations. In college I attended meetings of feminist groups and feminist rallies, but I was never a leader in any of those groups. I have never felt that I am not equal: I've done what I wanted to do, which is to live my life and have a career. Thanks to my mother and other feminist activists like her, so much has been accomplished in the last three decades. Obviously, a lot still needs to be done. The issue of abortion is very important, and the issue of child care has become very important; it's outrageous that there's not enough quality affordable child care in this country, nor adequate maternity leave. Until women are in a position where they can feel that their children are being well taken care of, and that they can work at the same time, how can they be equal to men?

Most of the daughters of feminists that I know are not activists themselves. I think that more of the women who are active these days are just discovering feminism for themselves. I had an experience at Oberlin where I was taking an anthropology course and I had to do an ethnography of a subculture. I chose to do a study of what I called the new feminist women, women who had discovered feminism for themselves when they left home for the first time. What I found was that these were the women who were actively involved in the big feminist organizations; they were the leaders. They had discovered something new and exciting. For me, on the other hand, feminism is part of the way I live my life; it is not a cause.

I think that the most important things my mother passed on to me are the sense of myself as a woman and the idea that women are equal to men. It is something I never even questioned. I don't think I ever had to come to a feminist realization; I never thought any other way. Although there was a struggle between my parents about whose work was more important, I never imagined that my mother was inferior to my father just because she was a woman. I can't quite conceive of a woman who says, "I would never call myself a feminist." Being a feminist is just what I am.

Deborah and Naomi, 1962.

Naomi and Deborah, 1990.

Deborah Wolf

and

Naomi Wolf

DEBORAH WOLF was born in Stockton, California, in 1938 and now lives in New York City where she is a psychotherapist in private practice specializing in the empowerment of women. She received her PhD in psychological anthropology from the University of California–Berkeley in 1977. Her dissertation on lesbian feminism as a social movement was published in 1980 as *The Lesbian Community.* She is married to the writer Leonard Wolf and has two grown children, Naomi and Aaron.

BORN IN SAN FRANCISCO in 1962, Naomi Wolf is well known for her books *The Beauty Myth* and *Fire With Fire: The New Female Power and How It Will Change the 21st Century.* She earned her BA in English in 1984 from Yale University and did coursework in English literature and feminist theory as a Rhodes scholar at New College, Oxford. She travels the country lecturing and offering her perspective on how feminism can improve women's lives. Wolf lives in Washington, D.C., with her husband, David Shipley, and new daughter, Rosa.

A Mother's Story

My daughter, Naomi, was born during the 1962 Cuban missile crisis. I prayed that I would live long enough to give birth and that she would have a chance to survive. When she arrived, I took one look at her and felt an incredible bond. At the time I was reading *The Second Sex,* so I was delighted to have a girl. I thought, "It's me and my little gypsy daughter against the world." I gave her a biblical name, Naomi Rebekah, which means "strong, visionary woman."

Perhaps I should have waited until I was older to have children— until I had lived in the world and knew how to run a household, until I was more stable. I have no regrets now, but at the age of twenty-two I lacked self-confidence and knowledge. I was not an especially welcoming birth mother, nor did I particularly like having infants. But as my babies became little people and started to talk and interact, I found them endlessly intriguing. My own mother had expected me to live up to her high standards. I was loose with my children, hugging them often and going out of my way to be affectionate. Over and over I told them they were beautiful, strong, and intelligent. As a mother I stood back and let them develop (though sometimes they needed more attention than I had energy to give them). We were, I felt, growing up together.

My grandparents were immigrants from Russia. My grandfather was a union organizer and my grandmother a social anarchist. Both were committed to the idea that people should make a difference in the world, and both believed in the importance of education. My mother was a sociology professor and a community organizer; my father, a professor of humanities who studied philology at Yale. He died the year Naomi was born, and I always felt she had an important connection with him. I grew up in Stockton, California, between two cultures: My parents were East Coast intellectuals; my high-school peers were *American Graffiti*—fast cars and fast food. Like any teenager creating an identity separate from parents, I wanted desperately to be part of the teen culture.

I entered the University of Chicago on scholarship and immediately went wrong. Being elected a fraternity queen automatically made me a pariah. Appearance, popularity, and politeness were not highly valued traits at Chicago; convoluted brilliance and cynicism were. In reaction to my experience, I got fat. Two years later—now cynical and political—I transferred to Berkeley, insecure about my intelligence and competence. I had a kind of breakdown and stayed depressed most of the time. After skipping finals and receiving all F's my junior year, I had no idea what I was going to do.

Serendipitously, I tripped over a rug at a wedding reception and fell into the arms of Leonard Wolf, a romantic figure in the Bay Area. Leonard, fifteen years my senior and a writer and professor of creative writing, had a daughter from a previous marriage. I found him incredibly interesting and sexy, and I felt safe with him, as I had not felt for a long time. "Live in sin if you want to," my radical friends urged, "but don't get married; it's so bourgeois." Nonetheless, we got married during my senior year. It was the right thing. I immediately began making straight A's and decided to major in anthropology.

The following year, Leonard received a Fulbright fellowship to teach in Iran, and I became pregnant with our son. On our travels, I discovered that people in different cultures react differently to pregnancy: Greeks patted my stomach for good luck, Londoners shied away. Aaron arrived in 1960 in Iran, and we took him everywhere. At three months he accompanied us on a boar-hunting expedition; at Persepolis I nursed him in the Hall of Mirrors. In Bali I had a revelation. Running down a beach one day, I saw some women emerging from the ocean with baskets of coral on their heads. Intrigued because their way of life was so different from mine, I wanted not only the knowledge but the physical experience of it. I had no idea that I was intelligent (after flunking out of school), but it seemed worthwhile to find out. Suddenly I was ready to go back to school.

In San Francisco after Naomi's birth, Leonard said, "You go back to school. I'll baby-sit while you take classes." I took a night course in folklore and loved it. When Berkely opened a department of folklore, I was accepted—considered at twenty-six an older student. Student activism at Berkeley was at its height, and on Mother's Day the children gave me an army jacket, a toothbrush, and a handkerchief to use in the event of tear gas. Police and tanks often appeared in the streets. During 1968 and 1969 I drove off to school each day wondering what revolutionary activity might occur.

From the time they were in strollers, Naomi and Aaron accompanied us to peace marches and demonstrations. Naomi was five when

> "Live in sin if you want to," my radical friends urged, "but don't get married; it's so bourgeois."

one march ended in a confrontation between Hell's Angels and peace marchers at the Oakland border. At a birthday party afterward, she announced that we had been to a war. Naomi was an extraordinary child and very much her own person. I put few restrictions on her. Once a stranger asked, "Whose little girl are you?" and she replied, "I'm my own little girl." Despite a strong sense of her own needs and destiny, she was enormously good-natured and kind.

Integrating feminism and motherhood was not especially difficult in San Francisco. During the late sixties and early seventies I belonged to a women's organization called Mothers for Peace. We took our babies and met in each other's houses to discuss ways to stop the Vietnam War and fight the draft. Most of my peers, however, had the flexibility and freedom that comes with being unmarried. Having children deepened me as a person, but at the same time I felt middle-aged and weighed down.

Fortunately, I had a strong framework of support. A graduate student would come in to help three hours a day, and Leonard helped enormously. He was more nurturing than I, and in many respects he was a model feminist father. He took the kids to Disneyland for three days so I could finish my master's thesis. When we lived in dire poverty in the South of France, he took the children for nature walks, awakened them to science, and taught them to read and write. We have had our share of conflict, but the intimate experience of living together as a small unit in strange cultures brought us together as a family.

I was loving but vague and absentminded. Hypoglycemia made me often lethargic and out of it, and thus inconsistent. Perhaps there were advantages in having a flaky, offbeat mother. I don't know. Naomi has felt, and she is right, that in some ways my attention to her was erratic when she was a little girl. Even now she would like me to be more there for her than I sometimes can. That is probably our biggest source of conflict.

In 1970 I entered a PhD program in urban anthropology at Berkeley. I wanted my dissertation to make a difference. Feminism was emerging, and San Francisco was a hotbed of lesbian activism. Lesbians saw themselves as the purest feminists, uncorrupted by heterosexual attachments, and lesbian mothers as those most likely to raise children in an egalitarian household. When lesbian friends said, "Why don't you, a straight woman, do this study so that lesbian mothers can retain custody of their kids?" I took them up on it. The subject was enormously exciting. Naomi grew up around my books and around my lesbian friends, who came to dinner and to her bat mitzvah with their children. I carried a magic velvet handkerchief, sewn by Naomi, into my oral exam. My dissertation about the lesbian community was published when I was thirty-nine years old. Confident of my own intelligence for the first time, I finally believed there was a place for my kind of intuitive thinking. That lack of confidence may be one of the biggest differences between my generation and my daughter's.

Two events gave me the sense of being a strong woman in the world. In 1971 Leonard and I were invited on a journey into the Israeli desert. I was the only woman in the group, and the trip was grueling. At one point I had an image that we were going in the wrong direction, which was critical because we were low on gas. When it turned out that indeed we were, I had a positive sense about my role as an intuitive woman in the all-male group. The second experience, also in Israel, occurred during the 1973 war. For six months I drove soldiers to the front, from Damascus Gate in Jerusalem to central command in Jericho. I again had a sense of myself as a warrior.

We tried to raise our children as equals, dressing them in unisex clothes and offering similar opportunities, such as art lessons. But gender was only one factor among many as each child unfolded with his or her own personality and character. Naomi dismissed both dolls and the Tonka toys Aaron loved. To teach egalitarianism, as the children got older we required each one to plan a meal, serve it, and clean up one day a week. We also sent them to public schools. We decided that knowing how to navigate in an urban situation would prove more useful than a private-school education. Unfortunately Naomi spent three years bored out of her mind.

Feminism and social justice played an important role in Naomi's life from a very early age. When she was seven, she wrote and illustrated a short novel about a strong feminist hero. At eleven, I think using an argument about affirmative action, she talked the local newspaper into hiring her as the paper girl. I don't think she enjoyed doing it much but she was concientious because she was doing it for feminism. At fourteen she was a dedicated volunteer for a battered women's shelter, the youngest one they had. Naomi taught me how influenced even very young children can be by ideology and how important it is to take them seriously.

I insisted that the family have dinner together, although cooking is not one of my strengths. Aaron got tired of the monotony of hamburger and became a vegetarian for seven years, but I did make wonderful salads, since I was always on a diet. I was the worst possible mother to prevent anorexia in a child because I was always frantic about food. As a hypoglycemic, I would overeat and become preoccupied. Had I lived in another era and known about nurturing and women's health, I would have been a better model. Naomi herself became anorectic when she was twelve. I was terrified. She was down to eighty-four pounds before she heard the doctor say the situation was dangerous and turned herself around.

It was hard to let Naomi go off to Yale in 1980 because she was so much a part of my life. Leonard was due for a sabbatical and didn't mind where we went as long as it was an island. I wanted to go to New York, so I said, "Okay, we'll go to an island, but let me choose which one." As it turned out, New York was right for Leonard as a writer and for me temperamentally and environmentally. We loved the city's fast pace and innumerable opportunities. Meanwhile, floods wrecked our San Francisco home, so we had to sell it, and Leonard took early retirement. We were ready for a new phase of our lives, but the move was hard on Naomi and Aaron. The childhood home is symbolically important, and they no longer had that.

Naomi came to visit often while she was at Yale, and we visited her in New Haven. My mother had been barred from the Yale library during my father's student days just because she was a woman. Her presence at Naomi's graduation was especially satisfying. After college, Naomi applied unsuccessfully for a Rhodes scholarship. I was proud when she tried again and succeeded. At Oxford she began the research that led to *The Beauty Myth*. I thought the manuscript was fantastic. I see *Fire With Fire* not as an about-face but as the growth of a sensibility.

I always told Naomi, "Don't get married until you've written a novel, been elected president, or figured out a way to make a living for yourself that you really like. Then get married and have children." She may have taken me a little too literally. Her marriage last year was a magical, memorable event. I loved the fact that Naomi wanted her wedding to have ritual. Marriage is an important step, and having the kind of ceremony with the community one wants is critical. Naomi's wedding reflected her belief that feminism should be about allowing women their individual choices. Unfortunately, the nature of her life makes it hard to be peaceful. She has been under constant pressure for years. I hope that she will let herself relax more, find a chance to spend more time just having fun with her husband, and nourish a part of herself that hasn't had a chance to be nourished.

Naomi's vision for social change was always her own. I was never a leader or spokesperson for the women's movement; I was just a mother getting her doctorate, and my activism lay in the subject I was writing about. I sat writing my dissertation at the dining room table so that my children would have a role model. Through the years, my work has changed and developed beyond my imaginings. For eight years I worked at various social-service jobs. In recent years my work in anthropology and life-stage development has led to an interest in spirituality. I specialize in holistic psychotherapy, particularly working with those who have AIDS. I concentrate on helping them live each day to the fullest.

The roles of women in my generation and my daughter's generation, the roles of mothers and daughters, are mixed up. Our daughters are teaching us many things, and we are charting new courses. The dialogue is really one between equals. Now she cautions me against giving my services away too freely and encourages me to ask for what I deserve. I believe that women of both generations will continue to grow and develop and become wise women—whatever direction we take. I see us as strong warriors in the world. In developmental terms, we will take on testosterone-associated qualities. As men become more nurturing and caring, the world will achieve a more effective balance.

This pattern of growing and becoming will affect not only our daughters but also our granddaughters. I want my granddaughters— Aaron and Naomi both had daughters this year—to have faith in their own development and to feel strength, love, and support from their families and communities. I want their hearts to be filled with enough love to take in and give out. I want them to walk freely in this life, whatever path they choose.

NAOMI WOLF
A Daughter's Story

I was born in San Francisco in 1962. San Francisco in the late sixties and early seventies was an exciting place, and I was lucky to be a part of it. It was ground zero, Haight-Ashbury. Feminism wasn't anything you debated; it was the air you breathed. I grew up thinking it was normal to be in peace marches; it was normal to go to the free store or the head shop or Hippie Hill, where everyone was playing bongo drums and getting high. There was such a mood in San Francisco at that time, a sense of hope that you could change the world. People were writing about this exciting new world, and saying that maybe it was being thought through in a way that could last. I read *Amazon Nation, The Advocate, Ms.* magazine, the whole range of texts about the gay and lesbian revolution and radical feminism that my mother kept around the house. Justice was the theme, and it was a joyful theme. It's that sense of joy that I keep looking for and haven't really found since. A sense of revolution that was a delight.

We were a pretty bohemian family. Cleanliness was not a big deal. One of my parents' favorite stories is about the time I waded in the mud in my brand-new Mary Janes and white lacy socks. Some bratty kid from the neighborhood went to my mother and said, "Mrs. Wolf, Mrs. Wolf, Naomi's wading in the mud!" My mother said, "Well, I hope she's having fun." She and my father were much more inclined to revel in our messy creation. We were always traveling. When I was four we spent three months in the South of France, living in a camper. We would go down to the beach and collect driftwood and sea glass. There was the feeling that our family was a little tribe of gypsies. When I was three, my parents let me take the bus a few city blocks in New York with my five-year-old brother, Aaron.

My parents were the psychic center of my life. I think that their child-rearing style was to give us everything we needed to go our own way but not to dictate any expectations to us. My mother's mother had been very disciplined and formal, so my mother was determined not to put limits and restrictions on us that would inhibit our creativity. On the one hand, that made me very independent; on the other hand, sometimes I think I yearned for limits against which to rebel.

In many ways my mother was not incredibly maternal. She was loving and supportive, but she was committed to her own studies and her own life. When Aaron and I were young, she went back to school to get her doctorate. Every afternoon there was a time when she would close the door and work on her thesis. Aaron and I had a baby-sitter, and I'm sure we whined and complained. But it allowed us to see that her work was as important as Dad's work, and it let me see that I too could close the door when I wanted to.

I admire my mother's self-creation, how she came out of sorority land and became a pioneer in her field. In midlife she went back to school and, with courage and autonomy, developed a new skill. My mother was always doing her own work, and that was important for me in a positive way. I never felt as if she was sacrificing her identity for me. That was an incredible gift she gave me. She worked intensely in the lesbian community in San Francisco. I grew up mostly around lesbians. A radical lesbian took care of my pet rat (my brother was allergic to larger animals) when I went away to Israel. When I had my bat mitzvah party, my mother invited a group of self-proclaimed "dykes on bikes."

I can't relate at all to the guilt and resentment some of my friends feel about having full-time mothers who lived out their lives through them. My mother gave me a lot of space. I didn't experience those weird, complicated knots people get into when they feel like their mother is always present and judging them. My mother was intent on being a person who had fun with her children; she rejected the enforced maternal role under which a lot of women labor. I loved her youth and vitality, but sometimes I just wanted her to be a grown-up. When you're an emerging sexual person, especially as an adolescent, you want your mom to be this fixed piece of furniture and not to stand out so much. Sometimes, I remember, I wanted her to act more like a conventional mom.

I'm so glad in retrospect that she didn't. Because she gave us space to grow up alongside her, instead of under her, I now feel that becoming an adult isn't about acting old, it's about reclaiming the innocence and enthusiasm my parents had. I have to remember this when I think about having children myself. I forget that being a successful parent doesn't necessarily have to mean acting like an adult all the time.

My parents' relationship was quite egalitarian, considering that my father is really of an earlier generation. My father took my mother's work more seriously sometimes than she had been raised to take it herself. He was way ahead of his time. I always knew that Dad was working and Mom was going to school but someday Mom would be working, too. The fact that my parents had such an equal relationship gave me a skewed sense of what was normal. I thought the whole world was going to be like that bubble of tolerance and progression in which I grew up. I was astonished to find that it wasn't true. I think that my entire life as an activist since then has been an attempt to convey the values with which I grew up, to explain why the hurdles that stand in women's way don't need to be there.

My father has a more maternal personality than my mother. I grew up expecting and accepting that he would assume at least half of the responsibility for child care. He was very involved in our upbringing, the caretaking and diapering. We had a number of baby-sitters while I was growing up, but none of them registered too deeply with me. My father always treated me like a very serious little person. He was committed to apprenticing me as a writer and would set up exercises for me. I think that the model of a man not only listening closely to a woman but listening closely to me helped.

My parents raised my brother to be a profeminist man, but that's such an inadequate term. We always expected that the men in our family would be caring, nurturing, strong, responsible, and responsive to women. That's the model I have of how men should be. Anything short of that seems odd to me. I think that is probably what makes me more optimistic about male-female relations than some feminist theorists.

My dad is crazy about my mother. That's been very good for me. The modeling in my family was that the women get to be the slightly self-absorbed, irrational ones, and the men are there and steady and do the emotional housework that keeps everything in place. Dad's moods were steadier than Mom's. I think that I am a bit more anxious than I would have been if my mother hadn't had her emotional ups and downs. In some ways I am like her. I tend to gravitate toward men like my husband, who are strong enough to let me be a little bit self-absorbed. Of course I give him support and caring, too, and we try to do things fifty-fifty. But, like my father with my mother, my husband is very responsive.

Between the ages of twelve and fifteen, I developed an eating disorder. A boy in my Sunday-school class had said, "Watch out, you're getting a little plump there." I was an average-sized child, but I took the warning to heart. I had seen that my mother, who was always a very beautiful woman, was conflicted about her weight, and I wanted to avoid that sense of anxiety. The irony is that I did it too successfully. I nearly killed myself. I got down to eighty-four pounds.

This was before there was much consciousness about anorexia, and nobody really understood what was going on. I had become incredibly self-absorbed—a typical anorectic. Finally my doctor told me that I had to gain weight. I think that ultimately my feminist upbringing allowed me to acknowledge that it was not okay to starve myself, and I began to force calories into my body to end the starvation. Feminism allowed me to break one of the ultimate taboos for women in this culture, to gain weight. I'm sure that my awareness of what having an eating disorder can do to a young woman's self-esteem helped propel me toward writing about women and body image in my first book, *The Beauty Myth.*

When I was growing up we were broke all the time. From a very early age I was aware of my parents' anxiety around paying bills. There was a sense that the end of the month was a scary time. As I became an adolescent that anxiety became more acute. It was clear to me that I couldn't always do what other kids in my peer group could do and that we didn't quite have the basic trappings of middle-class life. For example, everyone else had washing machines and we didn't. We used to trudge half a mile to the Laundromat, and the laundry was heavy. My brother's braces were a real stretch. It was an uncomfortable feeling. Kids don't want to feel that their financial needs are a burden.

When I became a teenager, it was clear to me that the public schools in San Francisco were pretty bad, and that was when being on the economic tail end of the middle class affected me. Some of my friends were beginning to go to private schools, where they were learning French and Latin, and I couldn't. I remember one depressing time when I was desperately trying to find out how I could get a scholarship to go to a different school. This became a constant theme: How was I going to pay for college? How was I going to pay for graduate school? It was pressure I put on myself, but I didn't feel that I had much alternative. Eventually I was able to piece together my tuition for Yale through a combination of scholarships, working, parents' savings, and going into debt.

In some ways I think that my parents' blitheness about being financially insecure was really good. It made us value things that weren't material. We didn't care about money for the sake of having money. But there was also an undercurrent of fear that could be damaging to a child. For that reason, I want to be more prudent about making sure there's money for my children's education.

> **I nearly killed myself. I got down to eighty-four pounds.**

There's nothing glamorous about not having enough money. I think it's crazy when financially stable, middle-class feminists celebrate poverty in feminism, as if there's something unfeminist about economic independence. There's nothing joyful about not being able to look after your kids, not being able to get winter boots, not being able to get your teeth fixed, or being terrified that you'll never get the education you need. I think it's antifeminism in the worst sense to glorify poverty when women's biggest problem is that they're poor.

Sometimes I find my work as an activist frustrating. I grew up in the heart of the second wave, when exciting things were happening, but as a young woman in the 1980s I saw that feminism for my generation was dead. I knew that I could convey information about feminism to women of my own age in a way that wasn't being done by women of my mother's generation. Historical circumstances change, and language has to change to match. I knew the second wave so well from the inside that I thought I could be a useful link.

My mother gave me a clear grounding in second-wave ideology, which I as an adult, like many of my generation, have been inclined to critique. I think that's how history works, how we move forward. Critiquing is a form of honor, of tribute—a form of love. One of the things I have been writing about, which has brought me into conflict with women of my mother's generation, is rephrasing feminism so that we can draw on the things that worked beautifully from the second wave and avoid some of the mistakes. I'm not attributing the mistakes to second-wave women specifically, but I think that feminism in the last ten years has moved off-center.

The majority of women today want feminism to be a civil rights movement that entitles every woman to determine her own life. Unfortunately, in the eighties the movement became an ideologically overloaded checklist of attitudes determined by one minority group. For instance, you can't be a feminist if you're not left-wing, if you're not a Democrat, if you're not a secular humanist, if you're not vegetarian, and all the way down the line. Really, what it comes down to is that we will let you into the club only if you follow the party line. What this does is exclude many of the women I've listened to in my travels who may be socially conservative, who may be Republican, who feel alienated from feminism, but who care about raising women's status. The status of feminism as a minority party is ensured when any one group claims to speak for all women.

What I've seen in many communities is that numbers of women feel paralyzed about engaging in any prowoman action. Judgmental attitudes about other women's choices is a big problem. A language about heterosexual relations that tends to demonize both men and sexuality is neither fair nor accurate. I believe everyone is elementally bisexual, though of course we tend to incline to one sex or the other. I call myself a practicing heterosexual, but I refuse to limit the way I define my own sexuality.

If anything good comes out of the legacy of postmodernism and the MTV mentality, it will be that we are rightly critical of any monolithic trend to define and limit our identity. In *Fire With Fire* I use the term "power feminism" to try to describe a humanistic, egalitarian civil rights movement that is open. If there is anything that characterizes the third wave, I hope to heaven it will be wit, playfulness, the will to use real power ethically, and resistance to fixed categories.

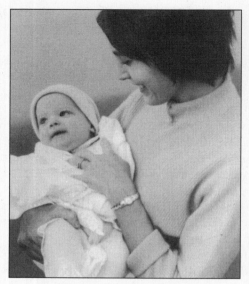

Michelle and Roxanne, 1962.

Michelle and Roxanne, 1994.

Roxanne Dunbar
and
Michelle Callarman

ROXANNE DUNBAR was born in San Antonio, Texas, in 1938 and raised in Oklahoma. In 1968 she launched a group called Female Liberation Front, eventually known as Cell 16, which published *No More Fun and Games: A Journal of Female Liberation*. She received her PhD in history from the University of California–Los Angeles in 1974. A professor in the Department of Ethnic Studies and Women's Studies at California State University, she has written widely on American Indians and other indigenous peoples. She resides in San Francisco.

MICHELLE CALLARMAN was born in San Francisco in 1962. She was raised by her father, Dan Callarman, and stepmother, Lili Dzenis, in Mill Valley, California. After receiving her BA in Fine Arts at the University of California–Berkeley, where she studied intaglio print-making, she attended the California College of Arts and Crafts. She has worked in a factory, waitressed, and been a buyer for a toy store. All the while, she has pursued her avocation as an artist. In 1989 she moved to Portland, Oregon, where she works in a pub for which she also does mural work. She lives with her fourteen-year-old pink cat, "my best and constant companion."

ROXANNE DUNBAR
A Mother's Story

My daughter, Michelle, was born on the second day of the Cuban missile crisis, October 20, 1962, when it seemed certain that we would all be destroyed by nuclear war. It was probably the most traumatic moment of my life. My husband thought we should go to the municipal auditorium, but I kept saying, "It's hopeless; no matter where we go, we're going to be killed." The irony of giving birth at the moment when the world might cease to exist had a profound effect on me, and I made two important decisions: First, I would never have any more children, ever; and second, if we survived, I would try to do something to stop this insanity. That day marked the beginning of my political involvement.

My ancestors were part of the frontier movement from Virginia and the Ohio Valley to Oklahoma when it opened up for settlement in 1890. Mainly Scotch-Irish, they claimed to be descended from Daniel Boone. My grandfather, a Wobbly (a member of the socialist Industrial Workers of the World) was beaten nearly to death by members of the Ku Klux Klan. My mother's Indian mother died when she was two, and she grew up as a half-breed on the streets. She started smoking when she was six years old and begged for food and cigarettes. At fifteen she was placed in a reformatory, where, required to attend church, she became a fervent Baptist convert. She stopped drinking and joined the Women's Christian Temperance Union but secretly continued to do the things she most loved in the world—playing cards and smoking.

On weekends and holidays my mother stayed in town with her sister, where she met and fell in love with my father, a teenage itinerant cowboy. Young and carefree, they married in the booming twenties and quickly had two children. When the Depression and drought hit, they joined the migrant workers, picking cotton in Texas and Oklahoma, living in dugouts. Without food crops or a milk cow, they nearly starved. During cold winters, my older brother and sister walked miles to school wearing makeshift shoes fashioned from cardboard strapped around their feet. Another son was born during the height of the dust bowl, followed two years later, in 1938, by me. Given my parents' circumstances, we were probably not wanted, but once born, we were well loved. I was named Roxy after a movie marquee my father had seen in New Orleans.

When I grew older and tried to judge what people were saying about their mothers, I realized mine didn't fit any of the categories. Leather-skinned, with big hands and muscles, she was strong as a horse and could do anything my father could. Yet she depended on him for her identity and security. In the mid-fifties he began teasing her about not drinking. She said, "Okay, I'll show you," and drank until she got drunk. For the next fourteen years, she was an alcoholic, constantly arrested (Oklahoma was prohibitionist until 1961). To the townspeople, she became known as the drunken Indian. The last year I lived at home, she abused me terribly. I was an adolescent at the time, and there was no way of working out ordinary teenage problems with her. My siblings refused to believe me until one of my older brothers actually walked in when my mother was knocking me down and stomping on me. He took me immediately to live with his family in Oklahoma City.

At sixteen I entered a trade school, and at that point I entered the world. I never intended to attend university, but with high grades I received a scholarship to the University of Oklahoma. My father warned, "Those are not our kind of people; those are rich people." He was right. No one I met at the university came from as poor a background as mine. When references were made to what was going on in the world, I felt intimidated and lost.

A month after I arrived, I met and fell in love with a rich young man who, like Pygmalion, took me in to develop me. Dan Callarman was a rebellious rich kid with long hair—a beatnik who read poetry. Anyone was acceptable in the beatnik underground, and Dan was impressed that I had read books, such as *War and Peace,* that he thought were great but had never read. He challenged my religious beliefs, and I encouraged him to read my heroine, Ayn Rand. *The Fountainhead* became the bond between us—a book I now consider fascistic.

The Callarman family saw me as a poor little hick urchin and "adopted" me into their estate outside Oklahoma City. Missing my own family terribly, broken up because of my mother's drunkenness, I was happy to be taken in. Dan and I married in 1957, when I was eighteen, a "child bride." Though we could have gotten support from the family for both of us to finish university, I insisted on working while Dan finished school, mainly as an excuse to avoid the foreign world of the university.

We moved to California, where Dan joined a structural engineering firm and I entered San Francisco State, a working-class university. Wonderful professors encouraged me, and I fell in love with history. I was learning and thriving, but Dan and I were in totally different worlds. He wanted me to be like his mother, who entertained for his father, but office functions gave me migraine headaches. He wanted a house and property in the suburbs; I had grown up with few possessions, and the idea of

> **Dan sometimes hit other men just for looking at me, so I always made sure my eyes were averted and downcast. During pregnancy, I was free for the first time of his jealousy.**

owning a house and furniture scared me. I was also assimilating the sixties' antimaterialist ideas at San Francisco State. I considered leaving Dan but decided to wait until I finished college.

Despite endometriosis, which the doctor told me would prevent conception, I became pregnant in early 1962. Abortion was illegal and single motherhood was beyond my comprehension, so I thought, "That's it. I'm stuck with it." My resignation provided me with an amazing freedom, however. Dan was a jealous man who sometimes hit other men just for looking at me, so I always made sure my eyes were averted and downcast. During pregnancy, I was free for the first time of his jealousy. He no longer objected to my going to a movie alone, and I realized how confined I had been.

Michelle was born into those traumatic Cold War circumstances that changed my political consciousness; then, when she was three weeks old, the pediatrician discovered that she had no fontanel (soft spot in the skull), and without brain surgery she would die. Even then she might die or be severely retarded. I refused to leave her with a baby-sitter until after the surgery, when she was three months old, because her head was like an eggshell; if anyone dropped her, I wanted to be sure it was me. During the weeks she was in intensive care, I slept in the hospital.

The surgery was successful, but instead of the terrible ordeal drawing us closer, it drove Dan and me further apart. I was the one who took Michelle to the doctor daily for examinations and X rays. Dan's response to the scientific information I gave him when he came home from work was, "How can you be so cold and rational? Don't you care about your child?" But I was raised to be staunch. If you have a crisis to face, you face the crisis: Get the grit and don't complain. Somebody had to take care of the baby. Dan's family came to help, but I ended up having to support them while they criticized me for being cold. I grew from admiring them and believing I was in the wrong to resenting and fearing them. After that I had to leave Dan; there was no getting around it.

During the summer of '63, someone handed me a copy of *The Second Sex* and said, "Read this." When I finished the book, I understood everything I had experienced. Three months later I left, and Dan won custody of Michelle. I had felt inhibited and limited by my husband and marriage, but I never felt burdened or restricted by Michelle. I didn't challenge the custody because I was terrified. I had never been to court or met a lawyer, and I didn't know that mothers were favored in custody cases. I simply thought, "That's it; he has the money and power, and I'm the one who left." It was painful, especially after going through the near-death crisis, but a working-class background so narrows the field of possibilities that I accepted what I assumed was reality.

From the beginning Dan allowed me to visit Michelle almost anytime I wanted, but it was always like a favor granted. For a long time I thought she would be better off growing up with the privileges that the Callarman family offered, whereas with no family to fall back on, I would have been totally alone with her. In 1968, when I decided that women's liberation was necessary, I decided to go back to court. The judge actually gave me custody, but by then Dan had remarried and Michelle was five years old; I didn't want to take her out of a stable home into an unknown situation.

Also, I had become completely involved in the movement. We were struggling for the hearts and minds of people then. I went east to Boston, where I formed a small group called Female Liberation. Abby Rockefeller, a member of the group, gave us her basement at 16 Lexington Avenue in Cambridge for an office. When one of us said, "I feel like we're in an underground secret cell meeting," we began calling ourselves Cell 16. We started a feminist journal called *No More Fun and Games,* and we raised consciousness, largely by satire and street theater.

Becoming involved in more radical aspects of the movement, I traveled south in 1970 to organize, and I began to experience the brunt of FBI repression. I was arrested several times and not allowed to get jobs. I entered law school, but the FBI intervened and I didn't finish. Finally, someone showed me my FBI file, which made me out to be not just a militant leftist, in which I could take some pride, but a weird, perverse psychotic.

Eventually I came to be alienated by the early feminist movement I had helped to form because it did not, and still does not, relate to working-class and minority women. That's the challenge for the future. I regret abandoning the women's movement for a time. However, I helped plan and participated in the United Nations project called Two Decades for Women. Now I am director of women's studies at my university and have completed a memoir, "Outlaw Woman."

During my time away from Michelle, I sent letters and called, but the separation weighed heavily. In 1972 I moved back to California, primarily in order to see her on a weekly basis. She had not forgotten me, and our first encounter was a happy one. Michelle had grown up as a privileged, suburban white girl in the richest county in the United States (Marin), completely opposite to my past or to my movement style of combat boots and dungarees. She had so much that I felt it best to keep my distance. I remained active in the movement, but I didn't discuss it. I dressed correctly in order not to threaten Dan and his wife, and tried to behave properly. They were impressed when I completed my doctorate in history at UCLA. I became a professor at California State University–Hayward in 1974.

With my political views, I knew I could easily lose custody and visitation rights if Dan decided to go back to court. Consequently, I hid a lot of myself from Michelle and made sure not to bring her into my life. For a long time she saw me as an auntie who was nice to have but not someone to miss. We did middle-class things acceptable to her father—Disneyland and the park and beach. Once I took her to Big Sur, unaware that it had turned into a nude beach. Michelle loved it, but I said, "Don't look!" and dragged her away. I could just hear her father: "Oooh, Roxy took her to a hippie naked beach!"

Protected and sheltered, Michelle absorbed many attitudes that I found offensive. I had no authority over her, but when she expressed prejudices or fears about blacks and other minorities, I talked to her. As she got older I told her more about my movement experiences and radical beliefs, and she came to respect them. Once she turned eighteen, no holds were barred. At UC–Berkeley she had her own studio, and we became best friends, doing everything together. I took her to New York to the United Nations when I lobbied and to Geneva when I did human-rights work. She had no interest in the UN, but she loved Geneva and New York, and she's a great traveling companion.

Michelle has had two mothers. I was always the shadow. She rebelled against her stepmother but not against me because I never had to be the disciplinarian—the person who made her go to bed at night or take her medicine. I became a kind of angel on her shoulder, giving her things without demanding of her. I was always the friend, which wasn't very fair to Lili. I regret the long period of time that I didn't see Michelle growing up. It's easy to make myself the victim and say her father didn't let me, but looking back, I think it was easier just to fall back into not seeing her.

Michelle and I are a lot alike in the stages we go through and the things we come to. We don't know whether our similarities are genetic or whether we just happen to be alike. I call myself an errant mother, but I have given her unconditional love 95 percent of the time. That's not easy for me, nor perhaps for anyone. And though she is more critical than I sometimes wish, she is probably the only person who loves me unconditionally. Michelle is just about the most sensitive, smart, and just person I have ever known. Alas, I can take little credit. She is very special.

A Daughter's Story

The first time I remember seeing my mother I was five years old. She came to visit for two hours with a boyfriend in a Volkswagen Bug. She had long hair and was wearing an Indian batik blouse, bell-bottoms, and sandals. I was really nervous and begged my father and stepmother not to let her come, but they said, "We have to let her see you when she wants to, or she might take you away." After my mother arrived, we ate cookies my stepmother had baked, and then we went for a walk to my elementary school. She didn't seem like my mother; she seemed like a stranger, but a nice stranger.

It took a long time for my mother to stop being a stranger. She was careful not to try to force a relationship; she just kept being there, and chipping away and seeing me, and doing things I wanted to do, and only answering questions instead of offering information. When I look back on it, I'm grateful for that. I think that's the only way our relationship could have grown. She knew she had to be cautious because I was uncertain and scared.

I was born in San Francisco in 1962, during the Cuban missile crisis. When I was two years old my mother left my father and me and went to Mexico, and while she was there my father started divorce proceedings. She says she didn't fight his custody of me because he was stable and she thought it would be best. My father remarried when I was three. Lili, my stepmother, a Latvian immigrant, is the opposite of my mother: a straitlaced, voluptuous blonde. My father and step-mother bought a house outside of San Francisco, in the suburbs—exactly what my mother didn't want to do.

I understand why my mother left, and I appreciate the fact that she gave me up for what she thought was a better life, but a part of me thinks: If you had an infant, especially one as sickly as I was, how could you go off to Mexico and leave her? I couldn't. I've never asked her that; I wouldn't want to hurt her. My mother didn't want a child. She was going to college and was uncertain about the future of her marriage. I know that if it had been legal, she would have had an abortion. I think she was confused and just convinced herself that she wasn't a fit mother and that she was doing the right thing.

When I was little I was very close to my father; I worshiped him. I used to be scared that I would turn out like my mother and disappoint him—that I would be wild and emotional and radical. Every time I lost my temper my father would say I was like her, and it scared me. His life was about stability, a house and family. My mother's life was about running from her family, running from her history, denying her past, never settling on any cause or place, just moving around.

I always felt different from other people. I was the only kid in my class from a divorced family. There was a show on TV called "The Courtship of Eddie's Father," and I thought that was like my life. In grade school I had one friend. The ones who excelled in the social strata of the school played a certain game, and I never knew how to interact. Kids can smell that—"Oh, here's somebody we can torture"—and I was tortured mercilessly. Just walking down the hall in school was a constant battle. My stepmother was outgoing and beautiful, and she had been voted most popular in high school. She expected me to be the same way, to be a popular girl, but I was a lot like my mother. In retrospect, I think that not being in Lili's image and fighting her was a good thing. In a world where I thought I was invisible and a nothing, fighting with her grounded me. It was the only thing I had confidence about: I was absolutely sure that I was right and she was wrong.

For a long time I never received any letters from my mother. I was five or six years old when one day, looking in a closet, I found a box full of letters and gifts from her from years back that I had never seen. One was a Chinese worker doll in blue. Perhaps my father intended to give the contents of the box to me later, but I don't know. After finding the box, I began getting cards and gifts. I felt terribly guilty accepting them, knowing how my father felt about my mother, but I wanted to. They made me feel good.

When I was six, my mother fought for custody of me and won, even though she didn't want it. My stepmother had tried to adopt me, and my mother said, "If this goes through, I'll have no right to her. You don't have to let me see her, and you could completely cut me off." After my mother was awarded custody, I had nightmares that she would come in the middle of the night and take me away because she had that right. I suppose that's from my father, but I don't remember. My father believed that my mother's behavior, whims, and motivations were completely irrational and unpredictable, and my mother may have unknowingly nurtured this fear to keep him in line. It was her bargaining chip in my upbringing.

My father and my stepmother began telling me I was fat when I was in the fifth grade. I started dieting then and screwed up my body forever. By the time I was fifteen I began starving myself, going for a couple of weeks at a time without eating. Once, my mother and I were driving across the Golden Gate Bridge, and I said something about how fat and gross I was. She turned to me and said, "What are you talking about? You're such a pretty girl!" That was the first time I had ever heard those words, and they just con-

> The first time I remember seeing my mother I was five years old. She had long hair and was wearing an Indian batik blouse, bell-bottoms, and sandals.

firmed the fact that she was crazy. Now I look at pictures of myself when I thought I was so fat and gross and ugly, and I *was* a pretty girl. Why didn't I know that? If I believed in myself the way my mother believes in me, I probably would be much more confident and less given to paralyzing bouts of insecurity.

Before going to college I believed that my father was perfect and that, in fact, men were better than women. Men were strong, smart, and cool; women were flighty, backstabbing, unstable creatures. But at Berkeley I had an epiphany. I realized that my father, who I thought was my champion against my stepmother's criticism, was undermining my confidence in deeper, more hurtful ways. My father raised me with "harmless" teasing, saying things like "You're spastic, you can't do anything right," "Stick to art, honey, you'll never excel at sports or math," etc. I found out later that he had belittled my mother in the same way. At first I was angry when I realized that thinking I had a big butt and couldn't catch a ball came from my father. I blamed him for all my insecurities and began to think I would have been better off had my mother raised me. Later I came to understand that this was probably how he had been treated by his father and he unknowingly passed it on to me. The good thing that came from this realization was that by taking blame off my stepmother and being more critical of my father's behavior, I had planted the seeds for what would become my feminism.

Sometimes I do wonder what I would have been like if my mother had raised me. Everything that I am today as a feminist—my world-view, how I think about politics and history, how I think about my-self—has come from her. My mother's feminism has opened my eyes and made me more critical. She taught me to be aware of day-to-day misogyny and not to tolerate it, and to value myself as much as I value men. My mother taught me that I can have dignity, and a voice and ego as strong and influential as a man's. I always thought that feminists were bitter, obnoxious, ugly shrews who couldn't attract men. When I got a taste of feminist anger I thought, "How could I not have seen this all along? How could I have been part of a world where you could tell me a sexist joke and I'd laugh?" Once my eyes were open, I could not stop seeing the unfairness everywhere.

I'm jealous of people who were raised in an atmosphere of open-mindedness and politics and talk. I think that would have been good for me. My mother is not afraid to jump headfirst into ice-cold water. She travels to foreign countries where she doesn't know anybody or speak the language, and she gives speeches to important people who will grill and criticize and sometimes ostracize her. It doesn't matter if something is risky or pointless or provocative or just plain foolhardy; she does it because she knows she has something to contribute, a per-spective that matters. I, on the other hand, lose conviction in my cause or task as soon as I come up against the first obstacle.

If I had some of my mother's confidence, I would be parading my portfolio all over town, trying to get art jobs, excitedly telling stone-faced strangers how I can benefit them. As it is, if I get an art job, it's almost by accident, being in the right place at the right time. I know in my heart that I have talent, but as soon as I show a piece to the out-side world, it suddenly shrinks to nothing. I apologize for it before my audience can form an opinion. I am not comfortable out on a limb; I would much rather hug the trunk. My mother dances on that limb and shakes the leaves down on her critics' heads.

Even with my mother's feminist strength and confidence-bolstering, though, I am fairly certain that I would be very much the same as I am today had she raised me. I believe genes play a much stronger role than environment in forming personality. My father's and stepmother's criticism may have worsened my insecurities, but I don't think my mother's support would have cured me of them. And the fact that I am so like my mother in so many ways without her presence—we're both very emotional and opinionated, and clear about how we feel about things—furthers my gene belief.

I know I look like a failure to my father and my stepmother. They sent me to college, and now I work in a pub. Throughout my childhood they always said, "You go to Berkeley, the world will roll out a red carpet for you." But that wasn't the reality of the world I walked out into in 1984 as a fine-arts major. My lifestyle has been partly a choice, but it's also economic. My mother has been very supportive and tells my father, "You're lucky that Michelle is a good person and has made her own way." She says I should go on welfare and do art full-time, but I've never had enough confidence in myself as an artist to be committed to it. It's something that will be a lifelong struggle for me.

The brewery I work for supports artists; all their pubs have paintings and murals. They're always opening pubs, so there's always artwork to do, and they pay me well. But though my niche here in Portland is comfortable and I like it, I also feel kind of stuck. Someday I would like to own a shop to display my own artwork and other people's. I'm interested in useful, practical art, folk art. I don't like anything pretentious. The kinds of things I like to do are small and private. I'm not interested in being successful; I've resigned myself to an unambitious career.

My mother says that she admires that I've never gotten married, because marriage is something that women are expected to do. That's another thing she has given me that is very important to me. I admire the way she has chosen to be alone. Denying family and pursuing her profession has been a very difficult life choice for her, but I've never heard her express regrets. A lot about my mother is very rigid and disciplined. She's frugal; she doesn't think that you should spend money on a lot of things. She lives a pretty simple life for somebody as complicated as she is.

I love children, and children love me, but I'm not ready to have one. To be ready means to be conscious enough of my behavior not to pass on the things that were given to me. To me, having a child is the most important and difficult thing one can do. I'm lucky that it's all right to be a single woman who chooses not to have children. I thank my mother and other feminists for this legacy.

My mother is my hero. She has taken knocks and seen setbacks as a political activist, but she just keeps getting out there and believing that it's all worth it, if just one opinion has been changed. If one person can be reached, that one person will talk to other people and pass the message. It is such a refreshing and beautiful idea. I think it's partly an innocence—an assumption that if you work hard at something, no matter what is in your way, you'll get somewhere, and you should keep working. None of my friends think that we can change anything. We believe, fatalistically, that the government is completely corrupt—lying to us about everything and up to no good, and there's nothing we can do about it.

But because of my mother's enthusiasm, I know I can be a dreamer until I am an old woman. I can keep changing and growing and shaking things up as long as I want to and I can do it without a man (or with a man, but not as a prerequisite). I can face my future and my choices because of the ground my mother broke thirty years ago. The most important thing my mother has given me is that I am valued for who I am and not for my looks or my financial success or my ability to beguile men. Thirty years ago, my success would have been measured by these meaningless attributes, and I would be doomed to misery trying to fit into the limited mold that once defined women.

Abigail, Robin, and Letty, 1974.

Robin, Letty, and Abigail, 1993.

Letty Cottin Pogrebin
and
Abigail Pogrebin
and
Robin Pogrebin

LETTY COTTIN POGREBIN, an acclaimed writer and a founding editor of *Ms.* magazine, was born in 1939 in New York City. She earned her BA in English and American literature from Brandeis University in 1959. Pogrebin has written articles for such publications as the *New York Times* and the *Washington Post* as well as many Jewish publications. Her books include *How to Make It in a Man's World; Family Politics; Deborah, Golda, and Me: Being Jewish and Female in America;* and, most recently, *Getting Over Getting Older.* The mother of three grown children, she lives in New York City with her husband, Bert Pogrebin, an attorney.

ABIGAIL POGREBIN is one minute older than her sister, Robin. They were born in New York City in 1965. Abigail received her BA from Yale University in 1987. She works at CBS News as an associate producer for "60 Minutes." She worked previously on Bill Moyers' election series, "Listening to America," and as a producer for Fred W. Friendly's Media and Society Seminars.

ROBIN POGREBIN, who also attended Yale, is a reporter for *The New York Times*. She has worked as an associate producer for Peter Jennings's documentary unit at ABC News, a staff reporter at the *New York Observer,* and a freelance writer for magazines—including *New York* and *Working Woman.* She is married and lives in Manhattan, 26 blocks from Abigail and her husband.

LETTY COTTIN POGREBIN
A Mother's Story

I will never forget the ecstasy I felt upon learning that I was pregnant with twins. It was as though I were carrying around an incredible secret. I don't remember much about the pregnancy except that I got big fast. I kept trying to convince the obstetrician that I was having more than one baby, but he didn't send me for X rays until my fifth month. I remember leaving the lab uptown and setting off to my obstetrician's office downtown with the X rays in a sealed envelope. I couldn't stand the suspense, so I broke the seal and pulled out the films to see if I could read them. The day was bright and sunny, and by holding the film up against the back window of the taxi, I could clearly make out two little spines and heads, one on either side of my spinal column. Upon arrival, I told the doctor I was having twins. "You weren't supposed to open the envelope," he chastised me. "That's absurd," I said. "This is my body; this is my pregnancy."

It was 1965, long before I became involved in the women's rights movement, yet in this instance I took control as if I were a veteran activist and seasoned protester. In fact, back then I was the most traditional woman you can imagine. In the early years of my marriage I was working as an executive in a book-publishing company, but I was also a good little wife. I baked bread; I went home during lunch hour to prepare dinner; I played with the kids after work. I assumed that if I wanted to "have it all," I had to be a superwoman.

I was born in New York City in 1939. My family lived briefly in the Bronx before moving to Queens—a giant step in upward mobility for a Jewish family. When I was fifteen my mother died. It was the most devastating, formative experience of my life. After her death I was on my own, thrown onto my resources in a way that was unusual for a young woman in the fifties. I had doubled up on my courses in order to graduate early from high school. At sixteen I entered Brandeis University, one of the few schools that had a bohemian and politicized student body in the apathetic fifties. I majored in English and American literature and wrote for the school newspaper, *The Justice.* I was also a cheerleader—the best game in town for a woman.

After graduating in 1959, I moved to New York City and lived in the Village for four years. I had a great job in book publishing, rode a motor scooter, had a dog, dated a lot, heard good jazz, and lived exactly the life I had always dreamed of. On my twenty-fourth birthday I met my husband, Bert, across a volleyball net on Fire Island. We were married in 1963.

> Upon arrival, I told the doctor I was having twins. "You weren't supposed to open the envelope," he chastised me. "That's absurd," I said. "This is my body; this is my pregnancy."

At the time few married women—and even fewer mothers of small children—had careers. So when I got pregnant, I said farewell to my job at the publishing house without even questioning my decision. Abigail and Robin were born on May 17, 1965. Bert wasn't allowed in the delivery room because the babies were delivered by cesarean, but he was with me through the labor.

Whenever we took the twins out in their carriage, they were like magnets; people constantly stopped to look at them. I remember one passerby saying to my husband, "Hey, man, you must be so virile," as if multiple births had something to do with the power of the sperm. The babies were the center of my universe but amazingly easy to care for. I nursed them for four months, which was immensely satisfying, and kept careful records of which twin had which breast at each feeding to be sure they were getting enough milk. When they weren't nursing, they gurgled or slept, and I read novels and did endless needlework projects. I know it sounds ridiculous, but I just didn't have enough to do. Bert saw the problem first. When the twins were six weeks old, he said, "Maybe you should go back to work."

I had loved my publishing job, so I called my former boss to see if I might return to my old post. "I thought you'd be back," he said; "I've held the position open." Thanks to inheriting a terrific child-care person from a friend whose kids were grown, I was able to return to work, but I chose to go into the office only three days a week. Of course, like many women who work part-time, I worked longer hours and took work home with me.

In 1968, pregnant with my son, David, I wrote a breezy, you-can-do-it book about my experiences in publishing—amusing encounters with famous authors, advice on how to succeed in business without really typing, that sort of thing. I never realized that having a boss who allowed me to combine motherhood with a three-day workweek was unusual. I was naive. My book *How to Make It in a Man's World* (1970) was a bit of a queen-bee treatise in that I wrote it without a scintilla of feminist consciousness, but its success allowed me to leave my job and become a full-time writer.

About six months before the book was published, my editor took me to lunch and told me: "You know, there is this new movement called women's liberation. Some of their women may attack you because your book doesn't acknowledge the systemic problems of patriarchy or economic issues affecting women under sexism." "What's patriarchy?" I asked. "What's sexism?" She handed me a manuscript by another author she was editing, Kate Millett. "Read this," she said. I took the manuscript home, and of course it was *Sexual Politics*. It opened my eyes to all the issues that are now so basic to feminist analysis but struck me then with great logical force.

I was determined to get my hands on everything published about this young movement. In 1969 there wasn't much available in bookstores other than Simone de Beauvoir's *The Second Sex* and Betty Friedan's *The Feminine Mystique,* which didn't speak to me, since I wasn't a housewife. So I beat the bushes for underground publications from Chicago Women's Liberation, Redstockings in New York, Bread and Roses in Boston, and various groups in San Francisco and Los Angeles. I read dozens of mimeographed position papers, political tracts, bulletins, newsletters printed on tissue paper and published in women's basements and garages. Through the writings of these trailblazing thinkers of the early women's movement, I raised my consciousness about gender bias, discrimination, and oppression, and read my way into feminism.

In 1971 *Ladies' Home Journal* asked me to do a monthly column called "The Working Woman," in which I reported on the breaking issues of the seventies when Title VII and the executive orders affecting job discrimination and women's work status first began to be seriously applied. (I wrote the column for ten years.) In 1971 I also became involved in the founding of the National Women's Political Caucus (NWPC). At the NWPC organizing conference in Washington, D.C., Gloria Steinem and I stayed up until 4 A.M. working on the group's statement of purpose, and by the end of the weekend we were friends. With Gloria, I also became involved in founding *Ms.* magazine. We had no idea if there would be enough interest in a feminist magazine to ever justify a second issue, so we decided that the first issue had to say it all. Gloria wrote about sisterhood. I wrote on nonsexist child-rearing; Judy Syfers wrote "I Want A Wife"; Barbara Seaman wrote on women's health, Susan Edmiston on the marriage contract, Anne Koedt on lesbian love, and Jane O'Reilly on housework. The illustration we finally selected for the cover, a drawing of a blue female figure with many arms doing all the things women do, evolved out of everything we were trying to say about women as full human beings. The figure, deriving from the Hindu symbol, represented the many responsibilities of women and the multiple roles we fulfill at home and in the world.

When *Ms.* hit the newsstands in December 1971, we expected the issue to be on sale for eight weeks, but all 250,000 copies sold out in eight days. People had predicted the magazine might do well in big cities, where the women's movement was making a few headlines, but when we sold out in places like Kansas and South Carolina, we realized we were onto a grassroots phenomenon, and we immediately began planning to publish the magazine on a monthly schedule, starting in July 1972.

Those were busy years for the movement and important years for me personally. From 1972 to 1976 I was part of a consciousness-raising group that met every week in women's homes. Our members included Betty Dodson, who contributed enormously to educating women about their own sexuality; Eleanor Perry, the screenwriter who wrote *David and Lisa;* Anselma Dell'Olio, a pioneering feminist thinker; and Gloria Steinem, among others. Whenever the group met at my house, my children wandered in and out of the living room and got a lot of love and attention from these radical feminists who were supposedly antichild and antifamily.

Also in the early seventies, I got involved in the creation of the children's record album, book, and TV show *Free to Be . . . You and Me.* Marlo Thomas conceived of this project after a fruitless search for non-sexist stories for her niece. Since such stories didn't exist, we commissioned them, subject by subject, cataloging the issues we cared about: girls' aspirations, boys' emotional lives, working moms, shared housework, children realizing their dreams without being held back by sex stereotypes. Then we called several well-known writers we admired and said, "We have all these subjects; which one interests you?" and the stories poured in. Abigail, Robin, and David were the test kitchens for the project. After listening to a song or story they would say, "This is too sad" or "This is great!" or "This is too silly" or "This talks down to us." We ended up with a wonderful anthology which became a record, book, and TV special. For seventeen years I also edited the "Stories for Free Children" section in *Ms.* and later put together a book-length collection of the best stories that had appeared in the magazine.

I've written eight books, but the hardest was *Growing Up Free,* a guide to nonsexist child-rearing, which took me eight years to research and write. It covers everything from theories of sex-role socialization to advice about toys, TV, books, school curricula, parental discipline, childhood sexuality, and children's friendships. Trying not to be doctrinaire, Bert and I raised our three children with the belief that they should be exposed to all kinds of opportunities and play materials so they could develop their own strengths, rather than have to conform to rigid masculine or feminine roles.

I think the biggest mistake we made as parents was not spending private time with each of our children, one-on-one. We went everywhere as a family. The Parents, the Children, the Family—those were the units; as a result, we didn't develop differentiated relationships with each of them until they were adults, and I think we missed many opportunities for mother-child or father-child intimacy. I would like to have more distinct memories of each child. I remember a day I spent alone with Robin and several with David (because he was left at home after the girls went to college), but I can't think of one day spent with just Abigail. The day with Robin was when she was invited to the White House in 1975 because of an essay she wrote in connection with International Women's Year. We went down to Washington together, and I remember it as a wonderful adventure. I should have learned from that experience that there is something very precious about private time together.

Nevertheless, I have gained so much pleasure from motherhood. I feel lucky to have the children I have. They are motivated by the right values, and all three have wonderful senses of humor. As parents, Bert and I always tried to maintain open communication with them. Even in their teenage years, they never created barriers, so we could always find out what was troubling them if they were upset. Abigail and I had serious issues when she was in her twenties, and I made mistakes that I paid for in a period of agonizing estrangement. But I believe the investment in the intimacy of the earlier years allowed us to get through difficult moments later on.

It means a lot to me that Abigail and Robin have both chosen terrific husbands who also happen to be Jewish. When Abigail was dating a non-Jewish man and moved to California to live with him, it was a sad time for me. Many of my relatives died in the Holocaust, so for my daughter to consider marrying out of the Jewish tradition (not to mention my general dislike of the young man in question) was extremely painful for me. At the same time, I was terrified of losing Abigail because of my objections, and I fought desperately to find a way to stay close. Looking back on this crisis period, I am of two minds: First, maybe I should have kept my objections to myself; on the other hand, I wonder if making noise made it clear how much her choice mattered to me. Not that you marry someone because of what your mother thinks, but I just couldn't fake it. I hope no scars are left.

Both my daughters view the world through a feminist lens, but they are not activists. Each generation has to choose its own battles, and I don't think Abigail and Robin have to do things as we did in the sixties, seventies, and eighties. The activist political style is a dwindling phenomenon. Today, to have an impact on the social scene requires so much more effort than it did in our time. One cannot command media attention so readily, nor raise moral imperatives with the same impact as when feminism was fresh and new and not yet distorted by the backlash. My generation did what we did so that our daughters could take their rights and entitlements for granted, and they do—and that's what we were fighting for in the first place. Activism should not have to be a lifelong profession; you do it in order not to have to do it.

A Daughter's Story

I never *learned* feminism: It was simply the context in which I was raised. I think that's the way the world should experience feminism—as something integrated into our lives. Feminism is practical; it makes sense. It's gotten a bad name for obvious, stupid reasons; people associate it with the clichéd image of a braless, man-hating, hairy woman shouting slogans and smashing a political hammer over someone's head. My mother, for example, is nothing like that. She is certainly strong and opinionated, but she is also maternal, domestic, "feminine"—all the things feminism embraces as well.

I don't take feminism's victories for granted. I realize how much my generation has profited from the work of my mother's generation—that we are riding their coattails. My mother had real battles to fight, and she fought them and they were largely won. My generation doesn't have to fight those battles the same way, and I think we sometimes take the windfall for granted.

The next hurdle for feminism, which my friends and I talk about, is the difficult balance between family and career. Women having kids right now are having a tough time. It's not clear how to handle all the demands or the conflicting pulls on them. There isn't much latitude for men to put child-rearing first, and women are still the ones staying home. And they want to—but they don't want to feel guilty for leaving work, and they don't want to feel guilty when they decide to go back. I hope that when my baby time comes, my feminism will kick in and allow me to feel fine about whatever I choose.

I was born in New York City on May 17, 1965, one minute ahead of my twin sister, Robin. We lived on St. Luke's Place in the Village until Robin and I were five. Then we moved to the Upper West Side, where my parents still live. I was very close to my father's mother, Esther, who was a bit of a curmudgeon. She was a character—caustic and yet loving. She took great joy in all our projects. When we were children, she always wanted us to put on a show, and Robin and I were happy to oblige. All she had to do was ask; we sang, choreographed dance numbers, and dressed up in Grandma's jewelry and high heels. I would characterize my grandma as a feminist. Certainly an activist. When there was a surge in Communist ideology in this country, she was involved and outspoken.

I remember my childhood only as happy. We were a close family and had fun together. Mom was always planning activities for us to do—everything from Spin Art to marionette shows. She defined *supermom.* Her level of energy and creativity were incredibly high—they still are. We were never bored. When we were young, Mom worked part-time, and we were looked after by Yvonne, who was very much a part of our lives. Yvonne came from Barbados and was warm and loving. I remember her sweet smile.

Both my parents led busy lives. There was a tremendous standard of achievement set by their example. They never overtly pushed us, but there was a sense that life has all these opportunities, and you might as well seize them—that they are in your reach. We grew up with the sense that we were entitled to the best and that we shouldn't settle for second-rate anything—a second-rate grade, a second-rate school, a second-rate boyfriend.

Robin and I responded to the atmosphere of achievement and followed in that vein. Our younger brother, David, just opted out. My parents were worried. They didn't know if they should push him, but they didn't want him to feel they'd given up on him. Finally he found his gift—he became a skilled chef—and the family breathed a sigh of relief. He attended the Culinary Institute of America (the Harvard of cooking schools, but of course), and he now manages a popular New York restaurant. I think it's wonderful that David found something he loves doing, but I hate to think of the pressure he must have felt to measure up. The fact is, Mom and Dad are an impressive team, and Robin and I are obviously also a kind of team, and it had to be difficult to be on your own in the face of that—no matter how close our family was.

Mom was and is always working on something. She takes vacations, has a social life, exercises, and goes to the occasional movie, but she's always in the middle of some writing project with a deadline hanging over her. I think it's especially hard to be a mother who works at home because the line gets blurred between when Mom is available and when she's not. When she was at *Ms.* magazine, it was fun to go there and be treated like celebrities and play with the typewriter. But when she wrote at home, she sometimes closed her door and put up a sign: MOM IS WRITING. It wasn't that we couldn't interrupt her, but we had to respect her work space.

Because she was busy, time with Mom was precious. She and I have talked about whether there's anything wrong with that. It's a hard call—especially when I look at friends who took their mothers for granted, whose moms were just always around, not having projects or pursuits of their own. When we talk about these issues, there's a wariness; I think Mom takes it personally. But there should be some room for addressing the pitfalls of the career-family balancing act—especially for the sake of my generation, which is making the next attempt. Maybe it's just not possible to have a husband, kids, career, and toned body all at the same time. There are costs, and I don't think it's terrible to acknowledge that. I think we'll feel less like failures if we realize some failure is inevitable.

I did not see any flaws in my parents until I was twenty-three years old—which is late. I went through my separation from them in an abrupt way. Robin didn't do it to the same extent. She had some of the same awakenings and struggles, but she always maintained a relationship with them that was P.C.—Pogrebin Correct. It was a temporary strain on my friendship with Robin, because I felt she let me be the black sheep for a while.

Several years ago, I dated a man who was not Jewish (strike one), somewhat conservative (strike two), and not ready to warm to a family that didn't want him in my life (strike three). It was a disaster. During the two years I was with Michael, there was a deep rift between my parents and me. I moved to California with him and didn't see them much. It was incredibly painful, and it's hard even to recall it now. They felt they'd lost me, and I felt they'd turned their backs. I was going through my own questioning process—realizing that I hadn't come to certain Pogrebin doctrines on my own, and that I should know why I believed the things I said I did. I wanted not just to adopt the dogma but to step back for a minute and consider the issues for myself—even if I ultimately came to the same conclusions. Michael never changed my mind; he just challenged my thinking. And I couldn't believe my parents had so little faith in the "independent" woman they raised to think I could be so easily swayed. My parents' liberal politics are an orthodoxy. There isn't much room for dissent—this despite the fact that the orthodoxy includes *tolerance of difference.* That seemed to me to be the great hypocrisy when it came to Michael. They didn't really try to get to know the person I cared for.

After two years I realized—on my own time, in my own head—that this match would never weather all the differences, which continued to surface and multiply. When I left California, I moved back in with Mom and Dad until I could find my own apartment. I couldn't help feeling like the prodigal daughter come home, proving her parents right. But Mom and Dad, to their credit, never even hinted an I-told-you-so. (Mom just left a synagogue flyer on my bed offering "Shabbat for Singles.")

> **I did not see any flaws in my parents until I was twenty-three years old.**

I met my husband, David Shapiro, in February of 1993. He works at a small investment banking firm that advises labor unions on restructuring and employee ownership. He has twin sisters and absolutely no pretensions. He is just good, intelligent, and fun, and he loves life. A lot like my father, he works hard, but he doesn't fret about things. I have the potential to get neurotic and bogged down, and he doesn't bring any of that out in me—he kind of keeps me buoyed. I feel like I am a better person with him.

Everyone says that there are going to be mountains ahead in marriage, and you might as well start from a place of commonality. I resisted the idea that you inevitably come around and marry someone familiar; I didn't want to feel like I was giving in or giving up. But I know now that in addition to falling in love with someone, it is important that they appreciate my family and what I come from. It's a relief not to have to constantly defend so much in my life.

Our family was fairly noncontentious. My parents never had arguments that scared us. Their fights were rare and always about the same things—who does the bills and who does more work around the house. Theirs was generally an egalitarian partnership, especially in terms of an emotional connection with us—my father was just as involved in our lives, and offered wise counsel and humor. But at the same time it wasn't an ideal feminist household, where all chores and all duties were equally shared. The house was equal in soul and in friendship, not in practice. When we were young, Dad made us Wheatina for breakfast, helped us on homework, taught us how to throw a baseball, and took us places, but managing life's logistics fell to my mother.

My father is my mother's biggest fan. Their relationship could have been, with all of her notoriety and accolades, fraught with land mines. But my father has a lot of quiet confidence, and he has found real contentment in his work, his kids, his summer house, and, above all, in his wife and her accomplishments. It's important to point out that in addition to his emotional support, he offered the financial support my mother needed to sustain her work. As an activist, she was not making much money for many years, and she says that without my father's income, she could never have managed to keep writing and keep us afloat. She's honest about the fact that you can't be a superwoman without help. Something is going to slip or drop.

I don't like conflict. That may be the only unhealthy by-product of my happy childhood. Witnessing no bumps in my parents' marriage, I came to think that if you had any, then the whole relationship or friendship was bad. Now that I am an adult, I can see that everybody has fights and problems, but my parents set a precedent of perfection. When people say, "Marriage is hard, marriage takes work," it doesn't ring true for my mother. That isn't that she intends to be smug about it, but it just hasn't been work for her. It set a high standard for us. People say it's hard to inherit a divorced relationship, but it's also complicated to inherit an ideal relationship. How can you possibly match it? And if you fall short in any way, you're bound to question the whole thing. Also, wanting to mirror your parents' relationship may mean you are seeking something that really isn't right for *you*. It is not necessarily a good thing to want what your parents have, but there was little that I could point to that I wanted different.

My friendship with my parents is as good now as it's ever been. That rough patch with Michael was a blip, but on some level I won't ever forget it. It showed me that their support is conditional in a way; that I could lose it; that there are things I could do that could cost me. I had never felt that before, and it's a lonely memory. But at the same time I know how scared they were. And I hate that I was the cause of such a sad time for them.

But there's no question that when all is said and done, my mother is a hero to me. I love her strength, her wholehearted and infectious enthusiasm. She loves celebration and ritual and making things beautiful. The family is so important to her, and it's the heart of who I am. She is incredibly loving and affectionate. I like that she is outspoken and accomplished. Mom's fame is a specific kind: When people know her, it means they know her work and they know what she stands for. And I am proud of that—proud when strangers recognize my last name and ask if I'm related.

My generation has seen so much activism in recent history that it's important to separate out what is worth yelling about now. There are clearly wars yet to be won, but I think it's important to isolate what they are. I don't think seventies activism, which worked in its time, is going to be effective now. My mother's work in those years was worthy of her attention and voice. Now there seems to be a lot of shouting for the sake of it. If someone asks me to, I will talk about feminism, but I don't see a need to add my voice. Maybe it's a cop-out, but for me, feminism hasn't been so much a cause as a way of life. It's about how you are at work, in your marriage and friendships. It's about feeling entitled to life's best, seeing how far you can go, getting your due. It's about loving those near to you and helping new daughters on the road my mother helped pave for them.

ROBIN POGREBIN
A Daughter's Story

To me, feminism means options. That's why I have trouble understanding why anyone would reject the term. If I have the slightest difficulty calling myself a feminist, it is because I haven't been more of an active one. I am a daughter of the women's movement in the literal sense; my mother was one of its most active leaders. Therefore I grew up with feminism as a way of life. And because I benefited so much from the battles fought by my mother and her sister activists, I haven't felt the imperative to keep fighting. Movements are organized in opposition to things, and the enemy lately seems harder to identify. In the world I move in day to day, women have made remarkable progress. They are the editors I report to as a journalist, the politicians I vote for, the public figures I look up to. But I also see that women remain scarce in the top ranks of corporations, and that sex discrimination, while more subtle, is no less pervasive or insidious.

When people say that I am following in my mother's footsteps, I have to disagree. Although we are both writers, my mother is an advocate, identified with the ideas she writes about. In my career as a news reporter, I aim to be as objective as I can. This professional distinction between my mother and myself is emblematic of our personal differences. I am more comfortable behind the scenes, telling other people's stories, conveying other people's ideas, keeping my thoughts to myself. My mother likes to speak her mind in public and doesn't worry about how her views will be received. I prefer to consider different perspectives on an issue and feel less eager to assert my own.

I was born in New York City on May 17, 1965. My twin sister, Abigail, and I had a very creative childhood. We made collages, improvised plays, kept journals, and filled empty books with stories. When I was ten years old, I started a magazine called *Brainstorm.* My mother made copies for me at her office, and I mailed them out to the relatives and friends on my subscription list.

Growing up, Abigail and I did just about everything together. We spent whole weekends in our own make-believe world, putting on elaborate costumes from closets filled with our extensive dress-up collection, inviting friends over to "act" with us.

Although I was close to my younger brother, David, our relationship developed less easily. He was three years our junior, which felt like a significant gulf at the time, and he had somewhat different interests. Because our parents constantly pressured my sister and me to be closer to my brother, we rebelled against that expectation. My relationship with David has grown more natural as we've grown older. We've had the chance to get to know each other in our own time and define our relationship on our terms.

My mother was always a powerful presence in my life. By her mid-twenties she had already established a solid career in publishing and been commissioned to write her first book, *How to Make It in a Man's World*. After she had children and became a founding editor of *Ms.* magazine, she worked at home a few days a week. When we were young, her desk was in the living room. She tried to create the illusion of an office, but we were never really able to leave her alone for long. Later she worked in a study and put a sign on the door when she didn't want to be disturbed.

Growing up, I was always aware that I had a celebrity mom and felt lucky because of it. Important things seemed to happen in our house. My mother was forever in the thick of political events, seminars, marches, countless meetings. Between turning out books, she wrote articles and lectured all over the country.

Because both of our parents were so professionally and socially active, I sensed that their time was precious—in some ways too precious. On the positive side, I never took them for granted and always felt as if their presence was special and worth savoring. On the other hand, I would have liked to be able to take them a little more for granted. I remember dinnertime with them being stimulating and meaningful but also something of a pressured performance—feeling as if I had to be lively and full of good news to keep their attention, to get it all in before they'd go away.

It's difficult just to shoot the breeze with my mother. She has never been someone with the air of, "Sure, drop by anytime." Being with her is about quality, not quantity. She always told us that we were her priority and that she would drop everything if we needed her for something important—which she often did. But it seems difficult to take on as much as my mother did and expect your children to feel wholly relaxed about your company. If a parent is doing a million things, a child is bound to feel like number million-and-one once in a while. Already seeing I have the same tendency as my mother to overextend myself, I hope I can remember that lesson when I have children. Ironically, now that I am older and need less of my mother's attention, she seems to have more of it to give.

> I remember dinnertime with them being stimulating and meaningful but also something of a pressured performance—feeling as if I had to be lively and full of good news to keep their attention, to get it all in before they'd go away.

To my mother's immense credit, she always carved time out of her overcrowded schedule to make special occasions feel festive and significant. She loves rituals, especially when they revolve around the family. Every Chanukah my mother used to host a big party for relatives and close friends at which every guest would receive a beautifully wrapped present. She organized our birthday parties around a particular theme; one year it was baseball—with my sister and me each captaining a team of our friends—and my mother gave our invited friends secondhand baseball shirts to wear as uniforms during the game and take home as party favors. Another year the motif was Paris; my mother put up pictures of the foreign city, and we all wore berets.

It feels mean-spirited to be anything but appreciative of my mother's painstaking efforts to make life's milestones beautiful and meaningful. But she is, in this and so many other ways, an almost impossible act to follow. Moreover, while I love my mother's enthusiasm for such events, her obvious stake in having them go well has sometimes translated as a demand to make sure they do. Like perhaps every mother, mine has always wanted our family to get along. But when we quarrel, she takes it especially hard, unable to just chalk it up to normal family tensions. It makes us feel as if we have let her down by being less than loving toward one another.

My mother's investment in the image of a happy, egalitarian family has caused her to cover for my father's inattention to household obligations, such as making social plans, keeping in touch with extended family members, and buying us kids birthday or holiday presents. While my father fully participates in our family get-togethers, he does not initiate them. Only once in my life has my father picked out a gift for me himself. My mother protects my father in these situations—saying presents she chose are from both of them, etc.—because she cares very much about projecting a united front, and because she knows he has only the best intentions.

I never doubted my father's intentions; I know he loves me and wants to come through. But I have also grown to realize that small efforts like making someone dinner or buying a gift or suggesting a lunch date—superficial as they may seem—can also be important. I have also seen how being the family organizer can backfire, given that I have become one myself. The men in the family rarely get blamed for being too lazy. Women in the family often get faulted for being uptight or overly controlling.

My mother has decided that the battle to make my father take more responsibility for his family and social obligations is not worth fighting. I forgive him his foibles also, mostly because it isn't worth agonizing over them. I appreciate the easygoing sensibility that makes him somewhat neglectful, and that my father is more involved in my life than most fathers. He is someone I feel I can turn to; his advice has often calmed me in moments of confusion.

Because of their commitment to avoid potential sources of conflict, my parents have what some describe as a perfect relationship. They don't bump up against the ways in which they might be failing each other. My mother has made peace with my father's lack of domestic organization; he indulges her occasional workaholic tendency to stay home and write on a Saturday night rather than go to the movies. My father admires my mother's intensifying religiosity; my mother accepts my father's religious indifference. It often amazes me that all the pressure my sister and I have felt from my mother's example—to be more actively Jewish, to juggle a thousand things at once—my father doesn't seem to feel at all.

My mother says one of the main reasons she and my father don't fight is that they never say the mean thing: You don't cut to the quick for the very reason that a spouse—more than anybody else—so easily can, she says. You know each other's vulnerabilities. You know how to hurt them. Don't use that knowledge against the ones you love most.

I think there can be a vitality to the occasional volatility of a relationship. But I cannot pretend I am ever free of the model that my parents' peaceful marriage represents. Perhaps worst of all, fighting scares me more than it should, because I have few tools for surviving it. I'm not saying my parents should have created conflict just to be instructive. But it would have helped if they had told me that life can be complicated and not all marriages are picture-perfect and it doesn't mean the world will fall apart if you argue.

To some extent, I may always resent my parents for setting such an impossible standard. On the other hand, I believe aspiring to some ideal is worthwhile. And I hope I'm getting closer to a place where I accept and appreciate my parents for who they are without demonizing them or idolizing them, where I acknowledge that it is more important to have a close and complex relationship with them than one that is detached or dishonest.

The struggle for me when I become a parent, of course, will be to take from my mother and father the attributes that I admire and to improve upon those things I think they might have done better. To encourage my children to aim high and explore every option, without making them feel as if they have to lead high-powered lives to be loved. To be available for my children, while at the same time pursuing my professional and personal interests apart from parenting. To somehow communicate to my children that even though their parents live one way, the world is full of many different versions that are equally valid.

And in the end, ironically, I imagine my struggle will prove to be just what my mother's has always been: knowing in practice it is impossible to have and do it all, but believing in principle that it is crucial to keep trying.

Eleanor and Lori, 1978.

Lori and Eleanor, 1995.

Eleanor Smeal
and
Lori Smeal

ELEANOR SMEAL, a leading advocate for women's rights and mother of two grown children, was born in Ohio in 1939. Known as both a political strategist and a grassroots organizer, she discovered the "gender gap" in voting, led the Equal Rights Amendment campaign from 1977 to 1992, organized the first national abortion rights march of over a hundred thousand people in Washington, D.C., and co-founded and became president of the Feminist Majority Fund and Foundation in 1987. She may be best known for the years she served as president of the National Organization for Women (NOW); under Smeal's leadership, NOW became the pre-eminent feminist organization in the country. Smeal holds a BA and an honorary law degree from Duke University and an MA from the University of Florida. She lives in Arlington, Virginia.

LORI SMEAL, a corporate associate with Pryor, Cashman, Sherman and Flynn in Manhattan, intends to combine her interest in women's rights with her career as a lawyer. Born in Pittsburgh, Pennsylvania, in

1968, she attended Boston University School of Management, where she received a BS in business administration with a concentration in accounting in 1990. In 1994 she earned her JD from the University of California, Hastings College of the Law, in San Francisco. While in law school she worked as a summer associate for the Center for Reproductive Law and Policy in New York and as an intern for a female judge at the California Court of Appeals. Smeal has been an American Jurisprudence Award recipient three times, executive editor of *Hastings' Communications and Entertainment Law Journal*, and a member of the Hastings Moot Court Board. She resides in New York City.

ELEANOR SMEAL
A Mother's Story

I had intended to wait until my children were around ten years old before beginning a career. With my son, Tod, I tried to be a perfect stay-at-home mother, the kind they used to feature in women's magazines, but my dad was dying, so I couldn't maintain it. When I was pregnant with my daughter, Lori, in 1968, I became ill with thalassemia minor, a form of Mediterranean anemia, which I inherited from my Italian-born father. Then I became even sicker with a slipped disk when Lori was ten months old. I decided that getting sick, loving, and dying are part of life. You don't take time out to have children; they have to become integrated in your life. I vowed that if I got well, I was not going to put off my career.

I'm an active person, and lying flat on my back for the best part of a year was hard to take. I had to do something, so I read every book I could get my hands on. My husband brought me feminist and women's history books from the library, and as a result I decided to do a doctoral dissertation on women and politics. At first my interest in the subject was academic. One day I was getting some material photocopied for Environment Pittsburgh, a group I volunteered for (air pollution was a real problem at the time), and the woman doing the copying asked, "Why is a woman like you not active in the women's movement?" I said I didn't know there was anything in Pittsburgh. She said, "Oh, yeah, there's a local chapter of the National Organization for Women; I belong to it." I said, "I'll go," and that was it. The year was 1970.

I am part of a transitional generation of women who made the jump from home to the workplace. The Rush Limbaughs of the world paint feminists as one-dimensional people, without families or knowledge of real life. I not only had a husband and children but also an extended Italian-American family with cousins and aunts and uncles. I grew up aware of the stigma against a first-generation Italian-American family. I was a homemaker without pay for fourteen years before becoming president of NOW. Considering my background, it wasn't such a big leap. I was educated, and I had volunteered for the Allegheny County League of Women Voters and a "junior" women's group in the South Hills of Pittsburgh.

My parents loved democracy and thought America was wonderful. My mother was traditional in some ways and progressive in others. In her lifetime, she went from riding in a horse and buggy to watching the first man on the moon. She talked about it all and could not get over it. Any new domestic innovation we learned about in Erie, Pennsylvania, she had to have. When permanent-press sheets came out, she got the permanent-press sheets; when Flako piecrust came out, she got the Flako piecrust. If there was a new way of doing a thing, she did it. The future was bright because the world was getting better. Science was better; knowledge was better. There was poverty in the world, but we were going to lick it. In the future, education would solve it all. Walking on the moon or Mrs. Smith's deep-dish apple pie—it was all progress.

My father was a born optimist. If things were bad today, they would get better tomorrow. World War II was the right thing. I remember staying up all night with my dad in 1948 listening to the Truman returns. My dad was ecstatic about Truman. On the school bus the next day I told everyone Truman had won, and they didn't even know who he was. (Ironically, my parents were the only non-high-school graduates in our neighborhood, as far as I knew.) Even after my father owned his own insurance agency, he worried about how less-fortunate people got paid. He and my mother gave me big doses of self-esteem. They told me and my three brothers that we were the smartest and the best.

I tried hard not to disappoint my parents and never really rebelled. They wanted me to go to Duke, and, frankly, I might have left when I discovered that Duke was racially segregated, but I could not disappoint them. They had sacrificed to get me to an elite, top school, and I felt a sense of duty and obligation, so I stayed. Duke was located midway between Erie and the Florida town where my parents had a second home, so I could easily go in either direction for school vacations. My husband, Charlie, and I went to my parents' home for most holidays as long as my mother was alive. We wanted to, and we also thought we should. I don't think my own children have rebelled, either. I know it is in fashion that kids are supposed to rebel, but it has not been our experience.

Some parts of my experience at Duke were very positive. I was president of my dorm and chair of the dorm presidents on the women's campus. I became an activist, working hard for integration and against discrimination. (My parents were proud of that; they hated discrimination.) We tried to integrate peacefully in the late fifties and early sixties. When the vote was taken, we had won on the women's campus and lost on the men's. In 1986, as the keynote speaker at my twenty-fifth college reunion, I recounted this experience and my current feminist struggles to end discrimination, and my former classmates responded with a standing ovation.

I had always wanted to be a lawyer. As a Phi Beta Kappa graduate in 1961, I could have gone to law school, but my political-science professor advised against it: "You'll become a lawyer, but you'll never practice law; you'll end up being a law librarian. Women can only be researchers." Two of my three chief advisors, Ruth McQuown and Gladys Kammerer at the University of Florida, were female (and feminist, I later learned), which was unusual. In 1963 I completed my master's degree, married Charlie Smeal, a PhD student in metallurgy, and continued in a doctoral program in political science at the University of Florida.

After completing the coursework for the PhD, I became ill with thalassemia and was ill for much of the next seven years. Tod was born in 1965 and Lori in 1968. Both pregnancies were difficult. We had little enough money, but at least I could afford help. There were no insurance programs for disabled homemakers, however. I asked one doctor what happened to those who could not afford help, and he said, "They have a lot of relapses." Women become chronically ill because they can never take time off. As it was, I had five relapses, the last when Tod was four and Lori was a baby.

As a result of my personal experience, I learned a lot about disability in pregnancy. In 1978, as president of NOW, I fought for the Pregnancy Discrimination Act, which ensured that disability in pregnancy would be treated as any other illness for women workers. In the early 1980s I testified on behalf of a broad coalition of women's groups for the Family and Medical Leave Act—an act considered an advance at the time, although it provided only unpaid leave. The women's groups had no consensus on unpaid leave, but I refused to testify unless I could depart from my remarks and say that family medical leave should be paid. Thirty percent of pregnancies have illnesses connected to them. What do people do? As an activist and a mother, my testimony was not just academic.

Being a housewife is good preparation for management because of the constant series of interruptions. When I worked at home, my children were around my feet. I don't know what a closed door means. We had a playroom, but the children wanted to be wherever I was. I had a desk in the family room, but I was always in the center of the chaos. My professional life has been like that, too.

> If you're visiting another mother with kids, what difference does it make whether you're doing a mailing or making cookies?

In the early days it was easy to combine motherhood and feminist activism. The more active I was, the better the kids did in everything, especially school. When Tod and Lori saw me testify, they could identify a new use for learning. They accompanied me to demonstrations, to courtrooms, and to letter-mailing parties. If you're visiting another mother with kids, what difference does it make whether you're doing a mailing or making cookies? Either way, the kids participate. Several NOW members in my community had children, and in 1971 we opened South Hills NOW nursery, an all-day nursery center with nonsexist education and high standards. Most of the kids could read well before kindergarten, not because we pushed them but because they had such high-quality care. It was there that Lori got a head start in her education.

When I became a national leader, I had to travel a lot. I don't believe in segmenting my life, however, so I sort of pulled it all together. I got my own mother involved in activism, and she came to marches and rallies. My nieces became involved, three of whom have worked for me and the feminist movement as full-time activists at various times. Bringing my children to the Supreme Court or to Congress or to state legislatures or to a NOW conference was just as important as taking them to a zoo. (I never liked zoos much, anyway, on principle.) I fought hard for NOW conferences to have child care, but not in the traditional baby-sitting sense. We had outings for the kids where they went out and *did* things. To this day, NOW has child care at all of its conferences.

Being active at the national level is physically demanding, and I often felt tired. But I didn't feel guilty about the time I spent away from Tod and Lori. Charlie made it immensely easier for me to do what I did—and probably made it possible. Believing my work was important for our children and for us, he was always supportive. He put a lot of time into raising the children. They never said, "Mom, I miss you. You're not home enough," I think, because he was able to be fully present when I wasn't around. Charlie left his work at the office, and when he was home, he was home. I can still see him on the floor playing board games with Tod and Lori for hours—from chess to checkers to Monopoly. If I mentioned the word *baby-sitting,* he had a fit. "I am not ever baby-sitting," he said. "These are my children. This is something I want to do." I never had to worry, because the kids were in good hands. My mom helped out, too. She came for a month at a time in the early years and took the kids for a couple of weeks every summer. She encouraged me to do it all. "We worked hard for you to get an education," she said. "Use it."

Charlie's steady salary enabled me to do the kind of work I did. Volunteering costs money—gas, travel, stamps, refreshments, phone bills—which many people can't afford. Charlie saw his support of my work as his contribution to improving the community and society. When I was elected president of NOW in 1977, I began to be paid for my work. The salary was nominal, but it paid my expenses. Since about 1980, I have made a living from my work.

Overall, I think that the second wave of feminism has been incredibly successful. I look at the legislation we have influenced, such as the Pregnancy Discrimination Act or the Violence Against Women Act, or at opening Little League to girls. The list goes on and on. On discouraging days, however, it seems that too much work has been done for too little progress. Women in Iran still wear veils; eighty million women in the world have had clitoridectomies; a small right wing is growing once again in Germany, where fascists destroyed the feminists, restricting women's roles to "children, kitchen, and church." A fundamentalist breeze is blowing throughout the world, and the position of women is not secure. Before I die, I would like to know that the successes of the feminist movement are stable, that they are integrated into the fabric of our society.

When I was younger I believed in a constant progress toward improvement; now I see that you have to fight every inch of the way. To be debating evolution versus creationism in the last decade of the twentieth century is ridiculous. Why are some reactionary viewpoints perpetuated generation after generation in our society? Why is society afraid of telling its children the truth? I believe that it is our responsibility to speak out against ignorance, wherever it is. I wouldn't be doing what I am doing if I didn't think it was possible to change institutions. The odds are against us, but it is our responsibility to try.

I do believe that a third wave of feminism is gaining momentum. Its members are young and strong, and they are more educated and more informed than we were. Until women have equality in the real sense—meaning an equal partnership with men—we need feminism. Women are not full, equal citizens under the law; the laws still favor men. We need to work for the Equal Rights Amendment; we need to get more women elected to office; we need to make a safer, nonviolent world where there is no place for poverty or human and environmental degradation.

Many daughters of activists hesitate to become activists because they have seen that it is a difficult way of life. I say that's fine. An activist is like a pianist: You've either got the impulse and the dedication or you don't. I've told Lori, "Charlie and I volunteered enough for at least five generations. You can have a break." Actually, Lori is more involved in activism than I thought she might be. But then, we are alike in many ways. We both love to live, and we love to be in the center of things. On the surface she appears to have it all: She is attractive, smart, and educated. At the same time, though, she has inherited some of my weaknesses and the same blood disease; we both worry too much and we overwork. If I could wave a magic wand, I might make both of us a little less conscientious.

I used to think it was silly for parents to be proud—after all, chance has a lot to do with it. You participate and help all you can, but there are many things over which you have no control. But I have to say I'm proud of my children, even though it's corny. I'm really pleased with the people they've become. When I think that Lori has finished law school and that Tod, who recently finished his PhD in molecular biology, is studying how cells change, I get excited about the future. I believe that their lives will make a difference.

A Daughter's Story

My mother has mentored me in every respect. Because she is a feminist, she has taught me that I am capable of doing any job—that I am capable of anything. She has influenced my thinking about furthering my career and raising children at the same time. People have asked me whether I plan to stay home when I have children. I look at my mother, who did a great job balancing her work and family life—with the help of my father and regular baby-sitters, of course. I plan to do the same.

I was born in Pittsburgh, Pennsylvania, on February 20, 1968. My father, a metallurgist, worked at Westinghouse. My mother was twenty-five years old when my brother, Tod, was born, and twenty-eight years old when I was born. Initially my mother stayed at home, but when I was still very young she became involved in volunteer work.

Unfortunately, shortly after my birth my mother slipped a disk in her back, causing her to be bedridden for almost one year. During the period in which she was confined to her bed, my father brought home feminist books for her to read. Although at that time she had already been interested in politics and particularly the women's movement, during her illness she became convinced that she wanted to devote her life to the advancement of women.

As a young child, I witnessed the early days of her grassroots involvement in the women's movement. She organized countless letter-writing campaigns at our house (in which we kids participated by addressing and stamping the envelopes) to obtain the support of members of state legislatures for the Equal Rights Amendment (ERA). I was proud of my mother, since I knew she was devoting her time and energy to helping women and girls, including myself. She became more and more active in the movement and soon began traveling throughout the country delivering public speeches and lobbying state legislators.

My mother became president of the National Organization for Women (NOW) when I was nine years old. Her new position required that she work in Washington, D.C. During her first year as president of NOW, my father, brother, and I remained in Pittsburgh. On weekends, either we would travel to Washington or she would return to Pittsburgh so that our family could spend time together. After about two years, my parents decided that the distance was too difficult and that the entire family should move to the Washington, D.C., area. While I was growing up in Washington, my mother often brought me along with her to Capitol Hill while she lobbied for extensions of time to pass the ERA. I loved the excitement; politics fascinated me.

> I'll never forget hearing my mother address the thousands of supporters on the Mall. When she began speaking, a feeling of pride overcame me, and I wanted to tell the world, "That's my mother!"

The first major women's rights event that I remember attending was the 1978 March on Washington in support of women's equality. It was about ninety degrees that day; over one hundred thousand people marched. It was exciting—I met actors and actresses, members of Congress, and leaders of major organizations. My mother was up in the front lines, but my brother, my father, and I decided to stay back in the crowd. I'll never forget my mother's address to the thousands of supporters on the Mall. When she began speaking, a feeling of pride overcame me, and I wanted to tell the world, "That's my mother!"

I have always been close to both of my parents, but I became very close to my father while my mother was traveling throughout the country rallying support for the ERA. Most husbands would not have been as understanding and supportive of their wife's career as my father was of my mother's. She was *always* busy; she worked extremely long hours. It was not unusual for her to work until three or four in the morning, and it was not unusual for her to be traveling for months at a time. I remember seeing my father's patience wane when she would get business calls at home during meals. My father would say, "Do you have to take every phone call?" My mother had a difficult time telling others no. It seemed like everyone wanted a piece of her, and she always wanted to give it. She never wanted to let anyone down. Although my father would get frustrated at times with her demanding schedule, he really believed in what my mother was fighting for.

My mother and father have very different personalities. My father is very quiet and my mother is extremely outgoing. He was an unusual father; not only was he always there for my brother and me, he also helped out at home by cleaning, doing laundry, and cooking. I don't know where my father got his feminist views from, since his family was rather conservative and did not share his progressive views.

I think my mother has done an incredible job of balancing her professional life and her personal life. Even during the days when she was traveling a lot, I felt close to her. My mother and I have a great relationship, even though we appear to be very different people. I am more quiet than she is and I am not as comfortable speaking to large groups of people. It always amazes me how my mother can speak to thousands of people with such ease and without a single note in front of her. I know she has more practice than most, but it comes to her so naturally. Her charismatic nature and ability to energize a crowd cannot just be the result of practice, as she claims. My mother and I are very similar in that we are extremely hard workers with great ambition. But I often wonder how she keeps going year after year at such an accelerated pace, and I wonder if I could do the same.

People who don't really know my mother probably think that she is just as aggressive and opinionated in her personal life as she is in her professional life. Quite the contrary. At home she is very easygoing. She never yelled at me or my brother. Like her parents, she didn't believe in disciplining her children through punishment. That doesn't mean that she never disapproved of anything we did as children; she just didn't punish us for our mistakes. Instead, she just let us know that she was disappointed or that she disagreed with what we had done. The only times I remember her raising her voice in the house were when she was expressing her opinion about a controversial political issue. There would be no stopping her then. She has such a strong passion for what she has spent her entire adult life fighting for—equality for women.

Growing up, I always felt protective of my mother and would feel hurt when her efforts were criticized, whether the criticism came from a friend, a relative, or someone I did not even know. She believed strongly, and still believes, that her efforts are the right thing for women and society as a whole. And so do I. But at the same time I realize that people have different values and view life differently based upon their own upbringing and personal experiences, and therefore may disagree with her ideas. Fortunately, however, the remarks made to me about my mother have been mostly positive. It is common to be at a restaurant or a public place and have someone approach us to thank my mother for all that she has done for women.

My parents helped me believe that I could succeed in anything. They didn't push me in any one direction; they wanted me to find out for myself what I would enjoy doing. I know my mother would like me to get more involved in the women's movement. I have always considered myself a feminist, and although I strongly support a woman's right to choose and other issues involving the rights of women, I have not been an activist like my mother. I have always felt a need to develop my own identity and be my own person. Although I am proud to be identified as her daughter, I want to be known as a person in my own right, too. I do want to devote time to women's issues, such as abortion rights. Recently I spent a summer working as a legal intern at the Center for Reproductive Law and Policy in New York City, where I helped challenge the constitutionality of various state statutes restricting abortion.

Although significant advances have been made for women, much more needs to be done. Through the efforts of my mother, in one generation graduate schools are now flooded with women. My law-school class was split along gender lines approximately fifty-fifty (as many law schools are today), while at the time my mother was contemplating law school only a handful of women attended law school. I attribute my ability to have a career as an attorney to my mother's successes.

Paula and Lauralee, 1977.

Paula and Lauralee, 1994.

Paula Gunn Allen
and
Lauralee Brown

PAULA GUNN ALLEN was born in 1939 and grew up in a small New Mexican village bordered by the Laguna Pueblo and Acoma reservations. Her mother was of Laguna Pueblo, Sioux, and Scottish descent, and her father is a Lebanese-American. She grew up in boarding school in Albuquerque, yet her connection to her mother's people and traditions remained a central part of her life. Since earning a BA in English literature, an MFA in creative writing, and a PhD in American studies, Gunn Allen has become a leading spokesperson for Native American culture. Now a professor of English at UCLA and an award-winning writer, she is best known for her book *The Sacred Hoop: Recovering the Feminine in American Indian Traditions.*

LAURALEE BROWN, an accomplished singer, musician, songwriter, and lyricist, was born in New Mexico in 1961 and, like her mother, is of Laguna Pueblo and Lebanese descent. After graduating from high school in 1979, she traveled extensively before settling in California. Today Brown resides in Mill Valley, California, where she studies music and voice, sings in a fifties and sixties rock band, and pursues her career as a featured vocalist performing at cabarets, supper clubs, and lounges in the Bay Area.

A Mother's Story

It took a long time for me to understand that I am a good mother. We learn to parent by watching parents, and I grew up with bad patterns of parenting. My dad hit me only twice, but Mom was violent. She smacked me around, then covered my nose and mouth and said, "Don't cry." I quieted myself as quickly as I could. I knew I had to stop crying or I was going to die. Mom used to tie me to my bed and tape my mouth. She did it to my sisters and brothers, too. I remember my youngest brother, born when I was nine, and that terrible cry of a newborn being hit. It is the most dreadful sound you have ever heard. It's like doom. Afterward I or my sisters would sneak in and try to console him.

I learned to keep myself quiet and calm by reading obsessively from my mother's library. I was nine when I first read *Jane Eyre,* my all-time favorite. I identified completely with Jane. From age six through high school, I attended a Catholic convent boarding school. I related to school the way I related to everything—in a dream. I got good grades, but I lived in my own world. I still think of home as somewhere you go to visit, not where you live. Until my mother died, it was wherever she was.

As a little girl, I heard about the women's suffrage movement because my mother's grandfather jokingly called her Susan B. Anthony. My parents met at a tea dance on the Fourth of July in Grants, fell in love, and eloped within the year. She was sixteen and he was nineteen. Her Jewish stepfather had wanted her to marry a nice Jewish boy, or at least an Anglo with prospects, while Daddy's sisters were upset that their darling brother had married anybody, especially a half-breed Indian.

I was born in Albuquerque on October 24, 1939, and brought home to Cubero, where I was raised within the intricacies of interracial, multicultural alliances. The conflicts were terrible, partly because nobody acknowledged them. My mother, fully aware of my Lebanese and New Mexican heritage, often said to me, as her Laguna grandmother had said to her, "Never forget that you are Indian. Never forget." In the United States you are expected to have one race and one culture, and although I have always identified myself as Indian (not Native American), I could not deny my father's side. On school forms, I wrote *mongrel* for nationality. When people ask, I say, "I'm Pueblo, Lakota, Lebanese, Scottish-American, and New Mexican—a multicultural event!"

In my family I was the scapegoat. My siblings, with the exception of my youngest brother, were hostile toward me, perhaps because I knew what was going on and could verbalize it to others. To maintain their own state of numb denial, they had to destroy my credibility, so I was known as the liar, the whiner, the oversensitive one who cried "if anyone looks at her cross-eyed." Ironically, their crusade to portray me as a liar created in me an obsession with the truth.

I think my directness frightened my mother, who had a lot of pain and abuse in her own life to deny. Her life was so dreadful there is no way I can blame her for her violent actions toward us. Nobody wanted her. She was viewed as a half-breed, a squaw, a disgusting creature. Actually she was a beautiful and intelligent woman who was treated like the Indian maid by her mother, a four-foot-six-inch Laguna woman who was busy passing for white. My grandmother molested me when I was small. I vividly remember being pinched and probed in the bathtub with my brother standing nearby. When I was sent across the yard to her house to get something, I felt utter terror.

By the time I was ten or eleven, my mother was drinking a lot, though I'm told she was drinking much earlier. My father, in addition to owning a general trading company, became the Republican lieutenant governor of New Mexico during the 1960s. He entered office at my mother's urging, but then she couldn't handle it. At night, in a sorrowful, drunken state, she would corner me and tell me how my dad was her white knight and how nobody had ever loved her. It created an enormous need in me to defend and protect her, but there was no getting the mothering I needed from her. I adored her from a quiet distance, and cried a lot.

My first sexual experience, at sixteen, was date rape. Afterward he said, accusingly, "You weren't a virgin!" That was the first clue that I was molested when quite young. My recollections aren't clear, and I know that memory can play tricks, but I remember being raped when I was three or four by a teenage cousin and molested in an ongoing way until I was postadolescent. I grew up feeling fat, ugly, sinful, and undeserving of love.

From the age of seven or eight, I fell in love obsessively. In college I had a boyfriend whom I adored, but my parents didn't want me to marry him, and I couldn't stand up to them. Instead, I became pregnant by someone else, broke up with my college love, and married my father's Lebanese cousin. I knew he was bad news even before we were married. When he told me his two dreams in life were to be either a Jesuit priest or a storm trooper in Nazi Germany, it was a good year before it dawned on me that he was serious. Two more years passed before I had the courage, born of terror and desolation, to leave. By that time I had a son, Gene, and a daughter, Lauralee.

Lauralee was born on June 6, 1961. Seeing her, I thought, "Babies are not a blank slate, and they are not born alike." From her first hours she responded to me and the world in her own unique way. Lauralee suffered from a difficulty caused by my gynecologist's well-intentioned attempts to "take care" of me. The diet pills he prescribed created a biochemical screw-up that caused her to cry for hours, sometimes all day, until at last we got in the car and drove her around Grants and up in the mountains, because she was happy in a moving vehicle.

Lauralee, with straight black hair and beautiful brown skin, was curious and bright. When she was two months old, it was clear that her father didn't like her because she was Indian and female. After he took to strutting around the house with a revolver or knife in hand, we fled—lucky to escape with our lives. When he sued for custody, I went to the doctor and said, "Okay, reveal the records." The records confirmed that he was not Gene's father, so he disowned both children in order to avoid being known as a man who sired only daughters. With the cash my father compelled him to provide me, I rented a tiny apartment in Albuquerque. There, jobless and nearly penniless, I struggled to survive.

I finally got a decent job in a bar, but after my estranged husband deceived some men who patronized the bar into thinking that I was a hooker, I was too humiliated and terrified to go back. Eventually I got a waitressing job, working until after midnight. One night my ex-husband broke into the house, scared the babies half to death, and left a threatening message that said adulterous women were to be killed. I quit the job and got daytime employment—first in a tourist shop and then for an optometrist. With government-subsidized commodities—cheese, peanut butter, and powdered milk—and a sitter who cared for my children in exchange for room and board, we survived.

I entered the University of New Mexico in 1964, with the help of a grant and my father. Several months later I married a white man from Kansas who adopted Gene and Lauralee. He was rigid in ways and we argued about the children, but he vacuumed and did laundry and would have been considered feminist for the times. With his support, I earned a bachelor's degree and an MFA at the University of Oregon. Twice I won English Department poetry prizes, but my creative-writing professor, refusing to believe that the woman with the beehive and the panty hose and the pumps could possibly have written such poetry, kept returning my papers to someone else.

After completing our degrees, my husband got a job in Sacramento, and I got one at a junior college down the coast. I saw my second husband as my rescuer, and he was a good husband, lover, father to my children, and friend. But he was alcoholic. When I was with him, we drank all the time. Realizing that something was wrong with a relationship that depended on chronic drunkenness, I eventually quit. Our seven-year marriage ended in 1971.

During this period, I wrote as Paula Brown. Later, when I moved to Albuquerque and married a third time, I became Paula Allen. Still unknown as a poet and writer, I turned to numerology to find a name that would attract publication. After fooling with every combination, I chose Paula Gunn Allen—a compilation of my given name, my grandmother's maiden name, and my married name. Soon I was publishing and receiving job offers. I took a job at San Francisco State when the chair, needing somebody to teach history, remembered my application because his cousin's name was Paul Allen.

Commonly, Native American parents value self-reliance and encourage it in the little ones from infancy, but Anglo schools don't expect children to be self-reliant or self-motivating, particularly if those children are neither male nor Anglo female. As a child, Lauralee was advanced verbally. I encouraged her to be friendly, open, strong, and stubborn. There was no way I was going to mess with her ability to say no, because I didn't want her to get raped or pushed around. All my kids suffered terribly from the conflict in social-cultural perspectives, but Lauralee's experience was particularly discouraging.

Once, in second grade, she brought home a piece of manila paper with intricately drawn flowers a bit to the right of and somewhat above the center, leaving the remaining expanse of paper empty. I said, "My God, this is beautiful!" And she said, "No, it's not; Miss N. didn't like it. She said it wasn't very good." The teacher had marked F on her drawing because Lauralee didn't fill in the page! Her first-grade teacher had dealt with her sternly because Lauralee insisted on writing her name in cursive rather than print. Gradually, before my horrified eyes, the vivacious, loquacious, charming human being named Lauralee Brown was buried under years of mindless, dehumanizing, soul-killing societal rubbish. I couldn't stop it no matter what I did.

During the seventies, while attending graduate school and working to support my family, I lost a child, Sulieman's twin, to Sudden Infant Death Syndrome. My marriage couldn't survive the blow, and two years later I divorced. That summer I got my PhD in American studies; alone ("an unwed mother," I used to quip), I taught, lectured, wrote and read from my work, marched, protested, raised my kids, tutored newer writers—mostly American Indian women—and tried to stay alive. I left my children with baby-sitters who, I later discovered, frightened and physically abused them. I learned early not to spank, hit, or threaten a child. I wish I had also learned not to withdraw and not to yell.

During that time the depression that haunted most of my life deepened, and even now I wonder how I survived. I think my children's need of me kept me from committing suicide. Lauralee was at that most vulnerable of times, early adolescence, as the lowest point of my life progressed, and my pain and deep depression indelibly marked her consciousness. She began writing music and participating in poetry festivals but refused to sleep in her bed or change from street or school clothes to sleep. A line from one of the songs she wrote then said, "Lights are out and Mama's crying."

Several months after my third marriage ended, I came out as a lesbian. Lauralee had worked with the anti-gay-bashing brigade in San Francisco in her early teens. At the same time I helped found and was advisor to Gay American Indians (now Gay and Lesbian American Indians). I had always thought I was straight, even though my only erotic fantasies had been about women. When I told Lauralee I was lesbian, she said, "Mother, I knew that. I wondered when you were going to figure it out." The next summer I was asked to read for the Gay Caucus at the Modern Language Association convention in New York City.

That reading marked the beginning of my career as a publicly recognized writer. It was my first experience with being heard without being dismissed as "nuts," "Indian," "female," "too academic," and (simultaneously) "a street poet."

It took me a long time to understand that I am bisexual. In all, I have married three men and two women, with boyfriends and girlfriends in between. If you are a double Scorpio, which I am, and trying to deal with a woman, you are in a pressure cooker. Men are another species entirely. Since coming into menopause, I like men as well as women. You would be surprised at what will turn my head, and it doesn't much matter which gender! I consider myself now as a person of gender-free sexual preference.

> The older I get, the more I love being a woman. I love going to the mall. I love women's magazines. I like being pretty and wearing makeup and buying beauty products.

If I can unsnarl the dreadful historical tangle of intergenerational dysfunction, then my children will not have to continue the cycle; we can all let go of it and do something else. That is a legacy I would like to leave my children and grandchildren. What I like best and respect most about my children and my parenting is that all three people I raised possess integrity and a fundamental sense of their own and others' humanity that is as multifaceted and nonlinear as possible. They don't always act on their sense of what constitutes truly human life, but it's there and they know when they are violating it. They can rebel, and they can conform. They are artists, able to function at all levels and classes.

I want Lauralee to live happily ever after. I hope she can find that brilliant beauty that is hers and trust it and love it. I wish she could see the incredible person she is. I would like to bequeath her strength, courage, persistence, stubbornness. I would like to leave her herself— not *my*self, *her*self—so that she can pass that on to others. That is the essence of feminism. Everything else—political correctness, acting holier-than-thou, hating men because it is all their fault—is a lie.

I see myself as a feminist, but a lot of feminists see me as a Native American lesbian woman of color, which is a way of dismissing what I have to say. When feminism is good, it is very, very good, but when it is bad, it is horrid. Bad feminism is women of privilege imposing their own internalized WASP standards (of which they are largely unaware) on everybody else. I am talking about that terrible tendency to say, "Do it our way because our way is good." Men are victims, too. I have seen my sons treated as cruelly as my daughter, Indian men and women treated too dreadfully for words to depict or emotions to grasp.

The older I get, the more I love being a woman. I love going to the mall. I love women's magazines. I like being pretty and wearing makeup and buying beauty products. I see the point of feminists who say that women's magazines oppress women, and sometimes I look at myself and I say, "Paula, what are you doing?" On the other hand, we live where we live and we live when we live. I don't want to go to my grave saying, "I forgot to participate in the world I was born into." I don't want to be so busy being noble and self-righteous that I forgot to enjoy what was given me.

I have an obligation to my children. They didn't ask to be born into this world, and I have to do what I can to change it. When I was young, I thought I could change it next year. Now that I am middle-aged, I hope it will be easier for my granddaughters.

I believe that beauty is the most important thing there is, and that if we cared more about beauty, we would have far less destruction. As women, we can learn to love our beauty and not be oppressed by it. That is what I want for all of us. The first time I heard Lauralee do a performance, I sat in the audience listening to what she wrote, and I knew I could quit. She will carry the message in her life and her work. And I can retire!

A Daughter's Story

My mother has been wonderful at helping me see who I am, ever since I was a little girl. She was very good about affirming my ethnicities, as a Native American and as a Lebanese. The first doll that she bought me was a black doll, and I named her Fatima. She didn't look like me, but she looked closer to me than the white dolls on the market.

My grandmother was a Laguna Pueblo. My mother's father, E. Lee Francis, was considered pretty radical because he married an Indian. He was from a wealthy family of Lebanese ranchers who ran hundreds of head of cattle in New Mexico, and he eventually became lieutenant governor of the state. My grandmother was very much the rebel; she spoke her mind constantly, though she still put up with my grandfather's belittling.

My mother was a housewife at the time I was born, though I can't imagine her ever being a housewife. The man who sired me—and I say *sired,* because he disowned me when I was two—is dead now, from what I have heard. I never knew him. My mother was not your average quiet woman, and my father, who was Catholic, had a problem with her wanting to have a say in things. Because she would not submit to his dictates, he made her crazy. They didn't even sleep in the same room after a while. He kept promising her that he wanted to work things out, but one day he just served her with divorce papers. He had to pay the church ten thousand dollars to annul the marriage, thereby disavowing any responsibility for me. He married again, and I have half-sisters and half-brothers I don't even know.

My father left my mother with nothing but two kids, me and my older brother. Her father was getting into politics, and my father's family threatened to ruin his reputation by calling his daughter a whore if she fought the annulment. So my mother's family swept it under the rug: "Hush, hush."

All my life I thought that there was something really wrong with me. In elementary school I used to tell the other kids that when my brother was born they planted a tree, and when I was born they cut it down. This didn't really happen, but I believed it did because of the incredible sense of rejection I felt. Growing up, I felt ugly, I felt worthless, I felt stupid, and it didn't matter what grades I got or what clothes I wore. For years I hated my hair. It is huge and obvious and out of control. I was trying to fit into somebody's image of what beauty is instead of just being beautiful and being myself. School became a battering experience. I was an outcast; I didn't fit in with the Chicanas, the sororities, the preppies, the children in my first grade class in Oregon called me "Negro," and ignored me; I didn't play any sports. I am a creative and outspoken person, and I consistently got in trouble for knowing too much. Kids used to make fun of me because of the big words I used, so I decided that I wouldn't learn. That way I would be safe. But I wasn't safe—I was still a target, for whatever reasons. I used to come home and gripe. I remember my mother telling me, "If you can't tell me something good that happened to you first, don't tell me anything."

I have memories of being in child care where abuses would happen. I was spanked by the caregivers for no reason, and once I was thrown into a toilet because I wet my pants when they wouldn't let me go potty. Sometimes, when my mom was working, I would sleep there overnight. Once they wouldn't let me go to the bathroom before bedtime, and of course I wet the bed. Luckily, my mom arrived before they could spank me. Another time they had us in a line and were systematically spanking us, and my mother walked in. They lied about what they were doing, which is a consistent experience I have had with abuse.

During this time, my mother met a businessman from the Midwest. They married and he adopted us. He was an alcoholic. My mom married him sooner than planned because she was sick and she needed his medical coverage. I remember my mom's sickness taking the form of depression and lethargy, but I didn't know she was sick with Epstein-Barr, and neither did she (or the doctors). She was a single, working mom; of course she was tired.

Dad was the one who administered discipline. He came up with all kinds of elaborate ways to teach us lessons. One time my brother got in trouble for playing with matches, so they removed everything from our bedroom and made us sleep without any toys or anything— like prison. Another time he wouldn't let me out of my high chair until I finished a hot dog. I sat there for hours—the sun went down and darkness fell—and I still couldn't deal with that hot dog. Alcohol was probably influencing his decisions, but I wouldn't have known it then.

I don't remember a lot about my mother at that time. She was often absent. I remember wanting more; I never seemed to be able to get enough attention from her. She had a studio and was painting and writing poetry, and I think she was starting to go to school. We kids were provided for, and I think that was her main concern. She knew we were safe and secure, so she didn't worry about us. Their marriage ended, when I was nine or ten and I felt like I was probably a burden for my mother. To get her attention was really difficult.

My early history is, for me, still jumbled up. My teenage years were a tough, trying time. Going through the divorce was very painful. I would say that is where my previous memories of how I felt about myself break off and become unclear. I started numbing out; my sense of myself was shaken and split into many different pieces. I would ask my mom, "What's going on? Are you and Daddy getting divorced?" And she would say, "Oh, no." I don't think she meant to lie, but she wanted to believe herself that it would work out. It got so that I didn't think I could trust my own intuition, my own feelings. Finally, my mother said, "Your dad and I are getting a divorce, and you have to make a decision about who you want to be with." I don't think she meant it to be as devastating as it was, but I felt I had no choice but to betray someone. Betrayal was something that scared me. Luckily, she made the decision to keep me.

I was a classic child from a broken home. I was mostly with my mother, but I got on a plane and flew across the country to Virginia for Christmas and a few weeks in the summer to see my dad and his new family. I felt betrayed by him; while he was living the American dream, buying his new daughter a car and sending her to college, he didn't send me presents or cards for years. I needed him to guide me, and he wasn't there for me. Meanwhile, my mother got married and divorced again. During this time her siblings became central adult figures in my life. Things eventually turned bad, because of their sibling rivalries. I didn't have anything to do with it; I just happened to be born into a family that fought. So that further split me and tore me down.

I wanted to find my real father when I was fourteen, and my mother's mother knew where he was. She never told me, "No, don't do it," but there was something in the way she looked at me that made me hesitate. I think she was gently trying to tell me that it would only bring pain and heartache, and I think now she was right; it is probably best that I didn't pursue it.

I don't think I am the marrying kind. After watching my mother go through three marriages, I decided I didn't want to go that route. I am involved in a caring and loving relationship now. My boyfriend is French-American. He is a waiter by profession, but he builds guitars. He has been very patient with me; our relationship is steady and quiet. Roland and I have been together twelve years—longer than any of my mother's relationships.

I never went to college, except for a few music classes at the College of Marin. I may eventually go back, but for now I have so much I want to do with my singing. I sing in a fifties and sixties rock band, and I also write. I am still defining myself with my music. I have built my voice up and I am very happy with where I am at, though I see lots of room for improvement. In my heart I am an outlaw, in my body I am an imposter, but in my soul is hidden my spirit. I am trying to get my heart, body, and soul in sync. That is what my work is about.

Today I am on new ground in my life. I didn't realize until recently that you have to have a conscious attitude about protecting yourself spiritually. Otherwise somebody will put a straw in you and suck you dry. What I am learning is that I have to stand up for myself, because the alternative—standing back in fear—is worse. I believe that a woman cannot go through this life as a gentle spirit without sacrificing something, but I can choose what it is I will sacrifice.

I am probably a feminist, though I don't choose to call myself one. I have a lot of negative pictures associated with the word. I see the problem for women in our culture as an intertwined thing; I could call it patriarchal, but I cannot assign a gender to it. I see it as race-motivated as much as it is gender-motivated; it is an overlapping problem for indigenous peoples of any area. I have been an active proponent of women's rights all my life. I have the propensity to speak up when things are not right. But my activism is personal; I'm not out in the streets marching and waving banners. I know that until I make the change inside myself, until I can assess my own value to myself, it doesn't matter how much marching I do.

In the sixties and seventies, my mother tried to instill in me a self-assurance and strength that she didn't have herself at the time. I'd tell my friends, "She's got me believing and behaving in ways that she doesn't even truly believe or behave in yet." Now, of course, she has surpassed me in her understanding and her behavior. But it has been a long, hard fight. At the University of New Mexico they wanted to devalue, underpay, and overwork her, and she just wouldn't accept it. She became a fighting woman. She did it her way, and now she is a tenured professor at UCLA. She is prominent and successful. She didn't do it by compromising. It was very difficult for her to be a woman in the pioneer stages of joining the workforce *and* take care of children. She helped forge the way by not breaking down, by going through therapy, and by enriching her own knowledge.

> You have to have a conscious attitude about protecting yourself spiritually. Otherwise somebody will put a straw in you and suck you dry.

I have never wanted to have children myself, for several reasons. First, I am terrified of childbearing pain. I have been, ever since I can remember. Second, my own childhood was so troubled. Because my mom worked so much, she wasn't available for me when I was little. I was good for cleaning up and staying quiet and out of the way. When she came home from work, I'd want her to read me a story and she'd say, "I read you one last week." She was tired, but I didn't know that—little girls don't know that. Third, because of the state of our planet and our resources and political situation, I just don't want to bring anyone into this world right now. But with all that said, I think I could be a very nurturing parent. I will have to nurture myself a little more before I make any decisions about having a child.

I love my mother deeply. I know that any actions she took and any choices she made when I was growing up were the best she could do. She placed a lot of responsibility on me at a young age, for my brother, my chores, my attitude. Certainly some of it was painful for me and I didn't understand it, but she has made every effort to heal that. She gave me a way of looking at the world that she had to learn herself. I talk to my mother about everything—my past drug experiences, my relationship experiences. I call her my mother, sister, friend, daughter, because certainly I have taught her things, too. She still struggles with self-esteem and issues around family and not being good enough.

At birth my mother was given the name Paula Marie Francis. Her name now is derived from her grandmother Agnes Gunn and her third husband, Joe Allen. It was when she changed her name that things started working for her. She has taught me that we can define ourselves, build ourselves, paint ourselves, construct ourselves.

I am amazed that my mother is my mother. I really lucked out with her. We have certainly had our problems, but we have learned to communicate, and I know that whatever I do, she loves me. She has gone through a lot of recovery and therapy to be a good mother. She has taught me more than I could ever put into words. For years to come I will be assimilating her wisdom and the things she has tried to open up inside of me.

Marie and Kirsten, 1975.

Kirsten and Marie, 1995.

Marie Wilson
and
Kirsten Wilson

MARIE WILSON was born in Atlanta, Georgia, in 1940, and now lives in New York City. She is an activist and author who has been president of the Ms. Foundation for Women, the only national multi-issue women's fund, for eleven years. Issues at the top of her agenda include economic empowerment, reproductive rights, and health and safety for women and girls. Wilson earned her MS in education from Drake University and has done everything from directing a university women's program to serving as vice president and director of education and human resources for the Iowa Bankers Association to becoming the first woman ever elected to an at-large seat on the Des Moines City Council. The mother of five grown children, she is a co-author of the book *Mother-Daughter Revolution: From Good Girls to Great Women.*

KIRSTEN WILSON, a performance artist, was born in 1966 in Wilmington, Delaware. She received her BA in English literature from Barnard College in 1990, and then attended the Institute of American Indian Arts in Santa Fe for a year. She is currently touring her

"Friendly Fire" trilogy of performance pieces which explore violence against women. The first piece, *There's No Place Like Home: A Case Study,* examines the violence hidden behind American myth and nostalgia. The second work, *The Amazing Magician's Beautiful Assistant Clara* probes how women control their bodies in order to control the violence of men. The final piece, *Odalisque,* explores how female desire is informed and deformed by the violence that surrounds us. Wilson also teaches performance monologue classes and Contact Improvisational Dance.

MARIE WILSON
A Mother's Story

Mothering is the hardest work I have ever done. It should be joyous work, but trying to raise children in isolation is crazy. Children need to connect to caring adults, lots of them. What saved people in the 1930s and 1940s were neighborhoods where many people looked out for the children. I believe the nuclear family alone is limiting for children. This idea comes not from reading feminist literature but from being at home with five children. Without the help of mothers, aunts, grandmothers, or anyone else nearby, I found motherhood to be an isolating institution. Speaking occasionally with other mothers, I learned that they too felt cooped up in small places with children. It's a wonder our children lived through those years. That is not the way to raise children. We live in a culture that neither appreciates nor rewards parenting, a culture where the difficulty—and hard work—of constantly being responsible for another life is enormously denied.

I was born in Atlanta, Georgia, in 1940 into a working-class home. My mother was a dental hygienist and my father a typesetter. My parents struggled to provide me with an education and a life not possible for themselves. My mother came from three generations of women whose mothers were too poor to raise them. I am the first child in four generations whose mother had a husband and had the money to raise a child. Because she was never nurtured, my mother had little knowledge about how to nurture. But she was strong and full of spirit and a model of energy and persistence.

The South helped shape her character. Southern mothers pass on complicated survival strategies to their daughters. They know that the "female impersonation" they teach their daughters is a game. Mothers tell girls they must impersonate the cultural construct of being women—which weakens but they must still be strong underneath.

There is such a bias against Southern women. I first experienced it when I moved to New York, and I continue to encounter it whenever remnants of my Southern accent emerge, which inevitably happens when I am under stress.

Growing up in the South in the 1940s, I knew something in the culture was terribly wrong. Black help was affordable even for poor white families, so while my mother was at work, a woman named Liz Brown raised me. Liz had two children of her own, but she stayed with me every day until 4:30 P.M. As a small child I remember worrying and asking about her children constantly. She was a mother to me and, frankly, to my parents as well. I wanted her time, so as I got older, I often cleaned the house and made breakfast before she got there. When my parents were away, she was the only person with whom I would stay. Seeing injustice done to Liz made me aware of racial injustice in Atlanta. As a young child, I always sat with her in the back of the segregated bus. One day the driver stopped the bus and told me to come to the front. I refused. Finally he dragged me, crying, to the front of the bus. As I looked back, I saw that Liz was crying, too.

> Southern mothers pass on complicated survival strategies to their daughters. They know that the female impersonation they teach their daughters is a game and that they can still be strong underneath.

After graduating from an Atlanta high school in 1959, I entered Vanderbilt with plans to major in philosophy and become a Christian-education director. Vanderbilt was full of young women making their social debuts in a scene that I found strange. Eventually I joined a sorority and even served as president of the pledge class, but I didn't believe in the sorority system. What I craved was a chance to try leadership—and this was one of the few venues open to women.

Later I found church-related groups that were becoming active in social change. The civil rights movement had begun in different parts of the South, and when Vanderbilt divinity student Jim Lawson joined a Nashville sit-in, I sat on a committee with Lamar Alexander to decide whether or not he should be expelled. We urged the committee not to expel him, but Lawson was expelled anyway.

After my junior year of college I married Eugene Wilson and moved to Delaware to work in the civil rights movement. Joined by a passion for justice, we settled in an African-American community in

Wilmington, where Gene was choral conductor in a Presbyterian church. Like many civil rights activists, we learned about leadership and justice in the church. In another era, I definitely would have been a minister. Many people currently in the forefront of justice movements may no longer work within the church, but that is where they heard about "justice rolling down like water." I admire the work that feminists are doing in the area of spirituality, but I wish the women's community had aspects of the church community to it. I left the church, but I remain a religious person in my heart.

I believe you can win people over. In that sense, I am a missionary. Gene used music to bring African-Americans and whites together, and I organized programs for inner-city youth. On Friday nights I scheduled coffeehouses or dances for community young people. I also ran huge carnivals. I didn't know there was anything I couldn't do.

At the same time, my first three children were born in rapid succession. Gene III was born in 1962, Renee in 1964, and Kirsten in 1966. My children were not planned; I used birth control, but it never worked. When I got pregnant for the fourth time, in 1968, I sat in the bathtub and cried. My health was horrible, and I didn't see how we could support another child. I considered an illegal abortion but couldn't do it. David was a great baby, but that pregnancy made me an advocate for women's right to abortion.

The 1960s were an especially difficult time to raise children. We were concerned parents trying hard to raise people who weren't as repressed as we were. My husband grew up as a minister's son; I grew up trying to be perfect and nice. Our intentions were good, but our methods were experimental. In allowing more freedom, we failed to give our children enough structure and discipline. Many children raised in that decade could have used a firmer sense of adult expectations. The pendulum swing was natural, but I would not raise my children the same way again.

Around 1970 I became a feminist over the issue of reproductive rights because I felt so strongly about what children need. I joined a group advocating medical control of abortion and worked with the slogan, "Every child has the right to be a wanted child, eagerly awaited by his or her parents." Personally, I still found my primary identity in being a mother. With four children at that stage in my life, I really couldn't do much as an activist, but I felt I could help one person, so we adopted a black child. As it turned out, he had cerebral palsy, so disability and not race became the biggest issue.

With the adoption of Martin, I felt especially overwhelmed. It was hard to be the kind of mother I had expected to be. I got sick and tired and depressed. I would help my husband with some retreat, carrying all the children along, and come back with strep throat or a staph infection. Once when I complained to my mother about having three children in diapers, she said, "Well, you wouldn't want to do it if it weren't a challenge." I actually liked a lot about being a mother, however, and would have enjoyed it more had I been less tired and had others around to help. I loved the nurturing parts—holding my children and nursing and rocking them. I liked the creative parts, and I even liked taking them to their games and swim meets. At night I read to them, and we put on records and danced.

Our marriage was difficult from the outset, and having so many children so quickly didn't help. I had never heard of job-sharing in my life, but in the late sixties I stood up in church and said, "I think we should share jobs. Men should be in the home part-time and women should be out part-time." People laughed and said it was the most ridiculous thing they had ever heard, but I knew that to be a complete person I needed to contribute in the home *and* in the world.

The day came when my husband said, "I am not a man who can afford a volunteer wife. I will help in the home in proportion to how much money you bring in." That was the first time I understood that in order for Gene to respect me and do his share, I had to contribute economically. It seemed harsh at the time, but the more honest contract with Gene helped me. We were living in Iowa in the late seventies when Drake University began a division of women's programming. I was offered the job of associate director and quickly learned how to write grants and raise money. With funds from the Women's Education Equity Act and Title IX, I was able to build every program I had ever wanted—for myself or for other women.

Aside from the current period at the Ms. Foundation for Women, the seventies were the most productive decade of my life. My work had been unacknowledged for so long that it was wonderful to get paid and be appreciated for changing things. The marriage finally fell apart, and I left the women's program to earn better money. From 1982 to 1984 I worked as an executive vice president of the Iowa Bankers Association and was elected to a seat on the Des Moines City Council.

My daughters, Renee and Kirsten, grew up with a feminist consciousness, which I gave them almost inadvertently. I was not a well-read feminist, so I didn't talk to them about feminism; I just talked about life. That was something I knew I did right. We watched television together, and when advertisements came on, I said, "Have you ever seen a woman dressed up like that doing housework?" or "Can you imagine that every car comes with a woman? We didn't get a woman with our last car." They laughed, and got doses of feminism by listening. They saw me working in the community, and when Drake colleagues began to come home with me, they had contact with wonderful women.

I am excited that my daughters are feminists—that they study political science and women's studies and try to stop violence against women with their talents. I feel fortunate that they care about human rights. I was afraid they would reject those values. It makes me proud that I can sit down and talk with them about women's issues. It makes me proud that even though they felt abandoned at certain points because of my work, they have picked the work up themselves and are part of a group of young women today who are engaged in a new kind of struggle against racism and sexism.

In the seventies and eighties, feminism dealt with overt sexism and flagrant economic issues; today the issues are more covert. I talk to many young women struggling with issues of marriage and children. In a sense they have choiceless choices. If they decide to be married, they have to wonder if there is a man out there who wants a truly egalitarian marriage. When push comes to shove, the woman is still the one having the child and working to maintain the relationship. Young women today have choices, but (they pay for them dearly.)

Looking back, I wish I had fought harder and more effectively for what I needed. That fight would have enabled me to be a better mother to my daughters. I wish I had been more confident about my right to certain things, such as time and money. I involved my older daughter too much in my life because of my husband's absence; she was more an ally than a daughter. I wish I had known better than to engage her like that. She should never have had to be a part of our struggle.

I believe daughters are aware of how much mothers can take. My own daughters have said that they knew I was unable to take their criticism when they were adolescents. Kirsten was in her mid-twenties before she told me that she had felt abandoned when I went back to work. A part of me said, "How could you possibly?" I felt I had worked night and day to be there for my kids, yet she experienced me as being consumed with the work of building women's programming. My daughters may have known I felt depressed for a good part of those years I stayed at home, but I also generated a great deal of positive energy. When I left the house and went to work, they felt the loss of that energy.

It is important that we tell the truth, that we not pretend to live in these we-can-have-it-all pictures. There are costs to being a feminist that many mothers are already paying and which must not be denied. That we abandoned our children in some ways while we did the work to save them in other ways is real. That our relationships are intense and powerful and that we struggle with them is necessary information. It is important not to gloss things over or to slip into the trap that because we are feminists we were perfect mothers who raised perfectly feminist daughters. We learn most from each other when we are honest about our own lives.

KIRSTEN WILSON
A Daughter's Story

The first time I remember hearing the word *feminist* was when an English teacher in high school asked how many of us were feminists, and I was the only one who raised my hand. Nobody had ever asked me that question before, but it seemed so basic. Of course I believed in equal rights. It wasn't until I went off to college at Barnard that the question became complicated. There were rules, and it was political; being a feminist implied that I was a man-hater, a lesbian, prochoice. Those were not the rules with which I had grown up.

My mother doesn't fit the stereotype of a feminist. She does not stick to politics as usual. The guys at her office in Iowa used to say, "She comes in like a Mack truck," because she stood up for what she believed in. I learned from her that you can be hated by the world, you can be ostracized, you can be not a good girl, and that is okay. I can tell that she is proud of the risks I have taken. It has given me great strength that my mother loves the rebel in me—the part that is inappropriate, that is too loud, that says the wrong things. I can dare to be different because I know I am worthy in her eyes.

I try to resist labels. When I think about whether I participate in organized feminism, my first impulse is to say, "No, of course not. I don't give to NOW." But then I think, "Yes, I do." I work for the rape crisis center as a performance artist. My work is completely feminist.

I was born on July 28, 1966, in Wilmington, Delaware, the third, and middle, child in my family. When I was almost two, I was sent to live with my father's mother for three months. My mother had become seriously ill with the birth of her fourth child, my brother David. I had a wonderful time at my grandmother's, where I was an adored only child, but it terrified me to be away from my mother.

I was afraid of death before I could speak. I could never get this idea across to my mother, who tried to protect me from thinking that she was going to die. She took me to ministers who tried to convince me that there was a God and I shouldn't fear death. I was an existential, weird kid, but I think my obsession with death stemmed from the period when my mother was sick and I was sent away from her. Because of this major disconnection, I grew up with a sense of fragility that my siblings didn't have.

My mother stayed home with us until my little brothers were in kindergarten. My father, a choral conductor, was absent much of the time. We lived in a two-bedroom house with two adults and five children on very little money. By the time I was out of second grade, my mother was working. All of the mothers in our working-class neighborhood had jobs outside the home; I didn't know mothers who stayed home.

For a time when I was growing up, my mother seemed depressed. While she wanted to save the world, she was very aware of her failures as a mother—that she couldn't always protect her own children, she couldn't save us from the meanness in the world. It was a hard situation for all of us, because on some level we all felt we had failed. My mother seemed sad and sometimes unreachable. She was happy when she was out of the house, and when she came home, at least for a while, she retained that happiness and energy.

My mother grew up believing that the only things that are important are peace, love, family, and God. In school, she was a top student, homecoming queen, Miss Atlanta Jr., and a cheerleader at Vanderbilt. Her fantasy was that she and my father would get married, he would sing to her, and they would have a perfect, lovely life, like the Fred Astaire–Ginger Rogers movies she watched as a child.

My parents were hippies; when we moved to Iowa, I went to kindergarten on the first day wearing a headband from a trip to Colorado, and the kids circled around me and sang, "Yippie, yippie, it's a hippie." In elementary school, you got free lunch if your parents were under a certain income, and I had this special lunch card. It was like a scarlet letter, because it was a different color. Every year we went to J. C. Penney or Sears and got outfits that we wore all year. My father's minister-father drilled into him that material goods were not important. It was a kind of righteous nonmaterialism. We always had socks and shoes, but we didn't go out to eat and we didn't go to movies.

When I was in elementary school, we kids started doing the cooking, our own laundry, and the housecleaning. Unlike the other kids at school, I had to come home and cook once a week. The cooking and cleaning weren't exactly fun. Making Hamburger Helper or cleaning house on Saturday mornings instead of watching cartoons didn't give me much of a feeling of accomplishment. It felt like punishment.

Early on, I gave up on being accepted by my peers. Not having money and living on the wrong side of town wasn't such a big deal; it was more than clothes that I was missing. In elementary school I was a social idiot. I was considered ugly; I was ridiculed and made fun of. Because of my teeth, I was called "beaver" and "bucktooth." At some point I began to feel more than just different; I felt martyred. I began to identify with my own drama and persecution. Strangely enough, my self-knowledge made me feel special.

> In elementary school, you got free lunch if your parents were under a certain income, and I had this special lunch card. It was like a scarlet letter, because it was a different color.

I felt I was my father's favorite, so I lived with the kind of tension that exists when you feel you are chosen by a parent. Since I felt so lost in the world, it was wonderful that my father recognized me and made me feel special. When people say to me, as occasionally they do, that I must not like men because I target them in my performance pieces on violence, I think, "You've got to be kidding." My relationship with my father is so important to me. He has been a touchstone in terms of my own self-worth. His love has helped to keep me alive, and I am grateful to be his daughter.

When I was fourteen, my mother moved out, and I decided to live with my father. In my eyes he was the one getting left, and I wanted to protect him. I think my mother felt betrayed because I chose to stay with him and that I was punishing her for leaving. Once she moved out, I saw her only on weekends. After about four months, desperate for her companionship, I moved in with my mother.

In some ways my parents' separation was a relief. I could ally with them as individuals in their separate homes instead of having to negotiate between them. Also, my mother's lover was very much a parent to me and was able to be more emotionally present than my mother could. My mother needed us to be strong and successful and functioning, which left us feeling that she couldn't take stress, she couldn't take it if we messed up, we needed to be together for her. Her partner was able to listen to us in our emotional traumas. On the other hand, it took some time for me to adjust to the idea that I was no longer needed to fill the role of being my mother's primary intimate relationship.

In many ways I feel I mothered my mother. I dealt with her depression by giving her attention, hoping to gain her attention and meet my own needs. She took long baths at night—this was her way of getting emotionally fed—sometimes, I went in and rubbed her back so that she could go to sleep after a tense day. Emotional boundaries were definitely crossed. We were all trying to comfort each other, get our needs met, and survive.

I always wanted to prove myself to my mother. At Barnard I was Phi Beta Kappa in English. I did it for myself but also for her. She always seemed beautiful and smart and perfect in so many ways. She has a charisma that pulls people toward her, and I wanted to have that. My sister used to be afraid to bring home her boyfriends because they always fell in love with my mother. When I was in college, my boyfriend, who had heard about every horrible thing my mother had ever done to me (I was at an age where I was furious at her for everything under the sun), still came home and met my mother and was smitten. He thought she was just so wonderful.

Throughout her career, my mother has chosen to focus on changing structures and systems. But while she focused on changing the world, she didn't focus on herself and what needed to be changed inside. I think that part of me has taken on areas my mother did not: the self, and individualized oppression. As a performance artist, I focus on how an individual's life influences her political expression. That is where change needs to happen. We can do studies on women's self-esteem, and we can make sure that abortion is an option and that laws protect women from sexual discrimination, but institutional change will not touch the way women react to society on a daily basis. Our reactions stem from sexual abuse, internalized misogyny, stress around our bodies.

As a performance artist, one piece I do is about women's New Year's resolutions. Generally, women resolve to eat less, exercise more, work harder, get more done. The underlying issue is discipline versus desire. It is about control. In the performance I do a tango between a woman and Life. The woman is trying to make these resolutions, and Life says, "No, you have to eat more, sleep more, work less, create more, make love. You have to get bigger and stronger if you are going to run hand in hand with your desire." I do a lot of work with gestures. And women's gestures usually communicate, "I will not have desire. I am in control. I will not take. My hands are in my lap, behind my back; I won't reach out and grab things." We are good girls, and we don't reach out. With desire comes punishment. If you reach out, you are asking to be slapped. Do not consume more, do not be loud, do not be threatening. Once you have reached out beyond the space of your own body, you have entered the male world.

A part of me wants to be bigger than my mother. When I say that I am doing what my mother didn't do, it is in part competitive. In a sense I am saying, "You didn't do this, so this is my ground. You didn't challenge yourself enough on the emotional front. You couldn't be the perfect mother, so you ran off into the world and didn't deal with it." As I challenge myself to deal with the personal and the private, I am also challenging her.

The women's movement didn't protect me from sexual violence. It didn't protect me from growing up in a society where women don't have a sense of their own authority. Sexism is still entrenched in our school systems and in our religion; it is deep, and it is in our own mothers. In my work I have been using a line my grandmother once said to my mother: "Don't walk that way in front of your father." In other words, you are asking for it. My mother hasn't chosen to deal with that, but I am.

Women like my mother, who have tried to build bridges in the women's movement, have had to be very careful. They had to convince people who were afraid of what it meant for women to step out of traditional roles that feminists aren't monsters; they just want to be seen, to be heard, to go to work, to study. These women had to do a careful dance: "Don't be afraid of me; I'm just trying to do my stuff." Women of my generation are trying to do things differently. We are trying to feel differently about our mothers and about ourselves as women. We are trying to envision ourselves and our bodies with confidence and authority and positive feelings.

Thanks to women like my mother, many of the big issues have been tackled. Major pieces of ideology about what it means to be a woman in society have been broken down. Nobody looks at me strangely when I say that I don't have children, for example, whereas they would have looked at my mother strangely. Perhaps now we can look at how we as women are invested in systems of oppression and can come up with a vision of how things can truly change.

Lisa, Maryann, and Kara, 1965.

Lisa and Maryann, 1995.

Maryann Napoli
and
Lisa Napoli

MARYANN NAPOLI was born in 1940 in Teaneck, New Jersey. While her daughters, Lisa and Kara, were growing up, she was a full-time mother and housewife. Now she is a consumer advocate, women's health advocate, and writer. Napoli is a cofounder and associate director of the Center for Medical Consumers, a public-interest organization that helps people make informed decisions about their medical care. She is also writer and editor of the center's monthly newsletter, *Health-Facts*. She lives with her husband, Richard, on the Upper West Side of Manhattan.

LISA NAPOLI was born in New York in 1962. She is a recent graduate of the Benjamin N. Cardozo School of Law. Like her mother, Napoli is a writer and has published two law review article: one on the right of armed Puerto Rican independence organizations to prisoner-of-war status and the other on women and the doctrine of informed consent. She lives on the Lower East Side of Manhattan with her husband, Sergio Borrero.

MARYANN NAPOLI
A Mother's Story

Shortly after getting married in 1961 and before I knew what I was doing, I became pregnant with my elder daughter, Lisa. "You are expected to have as many children as God sends," my mother said repeatedly. And with years of Catholic-school brainwashing, I was convinced that I would go to hell if I used birth control. Kara arrived two years after Lisa. I loved being a mother, but there was always something I wanted beyond. Why I ever thought of seeking advice from my mother, I'll never know. When I told her I wanted to do something outside the home, she said, "You don't have anything to offer on the outside; you should be at home."

I used to wonder why my mother, who seemed so independent before she married, became a subservient housewife and passed the ideal on to me. Perhaps class issues were involved. My mother was the daughter of Italian immigrants, and my father was a second-generation Irish-American who quit school in the eighth grade to work as a secretary for a steamship line. They married during the Depression and were the envy of their friends because both of them were employed. My father was a middle manager, and my mother taught school, having earned a college degree at Rutgers at night in the years before her marriage. In the mid-1930s, my parents moved from their working-class neighborhood to a suburban house in Teaneck, New Jersey. By the time I came along, in 1940, my mother was an always-smiling housewife in the Donna Reed mode.

My parents' marriage was long and happy but not one I ever wanted to emulate. Later in life, I realized they probably didn't like kids very much, though they had five (I was third). As Irish Catholics, they didn't have much choice. My mother went to morning Mass every day, and for years we knelt down together as a family each night to say the rosary. I remember how proud my mother was about having five children, and she was particularly proud of not looking like she had five children.

My mother waited on my father his entire life. In her era, the concept that men needed to be served was all-pervasive. When a woman in the neighborhood had a baby (which meant a hospital stay of a week or so), another woman, usually with five kids of her own, would cook the husband's dinner each night. My mother constantly drove home the point that men's work was far more important than women's: "A man works hard all week; he deserves relaxation once he gets home." For years my father played golf all day on Saturdays. Only with the benefit of hindsight did I see that my mother didn't quit work at five o'clock each weekday, nor did she have a weekend off. For fifty years she catered to and encouraged my father's self-centeredness.

My father's version of fatherhood was bringing home the paycheck. He didn't lift a finger to help with housework and child care; in fact, my mother once said he never even held us until we were about a year old. Demeaning remarks about women were part of life with Father. Even for a misogynist era, his comments were off the charts. The few powerful women of the time, like Eleanor Roosevelt, were referred to as "old bags" (a "dried-up old bag" if the woman was over sixty) who should stay home to mind their children. Women's illnesses were usually psychosomatic. Any girl who excelled in school was just a good memorizer. Women's bodies were to be commented on: A flat-chested woman was referred to as "Slats"; an unattractive woman had "a face that would stop a clock."

My husband, Dick, and I met at college. I was twenty-one and much in love when we married. Had I experienced a single woman's life and freedom, it would have been much harder, but I went from school and my father's house to marriage, or from shut-in to shut-in. I felt isolated in the suburbs, but I didn't know any better. When we married, I fell right into my parents' pattern: I actually tried to stop him when he went into the kitchen to cook, saying, "Don't do that; men don't cook." The old rules under which we married caused many marriages to fall apart in the early days of the women's movement because the men didn't want to change. I was fortunate because Dick was ahead of me. In 1966 we left the suburbs, afraid of becoming suburbanites like our parents, and moved to Manhattan, where I was much happier.

Dick was a feminist before I was, but without the label. It was not something he had to be converted to; he simply had a built-in sense of justice. He thought women should have the same rights as men. Nothing in his background accounted for this attitude, but it made his daughters sensitive to antimale sentiments in the early days of the women's movement. Walking down Fifth Avenue in the 1970 feminist march, we saw a woman holding a sign: STARVE A RAT TODAY; DON'T COOK YOUR HUSBAND DINNER, and Lisa and Kara cried, "Our daddy!"

I came to feminism slowly. When my brother gave me a copy of Betty Friedan's *The Feminine Mystique,* I had a negative reaction. I had totally bought the Catholic mother ideal and was threatened by what I perceived as an attack on it. I was greatly influenced by the "click" article in one of the first issues of *Ms.* magazine ("click" meaning the moment when one recognizes sexism). Then I read Kate Millett, Simone de Beauvoir, and Germaine Greer. Around this time, Catholicism experienced serious challenges over its position on birth control. A book entitled *What Modern Catholics Think About Birth Control,* containing writings by church fathers St. Thomas Aquinas and St. Augustine citing woman as "the gateway to the devil," had a powerful effect on me. Not being able to control my fertility put an enormous strain on my marriage and eventually led me away from Catholicism.

When Lisa and Kara got older, I wanted to earn money, but I thought that I should only work part-time because I wanted to be there when they came home from school. The early 1970s was the era of "just a housewife." If people asked, "What do you do?" you were embarrassed to say that you were a housewife. I wasn't bored with housework and cooking, but I felt I was boring. Dick encouraged me to do whatever I wanted, but until the women's movement it never occurred to me that I could be anything other than a teacher, nurse, or secretary. (You trained for one of those jobs for extra "pin money" or in case your husband died.) Lisa was around ten when I got a part-time job in an employment agency.

Around the same time I joined Consumer Action Now (CAN), an urban environmental organization formed by women. Half the group were career women; the rest were full-time mothers of young children (read: housewives)—two groups supposedly incompatible in those days. The women were high-powered, and for me Consumer Action Now was a training ground for the job market. Like many women, I had lost my confidence staying home. I was afraid to speak in public and certainly never thought of myself as a writer. At CAN I discovered I could do both. Volunteers at a time when volunteerism had fallen out of favor, we identified pesticides, additives, chemicals, and hormones that polluted the air, water, and food supply. We educated, lobbied, and took to the airways to get our message out.

CAN also functioned as a consciousness-raising group. Whenever the conversation turned to childbirth or medical care, there were the usual complaints. Here was an organization urging people to educate themselves, read labels, make informed decisions, and take responsibility for the consequences of their purchases; yet as consumers of medical care, we still functioned largely in the dark. The women's movement had already revealed that the scientific bases for medical interventions in the birthing process were shaky or nonexistent. But where do you go to find out whether your child really needs ear tube surgery and whether there are alternatives?

> When we married, I fell right into my parents' pattern: I actually tried to stop him when he went into the kitchen to cook, saying, "Don't do that; men don't cook."

Friend and fellow CAN member Rona Roberts and I decided to take the critical evaluation of medical care that the women's movement had initiated for women and apply it to everyone.

In 1976, together with Arthur Levin and Reverend Howard Moody, we formed the Center for Medical Consumers, now in its nineteenth year. Our first project was to open a medical library for the lay public. *HealthFacts,* the monthly newsletter I've written since the center opened, holds up common medical treatments to scientific scrutiny. In the early eighties, my work at the center led to an invitation to chair the National Women's Health Network's Breast Cancer Committee. Today I am a medical writer and consumer advocate. My recurring theme is: Don't take medical recommendations at face value; check out research for proof of safety and efficacy. The volunteerism begun at CAN remains a part of my life today: During Monday's lunch hour, I work at a soup kitchen, and I am on call two evenings a month at Mt. Sinai Hospital's Rape Crisis Intervention Program.

Our decision to live in the city meant that we had to consider sending our children to private schools. As a private-school teacher, Dick got tuition cuts for our daughters, but for years all our money went to tuition. We never went on vacations. It wasn't that we were steering our children to the Ivy League (we knew we'd never be able to afford it); we just felt that early education was the most important. With a good education as a basis, we reasoned, the girls could do what they wanted for college. The other part of the equation was the danger in public schools. That concern was naive, however, since women aren't safe anywhere. As it turned out, Lisa had a terrible experience with a violent male classmate at one of the top private schools in the city. She didn't tell us until after it was over. Only recently did we learn that the young man stalked her for a year.

Lisa has had many personality changes throughout her life. As a young child, she was cocky and bossy. Around the age of nine she went through a period of such shyness that her sister would have to tell the elevator man what floor they wanted. As a teenager, she became sullen and distant. She was so ashamed of her body that she walked around slumped over. Nothing Dick and I said in encouragement made a dent. Finally, her school needed a fourth person to play a part in *Who's Afraid of Virginia Woolf,* and Lisa got the role. She suddenly blossomed and began looking at colleges for their drama departments. Intelligent, articulate, and witty, Lisa says now that her sulky teen years were a depression.

Lisa also has incredible psychological and physical courage, which I can't take credit for. When she was fourteen she saw, from her bedroom window, a woman handcuffed, thrown facedown into the backseat of a police car, and beaten by two cops. Instead of telling us, she went to the police station (with her sister for moral support) and reported the incident. The officers threatened her, suggesting that if our family was in trouble, the police would not respond. The effect on Lisa has been lasting. If she sees injustice on the streets, she doesn't just walk by. Once she intervened when she saw a teenage boy hit his girl-friend. She doesn't tell me these things, but a friend of hers told me that she does things that terrify him, such as facing down cops during the Tompkins Square police riot several years ago.

For many years, I attributed Lisa pushing me away to teenage surli-ness. Kara didn't feel alienated in her teenage years the way Lisa did. Perhaps it is the difference between the first and second child: The first child has to push the boundaries and break in the parents. Kara was a cuddly baby and an affectionate little girl, with Dick's easy, unruffled confidence. Like Lisa, she has enormous courage. In college she was ar-rested for protesting against a nuclear-weapons company. The protest-ers were surrounded by cops in riot gear and offered the chance to go home or be arrested. Kara was among those taken to jail for three days, complete with prison uniforms and leg shackles during transport. I have such admiration for my daughters, but they scare me sometimes. Sure, Dick and I took them to many anti–Vietnam War protests, but nothing we ever did comes close to getting arrested.

My daughters have an incredible sense of the importance of public service. I am proud of what they have become. They are two terrific, intelligent, loving women doing important work for the public good. Lisa is in law school, aiming her work in the public interest. Kara is finishing her master's degree in public health, teaching health education to women in shelters. I hope that each will always be in a loving relationship. Their respective partners, reflecting the changes we see in men, do not consider their own jobs as more important.

Because of the women's movement, my daughters' options are a hundred times greater than mine were. I don't remember literally saying it, but I think they grew up knowing they could do anything. I have always encouraged them to do what makes them happy. If they choose to have children, my daughters will parent differently than I did in that they probably won't stay home as long as I did. I hope that their work lives will be what they enjoy, and that their choices will always be ones that move the world forward in some way.

LISA NAPOLI
A Daughter's Story

An awareness of being a woman and the social ramifications of that have always been part of my life. My mother took me and my sister to women's marches when we were little, and I was very proud to be at them. As a child, the images of the sixties and seventies—the Black Panther Party, war protests, the Young Lords, urban riots, Kent State, and women's marches—all seemed to be linked, even though in reality there was division. To me, women's rights are part of a spectrum of civil rights, and none can be divorced from the others. It is not enough to win equality as a woman only to find that you are still treated as a second-class citizen because of your race or religion or sexual orientation. Also, we diminish our power when we separate ourselves from those who are our natural allies, so from a strategy perspective it makes no sense for women to distance themselves from other groups when we all have the same basic goal of an equal society. I think the women's movement has been important and effective, but only up to a point. There are scores of women for whom these advances have not made one bit of difference.

I was born on June 10, 1962, in White Plains, New York. When I was little, my father worked and my mother stayed home with us. She had worked as a secretary but became a conventional housewife once my sister and I arrived on the scene. My mother never seemed to want to do anything besides be a housewife until I was about ten and she got involved with Consumer Action Now, a group of women who were environmental activists. This change in my mother really exemplified what the women's movement meant to me as a kid: that women no longer *had* to be housewives or work in crappy jobs; we could do anything we wanted to do—all of the limits had been lifted. (I later found out this wasn't reality.) In 1976 my mother cofounded her own organization, the Center for Medical Consumers.

Even though I would say that my family life was loving, I was not a happy kid. Most of the games I played were imaginary ones without toys, like playing store and house. As I grew older, I retreated more and more into an imaginary life. I was very withdrawn as a teenager; I read a lot. I read all of Shakespeare's plays, *Crime and Punishment,* and *Tess of the D'Urbervilles.* I read *The Stranger* when I was eleven because my mother told me that it began with "My mother died today—or was it yesterday" and that I would like it. I did. I loved how the oddness of it was so normal, and I identified with the dissonance. I was really into Russian history, especially the Russian Revolution. I would write short novels, like one I wrote about nihilists plotting the assassination of Alexander I. My parents encouraged my reading and writing, and they also conveyed to me the feeling that I had a very valuable intellect.

In retrospect, my increased withdrawal into an imaginary world and later into drugs was due to an alienation I felt that grew beyond my ability to manage it. The feeling of otherness and of being an outsider was probably why I liked *The Stranger* so much (and why my mother recommended that I read it). I felt like an outsider at the school I went to because it was for rich WASPs, and we weren't. I never fit into that world—and it wasn't like I rebelled and refused to; I tried like hell. It was immensely painful. Later in life, when I entered into a major depression, I wanted to jump out of my skin. I would cut myself with a razor—anything to get out of myself. Now I feel different. First of all, I no longer feel so bad about my otherness. Second, I have made it a point of comfort: I chose to go to a Jewish law school, I chose to live in a neighborhood that is primarily Latino. I have reached a point of integration where I don't feel the dissonance I used to.

I went to a Catholic school when I was little, mostly because I got a tuition break there, since my father taught at a related school. I considered myself Catholic and was religious. Mom became anti-Catholic and antireligion when I was around six. I made my First Communion and was really into it, but Mom wasn't, and she dressed me in red. I didn't get it; all I understood was that my classmates got new dresses and lots of gifts, like jewelry, and I got ten bucks. It hurt me that my First Communion wasn't a big deal to my family like it was to the other families.

I hated Catholic school; I was nauseated from the day I began, a psychosomatic illness that has never left me in times of duress. The school was very restrictive. Mom wasn't happy about my being there because she thought that a Catholic education was rote and not very challenging. She was right. My parents switched me to a mostly Protestant school, where I was shocked to learn that there were other religions besides Catholicism. The idea that there were other conceptions of God really made me question being religious. Later, when Martin Luther King was assassinated, I dropped religion altogether.

> When I was sixteen, my mother gave me a very frank talk on how women have orgasms.

My parents would identify themselves as agnostic. However, when I was in high school I reported that I had identified us as agnostic in an informal poll in my theology class, and my mother told me that *agnostic* was too active a term for what we are— "Basically, we just don't give a shit." This is more accurate.

Growing up, my sister, Kara, and I were very close. Until I was ten we shared the same room and played together constantly. I was sometimes jealous of her; she is more socially acceptable and socially adaptive than me and had a completely different experience of the WASPy school we went to. Whereas I was a zero and did practically nothing outside of school (and when I did it, I did it badly), she did gymnastics and won awards and went on a tour to Germany with her team. At the end of high school, however, I snapped out of whatever stupor I was in and found that I loved theater. Actually, I had always loved it and was constantly putting together productions in my head but was too shy to say anything or do anything about it.

My relationship with my parents and especially with my mother is very different from Kara's. As a teenager I would argue with my mother, whereas Kara would never argue with anybody. She just quietly did what she wanted and did not draw attention to herself. My existence was more operatic. My mother and I have frequently clashed because we are both strong-willed. It's hard to clash with my father: He's very sweet-tempered, and I have seen him angry only occasionally. Kara tends to be more like him in terms of temperament. My mother and I are both angry, driven people. If we don't like something, we are quick to point it out. This has its advantages if you are talking about something like inequality, but it can be fairly unpleasant when it comes to interpersonal relationships.

What I admire most about my mother is that she is very sharp. I think that I take after her in this regard—or at least I hope I do. As a layperson working in the medical world and often coming up against the medical profession, she knows she has to be absolutely detailed, thorough, and well researched on every issue she addresses. It is a quality that I try to emulate.

My father has always been feminist. He always communicated to us that girls were smart—in fact, he communicated to us that girls were smarter. My femaleness was celebrated: When I got my period for the first time, he brought me flowers to mark it as a very special occasion, and I dried some of the roses in a dictionary to commemorate it. When I was in high school, a friend of mine who had grown up in Italy told me that since my father is Sicilian, he must have wanted sons, because all Sicilian men want sons, and my father *must* have been disappointed. I didn't really put much stock in this, but I asked Dad anyhow if he had wanted sons. He didn't seem to give it much thought; he just said, "No. There is nothing I could do with a son that I couldn't do with you."

My parents were always open with us. When I was sixteen, my mother gave me a very frank talk on how women have orgasms. At the time I was a stinky teenager and I did *not* want to have a candid discussion of this with my mother, of all people. I had, amazingly enough, figured this one out and had already negotiated it with my boyfriend. Nonetheless, it was a remarkable thing that my mother did, and I will definitely have that talk with my children. Even though my mother's talk came a little late, my parents' prior openness had paved the way for me to figure out how I have orgasms and had led me to request and expect sexual satisfaction from my partners.

My parents never fostered our dependence on them, and I always knew that when I finished high school, I would be on my own; I would be an adult and responsible for myself. I decided to go to the University of Toronto because it was cheap and urban, and I could do my degree in three years. I knew college was important, but it seemed like a way to put off working and continue being a child.

I loved the University of Toronto and majored in theater. I wanted to see how far I could push the boundaries of expression; I did activist and experimental theater that pricked at people's consciences and disturbed them. When I got out of school, I wandered around the downtown experimental theater and performance art scene in New York and then set up my own theater company that operated primarily on the Lower East Side. Theater was a passion that I never thought would be dampened, no matter how difficult it was to survive doing it. But by 1988 there were hundreds of people living in the park down the block from my house, and this began to change how I felt. There had always been people living on the street, in lots, in doorways, and in hallways on the Lower East Side, but the magnitude and concentration of the Tompkins Square Park encampment was really astonishing. In August of 1988 there was a police riot, and after that, theater seemed self-indulgent. There was a lot going on in the neighborhood, and I chose to become part of that.

In May of 1989 I founded the Lower East Side Women's Center, which I envisioned as a means for women to begin to take control of their lives through access to information and support. The Women's Center would also be a meeting place where women could organize to take action on issues we decided were important. The center functioned for nearly five years, staffed by volunteers giving information, referrals, and support. In December of 1993 we closed the center. It was very difficult to run an all-volunteer organization without adequate financial support. Most funders want to see services; we were adamantly not a service organization because we wanted to be an alternative to the service provider–client dynamic that is so prevalent on the Lower East Side and in other communities where many residents are poor.

Given my history of feeling alienated from others, it is kind of surprising, and to no one more than myself, that I am married. I thought Sergio was a real find when I first met him: smart, handsome, interested in things outside of himself. I already had a lover, so I tried to fix him up with everyone I knew because I thought he was too good to let go by. Our feelings deepened, and we began a romantic relationship. Very early on, I knew Sergio was the one. It is interesting that he is the lover with whom I have felt the least amount of otherness. My parents' relationship has always been a model for me: They have a real partnership. Sergio and I have a partnership as well. We help each other out, we learn from each other, and our relationship continues to grow.

When I get out of law school, I want to do community-based legal services and eventually incorporate direct service with policy making. That way, grassroots community efforts can translate into systemwide changes that are lasting. I think that this will make community organizing more effective and give community initiatives more power. I do want to have children someday, but my maternal feelings aren't too strong at this point. Sergio and I are a family now, and if we choose to increase our numbers, I know I will pattern my parenting on that of my parents.

Barbara and Rosa, 1970.

Rosa and Barbara, 1991.

Barbara Ehrenreich
and
Rosa Ehrenreich

Barbara EHRENREICH, a novelist, essayist, lecturer, and mother of two grown children, was born in 1941 in Butte, Montana. She moved several times as a child, ending up in Los Angeles. In 1963 she graduated from Reed College in Portland, Oregon, then attended graduate school at Rockefeller University in New York City, where she studied cell biology. After her daughter, Rosa, was born, Ehrenreich spent some time teaching but eventually quit to become a full-time writer. Her articles have appeared in, among other places, *Ms., The Nation, Vogue, Time,* and the *New York Times.* Her books include *The Hearts of Men: American Dreams and the Flight From Commitment* and three books coauthored with Deirdre English on women healers and the sexual politics of health care. Ehrenreich's most recent book is *The Snarling Citizen,* a collection of essays.

As SHE TELLS IT, Rosa Ehrenreich, who was born in Manhattan in 1970, never officially graduated from high school due to a poor attendance record. Yet she earned a BA in history and literature from Harvard University in 1991 and an MS in social anthropology from Oxford in 1993, and she is now enrolled at Yale Law School. She expects to receive her JD in 1996. Her first book is titled *A Garden of Paper Flowers.*

BARBARA EHRENREICH
A Mother's Story

For my mother's generation, having babies wiped out the rest of a woman's life; for me, babies were a wonderful addition to the rest of my life. Motherhood and feminism did not clash for me. After my children were born, I wanted to change the world for them. I believed that staying home while my husband made the money would be a bad example for my daughter, Rosa. I wanted her to have a model of a woman she could be like, not a mother who existed only to propagate. I felt I wouldn't be a good mother if I wasn't stopping nuclear war while making a nutritional dinner. Of course, you have to be a superparent to raise children and make the world safe for them at the same time.

The big difference I see between women of my generation and young women today is their amazing degree of self-confidence. Rosa's generation doesn't start with the same sense of being damaged. After a prochoice march in Washington, Rosa and I were having coffee with a friend of hers whose mother is also a feminist, and I said to myself, "These young women are smart, courageous, talented, and they fear nothing. What is it? Was my generation just a practice model?" We had to pull ourselves out of something. We needed consciousness-raising and support groups desperately, just to establish that we weren't insane to find so much wrong with our lives.

My father was a copper miner in Butte, Montana, and my mother cleaned boardinghouses. After my birth in 1941, she quit her job to become a full-time homemaker. I wasn't close to my mother and I didn't want to be like her, so she was a confusing role model. My father did not respect her, and they fought all the time. Nobody was as smart as he was, and I was smart by association with him. Once, after I got into a fight with some neighborhood kids, my father said, "Don't play with those kids. They're dummies and you're smart." I guess that was ego-building. At least I wasn't a dummy.

My parents were always on the move. After Butte, we lived in Pittsburgh, Queens, and various towns in Massachusetts, finally ending up in Los Angeles. Along the way my father got an education and became a metallurgist. My parents divorced when I was in my early twenties. They were both alcoholics, though neither acknowledged it. Alcohol was a factor in my mother's early death at the age of fifty-four.

I was an odd child, a total nerd. I read the *Bhagavad Gita* and the *Upanishads;* I also read Kafka. I had pimples and I was flat-chested. Needless to say, I had few boyfriends. When I entered Reed College in 1959, I was finally in a place where everybody was weird, and I took off socially. I had more boyfriends than I could handle. To fulfill my father's wishes and become a scientist, I majored in chemistry and physics. Looking back, I realize that I was a budding feminist. Seeing all the girls (they were still girls in those days) in art history and French literature, I knew instinctively that I should stay away from those disciplines if I wanted to make a living.

Around 1965, when the United States increased its involvement in Vietnam, I awakened politically. I was a graduate student in Manhattan majoring in biology at Rockefeller University. Rockefeller was an indoctrination in upper-class behavior, with its luxurious quarters and dining hall servants. Everyone was supposed to be a gentleman and a scientist—even the girls. But the contrast I saw on long walks around Harlem caused me to question this world of privilege.

I met my husband through the antiwar movement. A group of us called a meeting because the draft was imminent, and John Ehrenreich showed up. John had been a disarmament activist at Harvard. The son of Communist parents, he seemed to understand what the world was about. That was important to me. We got married in 1966 at City Hall and then attended a demonstration where pacifist A. J. Muste spoke. Afterward we went up and told Muste we had just gotten married, and he gave us his blessing. For our honeymoon we went to Guatemala and made contact with the guerrilla movement there. As cover, we carried letters indicating that we planned to visit a nutritional center connected to Rockefeller University.

I was not part of the women's movement in the beginning. I thought Betty Friedan's *The Feminine Mystique* had to do with my mother's generation, not mine. I felt more connection to Helen Gurley Brown's *Sex and the Single Girl,* a book about young women in cities trying to make their own way. I remember one party in our apartment where Shulamith Firestone and Kathie Sarachild tried to tell me about women's liberation. "*I* don't have any problems," I said. "I'm a graduate student in science; nobody's ever discriminated against me." They probably left shaking their heads, saying, "What a jerk."

By 1970 I was reading feminist literature to gain an intellectual understanding of the issues. But it was pregnancy that changed me in an emotional way. For prenatal care, I attended a hospital clinic, the only white woman there. Most women at

> **I insisted that my Lamaze-trained husband be allowed in the delivery room. That was seen as a radical act.**

the clinic were black and Hispanic, and poor. The male doctors treated us in sexist and humiliating ways. When I asked the head obstetrician if my cervix was dilated, he looked at the nurse and said, "Where did such a nice girl learn to use words like that?" I had a PhD in biology, and he still treated me like a dummy.

My feminism rose from my experience with pregnancy, but giving birth radicalized me. To speed the delivery, the doctor gave me oxytocin. My labor was on schedule, but at ten o'clock at night the doctor wanted to go home. I didn't know enough to fight it, but I insisted that my Lamaze-trained husband be allowed in the delivery room. That was seen as a radical act. I wasn't allowed to hold Rosa the first night because the obstetrics ward was full and I was put in the gynecology ward with twenty sick women. It was infuriating. Those procedures probably produced a lot of feminists.

Rosa was an unusual child, and I don't say that just as her mother. She is objectively unusual. I knew it as soon as I saw her. From the beginning she was assertive, confident, analytical, and strong-willed. She was not a baby who cuddled up against you; Rosa was ramrod straight. When people stared at her, she looked back with great staring blue eyes. She could put words together in sentences when she was ten months old. People would look around to see where the voice was coming from, never suspecting it was the little person in the stroller.

After Rosa's birth, I continued working but shortened my hours. John, proficient at changing and bathing babies, took care of Rosa while I worked. From the start, he did more than half of the child-rearing. When Rosa was a year old, I got a job teaching and we moved to Long Island. Benjy was born when Rosa was two, nearly arriving on the hospital steps. When labor began, we raced to the hospital, but John, deciding he had to park the car, dropped me off at the entrance. A contraction began, and I lay down on the steps and did my Lamaze breathing. Benjy came so fast it was hair-raising.

In those days, children required less work than they seem to now. The baby was part of your life, not vice versa. We used to throw Rosa in a backpack and take her to demonstrations and meetings. If a conference provided day care, we left her at day care. Today, styles in middle-class child-raising have changed dramatically. Young mothers seem totally overwhelmed by their children. They can't manage them, and the children take over their lives. Part of it, I think, has to do with maternal guilt. Working mothers are with their children for such a limited amount of time that they believe there can be absolutely no unpleasantness when they're together.

I have always respected my children as people. When they were babies, I had the sense that they were their whole big selves, just in little packages. I felt privileged to be able to guide them through this helpless stage. It's difficult to be a baby and a little kid, because you start out small and incontinent and dumb, and you don't know anything. It's easy to patronize or humiliate people in that condition, which is the traditional method of child-raising. We need to treat children with dignity and respect their privacy. They deserve space and, of course, as much love as they can absorb.

By 1974 I was sick of the college faculty scene. Money meant little to us, so I quit teaching in order to write. We weren't exactly hippies, but we were part of a subculture that supported people who dropped out from the materialistic world, so we were poor and happily so. I did once dream that all the food at Finast was marked down. Then I realized we really were poor.

We always had other people living with us—friends and drifters. Rosa says that one of the best things about growing up in that house was learning to be around people of every color and sexual persuasion, from factory workers to professors. We had plenty of politically correct books, including the lesbian version of *Cinderella,* and we were open about the facts of life. I grew up in an environment where tampons and sanitary napkins were hidden in the bathroom, as if men never suspected that women menstruated and nobody could give the secret away. That seemed weird. At twelve you suddenly start to bleed, and it's terrifying. I thought it shouldn't be such a big deal, so I changed my tampons in front of the kids if they happened to be in the bathroom.

John and I were divorced in 1977, when Rosa was six. Various kinds of incompatibility led to the breakup. The divorce was traumatic for Rosa, but John lived in the city, so he was not just a weekend daddy. We thought it was important for the kids to see that they still had two parents present in their lives. John came to the house and cooked dinner for them three nights a week. He is a great guy and a true feminist. Without his encouragement, I could never have done my writing. Each of us has remarried, but we remain friends.

I believe that children should not have full-time parents, that they should see that adults of both sexes do things in the world. My kids knew that I had a grown-up life and work that was important to me, and they understood the causes that moved me. Most of the time I worked at home. As I became better known, I traveled a lot on speaking engagements. Even though I'd be away for several days at a stretch, which could be hard on kids, I was more likely than most working mothers to be home when they came in from school. Of course, if I had a deadline I'd have to say, "Door's shut." They understood, but I still got the little knocks.

My child-raising credo is spelled out in an article I wrote called "Stop Ironing the Diapers." As a parent, I tried to reverse many of the ways I was raised. I don't want to sound ungrateful to my mother, who was just a teenager when I was born. In some ways I have tried to emulate her. She and my father always took my questions seriously, saying that any question deserves a response.

I am proud that my kids are not only smart but good. I trust them. I also find them fascinating. Rosa is smart and funny and vivacious. We have a good time together—snorkeling, bike riding, or sitting around talking. It's hard to distinguish our opinions on a lot of things, although in some ways she's probably more socially conservative. Rosa will probably always have neater living quarters and better-organized drawers. She's more into clothes than I've ever been. She doesn't know it, but I'm still wearing clothes she wore as a teenager.

The year Rosa went from age thirteen to fourteen was difficult. She turned on me. Suddenly she devoted her life to the critique of Mommy. I could do nothing right, say nothing right, wear nothing appropriate. She told me later that she knew something was going on with her during that period, so she went to the library and read books about adolescent psychological development. For a thirteen-year-old, I thought that was remarkably self-aware.

Rosa is aware of her privileged position in society in attending Harvard, Oxford, and Yale. We laugh about what a good thing it is that I gave her the experience of poverty growing up in order to counteract her life today. One day her law class was discussing people who cheat on unemployment, and she said, "You don't understand; sometimes people have to do this just to eat. I remember when I was a little girl . . ." The students were dumbfounded.

Rosa is an activist. When she was in sixth grade and the antinuclear demonstrations were taking place in New York City, she led a disarmament rally at her school. She gets people together, gets them mobilized, and gets the job done. At Yale she organized a progressive student group to promote career alternatives in public-interest work. I wouldn't consider myself an activist right now. The last time I ran around like crazy was during the Gulf War. When issues such as abortion rights come up, I mobilize myself around them, but my day-to-day contributions are through writing.

Despite allegations that feminism is a white, middle-class movement, many women have picked up a sense of defiance from the movement and are applying it to their own lives. Today feminism has permeated our culture. You see it on television; it's on *Roseanne,* it's everywhere. In personal relations, however, I'm not sure we've come that far. Too often young women are afraid to say something that makes men nervous because the men might be less likely to ask them out. In addition, there is the campus phenomenon of not wanting to be seen as lesbian.

I worry that young middle-class feminists are not as involved in collective action as we were, but instead see feminism as an individual program for self-improvement. That's fine if you are fortunate and privileged, but what about the women who aren't? How do we make up for that? We need a collective movement. Patriarchy is an old way of organizing human societies—twelve thousand years old, more or less. That's quite a thing to overthrow. We still need a revolution.

ROSA EHRENREICH
A Daughter's Story

My mother's basic child-rearing philosophy seems to be that children should be treated like small and slightly handicapped adults. She always managed to act as though she respected me intellectually, even when I was just a babbling four-year-old. I got plenty of praise—if anything, I sometimes think my mother has an unrealistically positive view of me. I'd say, "Mom, I'm having trouble with this or that," and she'd laugh and say, "Oh, dear, you'll work things out. You're so wonderful; you always manage to work things out."

Having watched other people bring up their children, I find myself feeling that I would raise children the way my mother did. She always took us seriously and included us in her projects. Obviously there is a downside: Sometimes kids just want to be kids, and they don't want to have to act mature. But all things considered, I wouldn't swap her for any other mother I've met. My mother managed to bring up two children who like her a lot, who talk to her a lot, and who trust her a lot. That's more than I can say for most families I know.

When I was born in Manhattan in 1970, my mother was just starting her writing career. She had never planned to write; she started more or less by accident. She and a friend wrote a short article on women's health issues and, rather to their surprise, the article got a good reception. People began asking them to write for tiny, obscure journals, and after a while the journals weren't so obscure. I think my mother realized that she liked to write and that she was good at it, so why not try to do it for a living?

My mother's finest child-rearing achievement, I think, is that she taught me to get my own breakfast at the age of two. She said, "Dear, you know I like to sleep later than you do, so I'm going to put a bowl of cereal and a spoon on the table and a glass of milk on a low shelf in the fridge, and you can get yourself breakfast whenever you wake up."

And so I did. My younger brother and I weren't supposed to wake Mom before nine o'clock; we were expected to play by ourselves. Naturally, we figured out ways around this rule: We'd just play a little louder, right outside Mom's bedroom door.

My brother and I were never sent to ballet lessons or violin lessons or drama lessons. In part this was because there wasn't much money to spare, and in part, I think, it was because my mother viewed such things as nonessential. We were not pushed, except intellectually. If we wanted lessons in something, we had to ask. This is one of the few areas in which I might not imitate Mom's child-rearing tactics: Four-year-olds can't ask for things if they don't know what to ask for.

Although we didn't have much money when I was growing up, I was not aware of wanting things, except in a trivial sense, like wanting another ice cream cone. To some extent, our poverty was voluntary, something we were proud of because we weren't selling out. At least, that was how my mother presented it to us. We were taught to comparison shop very early. I think my mother succeeded in making it something of a game, recruiting my brother and me as bargain-hunting assistants. We went to rummage sales and to the Salvation Army to hunt through the old clothes. When I was small, this was fun. When I got to be twelve or thirteen, it was distinctly not fun. My mother was better off financially by then, so we didn't have to rely on thrift shops anymore, but we still had less money than most other families we knew.

My parents separated when I was about six. I don't remember the breakup. I'm told that I was upset about it, but I'm happy to say that I seem to have repressed the whole thing. I was lucky: The divorce was friendly, and my parents were firm about presenting a united front. I often heard sentences that began with "Your father and I have decided . . ." or "Your mother and I think . . ." After the divorce, both of my parents eventually remarried. Dad moved to an apartment in New York City, and my brother and I visited him whenever we wanted. Having a New York pied-à-terre made us the envy of our friends. This made up for a lot of other perceived deprivations.

My mother traveled a lot, but Dad was around the whole time I was growing up. He visited on some weekday afternoons each week, and we usually stayed with him on weekends and for parts of the summer. In some ways he has always been more domestic than my mother. He loves to cook. We occasionally had bizarre situations where Mom would be out of town, Dad would come over to make dinner, and my stepfather, my brother, and I would join him at the table. Our friends and neighbors got pretty confused.

Our house was in a working-class neighborhood, and after a short stint at a Quaker school I attended a little local elementary school with mostly Irish Catholic and Italian kids. Then the town experienced a boom, and I went to junior high school with children from very wealthy families. It was during the early and mid-1980s, the height of a nasty kind of materialism, and I was acutely conscious of not having the fashionable brand names that my classmates had. I was embarrassed when Mom picked me up from school in our battered old car. She wore jeans and a sweatshirt. The other mothers wore makeup and ritzy clothes. I wanted my mother to look like everybody else's mother, our car to look like everybody else's car, and our house to look like everybody else's house. One girl, critically inspecting my clothes, actually asked me what was wrong with my family. She said, "At least my mom's not some kind of *women's libber,* and she can afford to buy me designer jeans."

At the age of thirteen I went through a sulky, obnoxious adolescent stage. I wanted only to be left alone in my room and not have to talk to anybody, ever. My mother bore the brunt of my moodiness. My father, who wasn't around quite as much, missed the worst of it. I was just rebellious and angry at everything. It was partly because my mother had succeeded so well in making the world seem like such a good, fun place. She never prepared me for some of the things I had to face—like junior high, where suddenly I was confronting nasty, dog-eat-dog realities.

I was in a bad mood for two years. At some point I realized I wasn't really mad at my mother; I was mad at the world. I took it out on Mom because she was there. But eventually I learned the rules of being an American teenager, and I also discovered the unique advantages of having a "weird" family. I realized that my friends liked coming over to my house, strange as it was, because my mother took them seriously and would say things like, "What do you think about my article? Do you think I should change this paragraph here?" My friends were incredibly flattered to discover an adult who cared about their opinions. Their own mothers made them tiptoe around to avoid getting the furniture dirty; my mother said, "Put your feet up, make yourself at home!"

While I don't really see how my mother could have done a better parenting job than she did, this is not to say that there weren't things that bothered me. She sometimes expected me to police my brother when she was away, to make sure that he was doing his homework or eating a proper dinner. Of course, my brother just saw this as his big sister trying to boss him around. I often felt that I was in a no-win situation. I wanted to be responsible and hold the fort when Mom was away, but I didn't want to have to be the bad cop with my brother.

When I think realistically, however, I realize that I wouldn't have wanted my mother to stay home all the time. That would have made her unhappy, and I would have been miserable. If you're a working mother, your kids will inevitably resent you at some point; they'll want you there seeing to their needs every second of the day, not out having a career. If you stay home, on the other hand, there's a point at which your kids are going to say, "Damn it, why doesn't Mom go out and get a life? Why is she always on my case?" Ultimately, parents should do what they need to do—happy parents generally have happy kids, and no child wants a parent who goes around acting martyred.

In high school, I was bored silly and became a truant. I almost didn't graduate. I had always done well in school, and my mother was fairly lenient about letting me take a day off if I felt like I needed one. I began to feel like it every day, so I began to take a lot of days off. My mother has an anarchistic streak. She'd say, "Why should you go to school? You're bored. It's easy for you. Why should you go?" After those few years of fighting, this shared time helped to cement our relationship. I'd crawl out of bed at eleven-thirty, just as Mom was starting lunch, and sit with her for a few hours. Then she'd go work and I'd go read my novels. I spent a lot more time with my mother than I would have if I'd gone off to school every day.

My father is more rule-abiding than my mother, and he wasn't happy about her attitude. He'd tell me, "I know you're bored in school, but that's just the kind of thing you have to do in life. You have to deal with these things." At some point my school implemented an attendance policy. If you missed more than twenty days in any class, you couldn't get credit. Needless to say, I was way over the limit. I failed gym and health, dropped math, and came close to flunking French as a result of my absences. In the end, the school decided not to let me graduate. I had already gotten into Harvard, so I called the admissions office and said, "Look, my school is not going to let me graduate because of this technicality. How do you feel about that?" They said, "We don't care. Your recommendations are good, your grades are good, your essays are good. We could care less whether you graduate from high school."

Even so, my father made a last-ditch attempt to get the high school to let me walk in the graduation ceremony. The day before graduation, the vice principal, who was a nice guy, said to the principal, "Come on, let her walk. She's going to Harvard. What difference does it make?" So I got a diploma, but I have never been sure whether I really graduated from high school.

It didn't feel like a huge leap for me to go to Harvard, though I came from a different background than most other students there. My stepfather was a union organizer, my mother an activist and writer. All through my childhood, we had strikers in the dining room making signs and refugees living in the basement. It was a bohemian, leftist scene. In my family, activism was presented not as a choice but as a basic part of the ethical equipment you go out with into the world: You have to take stands on issues. It didn't really matter how you chose to become socially involved, but it was assumed that you would in one way or another.

At Harvard I became politically involved very quickly, working with the union drive, the anti-apartheid movement, and student public-service organizations. While an undergraduate, I thought the student body a bit apathetic politically. But now, having studied at Oxford, I appreciate Harvard much more. Compared to Oxford, it was downright activist. At Yale Law School, I've been disappointed to find relatively little concern about making the world a better place. Feminism at Yale seems to be more about a sense of entitlement and a set of symbols than anything else, which saddens me. Upper-middle-class women seem to assume equality, partly because of the work people like my mother did.

My mother made few compromises in her life that I would be unwilling to make. I would rather not have as little money as she had when I was young, but one can manage without too much money. My mother is about as nonmaterialistic as you can be. She is also straightforward, but in a way that's respectful of other people. She's a fighter who doesn't let herself be intimidated intellectually or politically. And she's kind. She has a sense of humor, but she doesn't use her intellectual skills or her sense of humor to intimidate others. She can make radical things sound like common sense, and she states her opinions in ways that are provocative but don't make people feel attacked. She uses humor to be inclusive, an ability I don't see in a lot of other people.

Sometimes it can be a burden to have such a well-known mother.

People read her work and assume automatically that I share every view. Often I do share her views—but all the same, we're different people. For example, people have often assumed that I'll do the same kind of writing she does. But I've discovered that I don't really like to do her kind of writing. From time to time, when I care about an issue a lot, I decide that maybe I should write about it, but generally I don't have a burning desire to comment on every public issue. I've been a fanatical fiction reader all my life, and writing fiction is something I've always wanted to do.

> All through my childhood, we had strikers in the dining room making signs and refugees living in the basement.

People say, "I admire your mother so much," and I don't quite know how to respond. I don't want to say, "Oh, she's nothing special," but it seems a bit smug to say, "Oh, yes, isn't she?" I do sometimes feel that my mother is wonderful and perfect, and I don't know if I can do the things she's done. She has a tremendous amount of confidence in me. It's a little worrisome, because I sometimes feel that my mother expects that I will do everything she has done, only better. I'll be happy if I can do what she does 50 percent as well.

Carol and Elizabeth, 1981.

Carol and Elizabeth, 1995.

Carol Jenkins

and

Elizabeth Hines

CAROL JENKINS is a television reporter and anchor for WNBC News in New York City. Jenkins was born in Alabama in 1944 but moved from there before she was old enough to understand racial discrimination. She grew up in New York and attended Boston University, where she received her BA in liberal arts and speech pathology. She earned her MA in speech pathology from New York University, where she later returned to take classes in journalism. After beginning her career as a secretary at CBS, she became a street reporter for ABC. In 1970 she took a position at NBC as a reporter, and she has worked there ever since. Jenkins lives in Westchester, New York, and has two children.

ELIZABETH HINES, a student at Yale University, was born in 1975 in Manhattan. At the time of her interview, she was eighteen years old. Hines has had a lot of work and volunteer experience, including an internship in the office of the editor-in-chief of *Ms.* magazine; participation in the day-to-day management of PTS, a family-owned graphic-arts school; and volunteering with God's Love We Deliver, delivering Thanksgiving meals to homebound people with AIDS, and Hale House, working with drug-addicted and HIV-positive babies. Hines was also a convention aide at the 1992 Democratic National Convention and an office assistant and street campaigner for Liz Abzug's campaign for the New York City Council in 1991.

CAROL JENKINS
A Mother's Story

When I gave birth to my daughter, Elizabeth, I felt as if I had become me. Creating this little girl was the highlight of my life. I fell in love with her. She was the easiest baby—bright and loving, gorgeous and smart. She made my life complete. I took three weeks off from work when she was born. Then I found a woman from Jamaica, Louise Thompson, who stayed with us for the next thirteen years. Elizabeth became my little partner. I took her everywhere I could, including work. She simply became part of my working life. When I did the news, she would stretch out under the anchor's desk and color. The network let her stay because she was so trustworthy. She was quiet until the commercial break; then she would sit up and talk to people.

I worked every Saturday and Sunday while Elizabeth was growing up. The table in my office was where we had our dinner, where she did her homework, where she brought her friends. It was highly irregular, but that is what a reporter's life is like. On an average weekend we spent the morning together and went into the studio around 2:00 P.M. I did my writing and then went on the air. Afterward we had dinner and went to a movie or saw a play or read. Elizabeth stayed with me until 11:30 P.M., when I got off. She did not have a regular childhood with regular hours because I felt it was important for her to be with me.

There were many times, however, when I could not be available for her. I don't have vivid memories of her day-to-day life because of work. In hindsight, I regret the time I spent away from her when she was growing up. I'd love to have more memories of when changes took place in her development, when she crossed certain lines. I'm afraid she lost a sense of security because she couldn't be with me when she might have wanted to. I wish she had come home knowing I would be there, instead of having to go through an elaborate phone or beeper system to connect with me. I wasn't the kind of mother who cooked, which I regret, because food is so associated with love. I think there were some middle years when Elizabeth was unhappy at not having a normal life with her mother.

I was always aware of a community of strong women. I was born in Alabama in 1944 into what I now consider a feminist family. My mother, one of fifteen children, was born on the family farm in Montgomery, where I spent my early years. She had eight sisters and six brothers. None of the sons went to college, because they were expected to take care of the farm, but all nine daughters did. The legacy of the family traveled through these strong, educated women. When my grandmother died, a sister took over the leadership of the family and kept everyone together. This aunt helped to educate all of us. If we needed clothes, she got out her sewing machine and sewed.

My mother has evolved into a feminist. She was married twice, first to my real father and then to my stepfather, who raised me. My mother was the nurturing, loving parent, my stepfather the disciplinarian. He and my mother began a vocational school called the Printing Trade School, where they spent eighteen hours a day training thousands of printers. They were true workaholics. Nonetheless, they had a traditional marriage, which meant that my mother catered to my stepfather. She spent years being the core strength of his business. After he died ten years ago, she became a truly effective and powerful woman. Today, at seventy-two, she still runs the business.

My family was middle-class, but middle-class black always seemed a few notches below middle-class white. Middle-class black meant that you could pay for your home and you had clothes. My mother and stepfather moved north in 1949. Until they got settled, I lived with my grandmother, who was very strong. When I moved to New York, my stepfather's mother, another powerful woman, came to live with us. In the New York community where I grew up, we didn't lock our doors. We roller-skated, sat on the stoop at night, caught fireflies, and ran from house to house. I had security with my grandmother, security in the neighborhood, and parents who loved me to death.

As an only child, I was adored, but the full expectation of the family rested on me. My intelligence was nurtured in that I was always expected to achieve. My parents were too busy to read to me, but I loved books and taught myself to read early on. We had the first television on the block, and I watched whatever was on from the very beginning. It occupied me as a child and gave me a great deal of stimulation. It was a friend, a window to the outside world, when I came home from school. In sixth grade, I scored so high on a reading test that my parents were advised to put me in private school, which they did at great sacrifice to themselves. I attended the Rhodes School and then a Lutheran school in the Bronx. From there I went to a tiny private school in Queens. To this day, I do not know how my parents managed to pay for it.

In 1967, at the height of the civil rights movement, I entered Boston University. During college I marched constantly, signed petitions, raised money, and protested. My biggest regret is that I didn't return to the South to work in the movement there. At the time I thought the most important thing was to finish my education. I majored in liberal arts and speech pathology in college and did a master's degree at New York University in speech pathology. I later returned to NYU for journalism courses. I began my career at CBS as a secretary, which infuriated my parents beyond all reason. Fortunately I didn't stay there very long. I soon went to work for ABC as a street reporter.

I always considered myself a feminist, but I don't think anybody would pick me out of a crowd and say, "That's a feminist." I wasn't organizing and marching in the early seventies; I was busy breaking into a male-dominated profession. I was out there being a television reporter, running stories from a woman's perspective. After my experiences at CBS and ABC, however, I decided that television journalism was too cutthroat, and vowed not to try it again. But in 1970 the NBC news director persuaded me to take an interesting position. It was an unusual opportunity: The industry was suddenly hiring women and minorities as window dressing. Several other women who are now prominent also came into the business at that time.

I met my husband, Carlos Hines, shortly after I went to work for NBC. I was twenty-eight, considered old to be unmarried and childless in those days. I was working hard, had my own apartment and money, and was having a ball. He was a Jamaican, fourteen years my senior, a charming, gentle man who had come to this country with nothing and had become the owner of a New York restaurant. I swore

I would never marry someone who had his own business, because it was too tough, but my parents liked Carlos and persuaded me to marry him. Immediately I began to fall into my mother's pattern. The restaurant was struggling, and I was expected to help out. When I found my life and career being swept under by trying to make his business succeed, I began to chafe. After three years I bailed out of the marriage. Elizabeth was a year old. To this day I have the utmost admiration for Carlos, but we were not meant to be married.

I did not want Elizabeth to be an only child. I wanted her to have company, and she wanted a brother. It was clear that I wasn't going to get married and have another child right away, because I was too busy working. We had talked about adopting a little boy, but not until I was sent to do a story on Mother Hale, who many years ago started taking in babies of addicts, did the dream become reality. I had covered Mother Hale many times before and was reluctant to go again, but I went. As she and I talked she handed me the baby she was holding in her arms. I took the little girl and said, "Hi, how are you?"

Mother Hale said, "That baby usually cries when she is held. Maybe you should think about adopting her."

I said, "I have a daughter, and she is perfect. I don't want another daughter, but I have been thinking about a little boy."

"I have just the little boy for you," she told me. Turning to one of her assistants, she said, "Go get Mikey." The aide went upstairs and came down with Mikey. Just as I fell in love with Elizabeth the first time I saw her, I fell in love with Mikey. I knew that he was my son. It was as if I had given birth to him—the same feeling and connection. I felt that he belonged with me. I went back to NBC and edited the story, and after the broadcast I returned to Hale House until Mikey went to sleep. He was eighteen months old and had no language. The only thing that he could do was bark like a dog. I took Elizabeth to Hale House so she could meet him. On Friday I told Mrs. Hale I wanted to take Mikey home for the weekend. He's been with us ever since.

Elizabeth was delighted at first. Later, when she realized that Mikey was never going away, she had difficulty adjusting to his being the center of attention. But for a ten-year-old, she handled it marvelously. Mikey was and is hyperactive. He had been at Hale House all of his life and had bonded with one of the caretakers. I hired her to work with us so that Mikey could have some continuity. She is still part of our extended family.

Mikey and I moved back with my mother when Elizabeth went to boarding school. It was hard to send her off to Hotchkiss. I did not want her to go, but I also knew that for her independence she had to be away at school. Our family is so turned inward; we are much too close. I didn't want Elizabeth to be caught in this cycle, to be the third generation of women who talked to their mothers every day and lived with their mothers.

Once when I went to visit Elizabeth at boarding school, I arrived at her door to be faced with a Nike advertisement that said, essentially, "You don't have to be your mother." I was extremely offended. I said, "Elizabeth, they would never do an ad that said you don't have to be your father." It is still okay in our society to put mothers down. We're vulnerable because we're responsible for nurturing and raising children, and we get the rap for anything that goes wrong. We need more positive images of motherhood, but we also need to understand that it's a struggle and that usually mothers do the best they can. In almost every case, the children survive and are stronger for some of the difficulty.

I believe that Elizabeth will be careful not to live her life as I have. The cost has been enormous in terms of things I have wanted to do or could have done. Short of abandoning the children, if you are a single parent you don't get much relief. I think that Elizabeth is somewhat wary, having watched me struggle. I think she will probably pace her life a little better. If I could live my life again, I would try to make as much money as possible early on. Had I known more about money, I could have built a secure base. Compared to women in most jobs, I make a lot of money, but my job is always tenuous. Television is a young industry, and a woman over forty who has achieved a certain stature and earns a substantial salary is at risk of being replaced by a younger woman who makes a tenth of her salary.

For Christmas I gave Elizabeth a subscription to the *Wall Street Journal* so she could begin to understand finances. I see that as the key. Women don't like to talk about money. Only now are we beginning to realize that we deserve it. Despite working all of my life, somewhere in the back of my mind I always assumed that some man would ultimately take care of me and my family. Now I realize that in order to be truly independent, you have to take care of yourself. I've never taken money for speaking engagements, but in truth, had I taken the money and invested it wisely, I would have had more to give to the organization to which I was speaking. That would have been a truly feminist act.

Elizabeth has recently had her own awakening as a feminist. I remember that when she was in junior high school I worried because she was getting the traditional old-boy education. I looked at the reading list and said, "Elizabeth, this is horrible. There are no women here. Go ask your teacher, 'What about the women?' "

> **W**omen don't like to talk about money. Only now are we beginning to realize that we deserve it.

Elizabeth came back saying, "The teacher said if we had to include some women, we would have to leave out some good men."

"Aren't you bothered by this?" I asked.

In the beginning she wasn't. But a trip she took in the summer of 1992 changed all that. With a group called Freedom Riders, Elizabeth spent a month traveling across the country registering people to vote. Riding buses and staying in YWCA's, the young people went all the way to the West Coast by a northern route and returned by way of the South. I flew down to Birmingham and did a story on them. After spending a month with these young women and men, all of whom called themselves feminists (and some of whom were lesbians and gays), Elizabeth came back totally radicalized.

We have gained so much from our daughters. Because of the limitations that were imposed on us, we often don't even know when we are confining and limiting ourselves. Elizabeth has no sense of limitation. When I tell her that women weren't allowed to do one thing or another when I was her age, she says, "That's the most ridiculous thing I've ever heard." My colleagues at WNBC News in New York tease me, saying, "Here comes Carol with another babe story," because I try to do as many pieces on women as I can. My hope for feminism is that we will get to a point where paying attention to girls in school will be as natural as paying attention to boys, where one reporter won't say to another, "Oh, you're doing another babe story." My dream is that sexism will no longer be part of our consciousness.

Seeing our daughters striking out gives us new energy and hope that we can do it, too—that even at fifty or sixty, our lives do not have to be over. Now that my son is older, I am ready to think seriously about dating men again. I'm beginning to pursue film production, and I sit on the *Ms.* Foundation board. I expect the next two decades to be the most productive in my life so far. To me, that's what feminism means: that women can do anything. We can live a full life without setting limitations on ourselves, and we can break through the limitations others put on us because we believe we can.

A Daughter's Story

If my mother hadn't thrown me on the bus for a Freedom Summer '92 cross-country voter registration drive, I probably wouldn't call myself a feminist now. I was one of the youngest people on the trip—I was seventeen—and it ended up being one of the best experiences of my life. Being with young men and women who talked intelligently and were starting to do what they wanted to with their lives pushed me to think about certain issues and where I stood on them. Most of the ideas and attitudes I have now were solidified during that month on the road.

I was born in New York City on April 8, 1975, at Roosevelt Hospital. At the time my mother was a reporter for NBC News, where she has worked my entire life. My father was a restaurateur from Jamaica. My mother and he actually met in one of his restaurants. After they got married they lived above one of his restaurants until my mother became pregnant with me; then they moved to a place near Central Park. My mother was thirty and my father was forty-four when I was born. I have an older half-brother and half-sister from his first marriage, but I don't have much contact with them.

My parents divorced when I was very young. My father moved down to Greenwich Village, but I saw him often and spent some weekends with him. When I was with him I got everything I wanted; my mother was the parental one, the one who really raised me. If I wasn't with my mother, I was with my nanny, T.T. She came from Jamaica, which I think was important to my father. From her I gained some of my toughness and my cynicism. After T.T. left, when I was thirteen, we had a number of different nannies. Finding someone you actually trust with your children can be difficult. Some nannies were immature and didn't know how to be nurturing.

When I was four or five we moved in with my mother's parents.

My grandmother became like a second mother and played an enormous role in my upbringing. She represented security to me. We still have a very close relationship. My grandfather was also a big part of my life; he told me great stories, played with me, and spoiled me to death. I absolutely adored him and felt very close to him. When we moved in with them, my grandfather, a diabetic, was already beginning to get very ill. He died when I was seven.

When I was nine my father died of colon cancer. At the time, it felt like everyone around me was disappearing. I was terrified that my mother and my grandmother would disappear, too. I was unable to spend a night away from home, sure that I would come back and find something wrong. Between the ages of seven and ten I was consumed with death. It was difficult coming to terms with the fact that I didn't have a father anymore. Occasionally it still feels like a piece is missing, and there are things I would like to know from his perspective.

My mother was an only child, and I spent my first ten years as an only child. By the age of ten I wanted a sibling. I actually called adoption agencies. When I told my mother about the calls and asked her if we could adopt a baby, she agreed to think about it. I guess she must have thought about it, because one day she took me to Hale House to see a little boy. We took him home for the weekend, and on Monday morning I sat on my mother's bed crying, trying to convince her that we couldn't take him back. He's been with us ever since.

After adopting Mikey, my mother moved us to Westchester County and commuted in to work. At first I missed being the only child. For ten years I had been the center of attention. I got all the presents. It was tough suddenly to have all these people come over and shower affection on someone else, but I learned to adjust. Mikey is one of the most important people in my life. He is a wonderful kid, and this year he has made incredible leaps at the Gateway School, a private school for children with learning disabilities.

For much of my life I have been known as Carol Jenkins's daughter. My mother is a great journalist and avid activist. She has rooms full of awards. I went through a period where I used to fear that in my lifetime I could not possibly win as many awards as my mother, even if I lived twice as long. I still worry about it sometimes. But I have come to realize that the sacrifices she made are not necessarily sacrifices I want to make. Television is not something I want to give my life to. It is a huge commitment; to a large extent, your life is not your own. Also, the age issue is not pleasant. As women get older they are considered less attractive, while men become distinguished. Polls can be very hurtful. It's easy for me to say, "You know, Mom, it doesn't matter," but she has to pay attention to the criticism. She has to think about it a lot.

One of the difficulties about having my mother in the spotlight is that it is not something I would necessarily choose for myself. I have had to get involved in her life in minor ways—newspaper profiles, family promotions that the station likes to do—though my mother has been good about not making me do those things. We are developing an understanding that my life is my own, and I don't necessarily want it to be a part of her public life. At the same time, being a celebrity has its perks, and I can't complain about the lifestyle it has provided me with. Because of my mother's career, I've grown up financially privileged; I've received a good education and met interesting people. There are definitely things I take for granted, like the fact that we often don't have to wait on line at restaurants and movies. Sometimes I think it would be hard for me to move back into an ordinary existence.

I was fifteen when I entered the Hotchkiss School in Lakefield, Connecticut. My mother didn't want me to go. She kept saying, "Elizabeth, you can't stay away for a week. How are you going to spend three years at that place?" I wanted to prove to myself that I could do it, and I wanted to get a great education. In the end, my mother allowed me to apply to two boarding schools, but she wouldn't let me go farther than two hours from home.

At Hotchkiss I grew up and learned a lot about who I am. At times I missed my mother, but we talked on the phone almost every day. I could go home anytime I wanted to, and often did, but I was also excited to be out on my own. The work and the demands tested my limits and gave me an incredible feeling of accomplishment. It was an intense environment. Without the support of several mentors, I don't know if I would have made it.

Because of my upbringing, I had a different experience from many other African-Americans at Hotchkiss. I had attended private schools my entire life and was always one of the few black children in these schools. I first became aware of race when I was in the second grade. I attended the Friends Seminary in New York City, and in class one day we were talking about race and how people are classified. I was sitting next to my friend Joanna, who is white. When the subject of black people came up, she raised her hand and said, "But Elizabeth isn't black—she's brown." Then we got into a huge debate about race. When we moved to Westchester, I was the only black student in my entire grade. Many of my mother's friends are white, and 85 percent of my friends are white. At Hotchkiss, many of the African-American kids would sit at separate tables, and although I sometimes sat with them and many of them were my friends, many of my close friends were also white. I absolutely understood why they sat together, but I had a hard time limiting myself that way.

All my life I've been aware of looking different from the majority, but I've usually thought of it as a good difference. Perhaps because my mother is something of a celebrity, I've had to deal with acceptance in terms of my race to a lesser degree than many other African-Americans. One of my mother's friends thinks I should date only black men, but my mother doesn't agree. She herself has dated men of different races. My brother's godfather is white, and there have been other white men in my mother's life. As for myself, I have chosen to date and hang out with open, liberal people of any race. I'm simply not attracted to people who aren't that way.

My mother has always been open with me about sexuality, but Hotchkiss is where I learned that sex can be a destructive component of a relationship. At Hotchkiss, sex was rampant. People got caught up in it and focused on it as a way to define themselves. It was just as often the guys who ended up getting hurt as the girls. Over and over again, I'd see a guy start a relationship with one of my friends and then get thrown aside, completely crushed. It was an interesting break from the norm. At the same time, though, I was very aware of sexual discrimination and sex stereotyping at Hotchkiss. I saw girls go from being just as outgoing as boys to sort of falling apart. That happened to me and to many of my friends, and I watch it happening now to my brother's female friends.

I have, for a long time now, been very interested in feminist activism, and I hope that it will continue to be a major part of my life. As a student at Yale I volunteer with drug-addicted pregnant women in New Haven, and I am a board member of the Third Wave Direct Action Corporation. Women's issues have also been a passionate cause for my mother. Now she belongs to a coven (with three of her best friends) that comes together on the solstices and the equinoxes to celebrate being women. I went to one of their meetings, and there was such intelligence and energy and focus in the room that it was magical. These strong women have all been wonderful role models throughout my life.

In the way she has lived her life and raised her children, in the decisions she has made and who she is, I think that my mother embodies the hope and the paradoxes of feminism. I am proud that she works and that she is successful at what she does. I love that she is strong and intelligent. I love that she cares so much about my brother and me, and that she would carry the world on her shoulders for us. She combines motherhood and a career with incredible grace. But I sometimes feel that she spends too little time thinking about herself and caring for herself. That bothers me. She gets so involved with making things right for everybody else that sometimes she forgets to make things right for herself. She has often sacrificed her own happiness for her work, her children, her mother, and her friends. I want her to step back and say, "I am going to do this just for me."

> **M**y mother has never missed an important moment in my life. She may have been a little late, but she has always been there.

My mother has never missed an important moment in my life. She may have been a little late, but she has always been there. It can be difficult to get in touch with her due to her job, but she has always made every attempt to be accessible. Sometimes it just takes a little extra effort—effort we are all willing to make. There are a few drawbacks to not having a stay-at-home mom. My mother doesn't cook; we're a take-out family. When I was two and a half, I knew the number for the deli and could order things in. My mother's friend's daughter wrote a book in which she said that she was depressed about the fact that her mother never baked her chocolate-chip cookies. Another of my mother's friends said, "If Elizabeth ever writes that in a book, you can slap her! You taught her how to order out, and you taught her how to live her life. Who cares if you never baked her cookies? It doesn't matter." And it really doesn't. Nobody lives a perfect life, and we all make sacrifices. In the larger scheme of things, baking cookies is rather insignificant. More important were the times I did spend with my mother, in the office and at home. Now I bake cookies. But to be honest, I still prefer to eat out rather than to make dinner.

In the last few years, I have come to see my mother as a friend as well as a parent. Listening to and helping people is a role I generally enjoy, and to a certain extent it is a role I have played with my mother. But I am still aware that there is that boundary of parent/child between us. There are some things we still don't talk about, and occasionally we have misunderstandings. In general, though, I cherish the relationship I have with her. I would love it if my children and I could be as close as my mother and I have been. She has shown me that it is possible to be a career woman and an attentive mother. I admire her for her commitment both to her family and to feminism, and I hope that I will become as accomplished and incredible a person as she is. But though I know I want to work, I would also like to take time off from work to be with my children.

I feel tremendously lucky and proud of my mother. I have big footsteps to follow in, but I am confident that I'll be successful in my pursuits. I am, after all, my mother's daughter.

Clarissa and Tíaja, 1971.

Tíaja and Clarissa, 1994.

Clarissa Pinkola Estés
and
Tiaja Kaplinski Pinkola de Dimas Villagomez

CLARISSA PINKOLA ESTÉS, PhD, Jungian psychoanalyst, award-winning poet and *cantadora* (keeper of the old stories in the Latina tradition), is the author of *The Faithful Gardener: A Wise Tale About That Which Can Never Die* (HarperCollins), and *Women Who Run With the Wolves* (Ballantine), translated into twenty languages. She is the author of an eleven-volume audio series of her signature stories and psychological commentary (Sounds True). *The Radiant Coat,* an audio originally created to comfort her AIDS patients, is now used by hospices worldwide. She is a commentator for community public radio, and *Theatre of the Imagination,* her 13-part performance series, is broadcast on many NPR radio network stations nationwide. The former co-coordinator of one of the first safe houses for battered women in the United States, she is now founder and director of the C. P. Estés Guadalupe Foundation which has as one of its missions the broadcasting of strengthening stories to trouble spots throughout the world. For her lifetime activism, writing, and expertise about the psychology of creativity, she is the recipient of the *Las Primeras* Award from the Mexican-American Women's Foundation, the Joseph Campbell festival "Keeper of the Lore" Award, and the Gradiva Award from the National

Association for the Advancement of Psychoanalysis. Her collected poetry and her next collection of myths and stories are forthcoming in 1996 from Alfred A. Knopf. Dr. Estés is married and has three grown daughters.

TIAJA KAPLINSKI PINKOLA DE DIMAS VILLAGOMEZ, twenty-three years old, grew up in the Rocky Mountains. She spent her nineteenth and twentieth years in Japan teaching English. She earned her way there and back by saving money from her after-school job during high school. She speaks Japanese and is in her fourth year at university majoring in international business while working full-time in retail sales. In the family tradition of educating both mind and hands, she will soon be a certified arc welder. She is married and will soon seek a publisher for her two children's books on perseverance.

CLARISSA PINKOLA ESTÉS
A Mother's Story

Raising our children today, as in recent decades, is like floating down a river overflowing with filth and garbage set afire. There are snipers of many kinds on both shores. We and our children are crouched in dugout canoes, ducking and weaving our way downriver. A person who says this is not so, or that it is only a recent phenomenon, is not yet awake.

Yet I have known since childhood that we are traversing another watercourse at the same time. The other one I call in my books *el rio abajo rio,* "the river beneath the river." It is an old, righteous waterway, powerful straight, and filled with Life Itself, clear, fully alive, vital and fresh. In *this* clear water in which raging pain is cooled and wounds tended to, we find our souls have never been irretrievably harmed, none are lost forever. I tell you as my grandmothers taught me: Draw from *this* water. Watch over your children with your lives. Take nothing for granted. Be vigilant. Protect them, strengthen them, particularly in spirit, in insight. World has lessons enough that will wound them; let their homes be places of safety, loyalty, learning.

At the same time, I worry that many of our contemporary families seem not to have enough people in them. My foster parents between them had seventeen brothers and sisters. How else will a child learn the tortures of being courteous if there are no testy relatives to practice on? How will a child ever learn devotion without at least one saintly aunt? Who will a girlchild dream of growing up to marry without at least one winsome older cousin to tell her she is pretty? How will a boychild and girlchild learn to throw balls until it is too dark to see, if there is no old uncle who never grew up? If the family's too small, everyone ought adopt enough non-blood family members until forced to borrow at least ten extra chairs for Thanksgiving dinner.

There is not just one chance to be family, but many. To become a true, loving family takes innumerable tries. In our families—I've two, one natal, one foster—we have withstood any number of exasperations and failures of many kinds. But "being family" is not a *fait accompli*. We practiced and practiced over the decades until many of us are now silver-haired, our elders completely white-haired. *Knowing how* to be family is one thing. *Practicing, perfecting* such is a many-decades-long work—except for those who are born semidivine.

My family men and women—those who have gone before me—are my headwaters. In our working-class community in upper Midwest rural northwoods Michiana in the later 1940s, 1950s, and 1960s, we did not have "feminists" per se, but we did have *las mujeres fuertes*, "strong women"—they who rise at first light and do not sleep till long after midnight. We had *á nagyhatalmak*, "the great powers"—old ones who knew how to spit, and were especially gruff and loving. We had *las machismas*, "the fierce ones," our girlfriend gang of young women: strong on the outside, soft on the inside. We had matriarchs—women who, by virtue of "having truly lived a hard, deep life," won the title of *leader*. Many family women who arrived at a certain age, having completed certain tasks, who are still standing foursquare and bright-eyed, these became *las únicas*—those who are one-of-a-kind—the greatest compliment any women living or deceased could ever receive.

On all sides of my families, we are refugees, deportees, immigrants, grafted from pillar to post—not far away in the past, but in our current three living generations. As a family, we remain interdependent, like a small sovereign nation rather than a "nuclear winter" family living in a pod. We are strong-faithed peasant Católicos deriving from 450 years of the postconquest merging of Indian and Spanish in Mexico, commencing also from the post-Hunnish reign of King Stephen on the Magyar side. Our rites and rituals reflect strong admixtures from our indigenous heritages. Our devotions, rituals, wild weddings, three-day funerals, our insistence on observing certain feast days and performing ablutions—these constitute our taproots, these keep us from blowing away in a high wind. When I was an older child, eighteen more souls from my family were plucked from slave labor and refugee camps in eastern Europe and brought to America along with their poor broken bodies and their broken hearts. They all helped to raise me, and I helped to raise them in return—back from the dead.

I was raised not by two people but by over thirty adults—extended family who all lived within kissing and singing distance of each other.

We were all related as much by wit and humor—through shared beliefs, traditions, a deep love for music, dancing, joking, and wine-making contests—as by hard times, hard work. Through daily injustices of every magnitude that were visited on the lower classes in this country then, as now, I learned to shelter living spirit. This prepared me, if one can ever be prepared, for shattering personal losses—a disfiguring accident in childhood that nearly cost me my leg; later, painful grafts and surgeries; later, loss of most of my childhood writing to a fire; later, loss of a beloved child over which my heart broke into a thousand pieces; later, divorcing a soul I'd deeply loved; later, being "detained" by guerrilla paramilitary forces in Central America; later, a crisis surgery at age thirty-two, which ended my childbearing years; later, a profound and prolonged meeting with death, carrying more irony than the knight's meeting the chessmaster Death in Bergman's film *Seventh Seal.* There is more to this list. But this is enough.

There have been long periods in my life when I awakened each morning weary to find that God had still found good reason for me to live through the night. While certain folk and certain fates have tested me sorely, my strongest protection has been, continues to be, will always be, my prayers to *mi reina, mi Guadalupe,* to whom I was consecrated when I was seven. I will say it as simply, as straightforwardly as I can: I am hers, and she is mine—in lifelong devotion.

During my teenage years I was mandated by destiny to become a tormented poet. *Writing* words was not valued in our milieu, so much of my writing had to be done secretly. This, and the reality of, "a woman's work is never done" gripped me daily. As I quoted my grandmother Katerín in one of my teenage poems: *Here everything is always hot, heavy or hungry . . . something always needs handling, hauling or pouring.* I trained myself to compose in my head while walking from tub to wringer, from kitchen to incinerator, from root cellar to sump pump. Eking time to write, scrounging something to write upon—and with—was a daily challenge. That is why today, I so cherish pens—of any and every kind—and papers of all sorts.

We lacked "connections" to power in the outer culture. We were sorely lacking in opportunities for superior education, good jobs, fair treatment. But there was a slim pathway—Catholic school. Late at night my mother slowly counted quarters, dimes, nickels, squirreling back enough to pay another semester's tuition at "the school of the women in black." To me, my Sisters of the Holy Cross were fountains of knowledge. Gentle black missionary sisters, told us of people with leprosy, taught us the Benares prayer for healing. Many nuns visited from Ethiopia, Egypt, Central America. Though most of us would never have good reason in our lifetimes to go past the last post in the road, here was the world come to us. It is true we were overcrowded—sixty-four children sharing thirty-two desks in early-grade classes. It is true, some few nuns seemed a little high-strung. One teacher gave me an F in English because I wrote a paper all in poetry. She harrumphed, "This is not mysticism class, this is English class!" Another tore my secret poetry journal in half when she caught me writing in it during class. But also, there was the kind young postulant who used a whole roll of very scarce Scotch tape to help me piece it back together again.

> Watch over your children with your lives. . . . World has lessons enough that will wound them; let their homes be places of safety, loyalty, learning.

I loved several nuns like family—they were my earliest nonfamilial models for bravery. We marched for civil rights together. In service of sacred life we built altars; I created a liturgy for the "spiritually gutshot" adolescent; we walked the sacred spiral in meditation. In service of living revolution I met Dorothy Day and my teenage self recognized her as a soul whose heart remained unruined in spite of immense sacrifice and suffering. She and several teachers continue to influence my life.

Growing up, we struggled to mediate abuse at the hands and fists of field and factory owners, sometimes by our own or other people's family members. There was much being run down in the fields for reasons that were never good. There were clashes to oppose capricious and immoral repatriations of immigrant workers; to bring to light employers who cheated on wages and those usurious merchants who cheated purchasers who could not even read the contracts. There were miles and miles of having one's words and concerns not listened to, not met in any way; having one's ideas twisted by those in power. We were "colonized" in many ways, that is, living under the unwritten law that whatever belongs to the underclass must be surrendered to the overclass, whether it be a toll road cut through our quiet rural village, or anthropology students who came down to "study" us.

I married at the end of my nineteenth year and continued working the jobs of the rural undereducated—those that use up the body and the bones. A good living wage was hard to come by and I was grateful for the work. Family members had taken severe risks to belong to nascent labor unions. Their work conditions were abysmal. The broken backs, broken feet of men and women line workers, the missing fingers, the broken bones, the deformed hands—these I can never forget. Several of my women kin had gone from field to factory—O glory days, we all thought. But the rubber-shoe factory and its brain-searing fumes accounted for their premature deaths. We suffer still from the loss of their lives.

When Tiaja was just a babe, and I a newly divorced young mother determined to go to college to lead my family onto a new road, she came to college with me in a little canvas carrier on my back. She was with me when I stood in food-stamp lines, at public "well-baby" clinics, at the house I co-coordinated for battered women. She was with me when I delivered books to the sick and food to the homeless, distributing flyers, walking picket lines, marching. She fell asleep in my arms at night meetings of grassroots activists. My Magyar grandmother, Victoriá, shortly before she died at ninety-six, said to me in her broken English, "That's a nize college you go for. Will dey giff a little diploma to babay too?"

When Tiaja was fourteen, in addition to the baby-sitting she had done since she was ten and the unpaid labor she gave to family and neighbors, she began working a twenty-hour-a-week job after school. This was not to earn "spending money." This was "to learn to work"— to really work, on time, without slacking, till the job was done. She is a hard worker and has accomplished much as a result.

I home-schooled Tiaja and several of our friends' children—sometimes their mothers too—in order to supplement the abominable education the children were receiving at a broken-down public school. I read to the children from Buber, from Heschel, and taught the pragmatics of life, as well as how all things have a human's or God's hands, sometimes both, behind them. I would say, "A cup is not 'just a cup,' but clay from the earth, shaped by a man's hands, who had a mother who probably loved him, and maybe a black dog. A piece of clothing is not 'just a piece of cloth,' but threads that were once cotton that sun and moon shined down upon in a field where the cotton-choppers were likely to have known some really good songs."

When Tiaja was one year old, I began writing one hundred literary tales on the inner life, a series of five books drawing from the pure oral tradition of my family stories. *Women Who Run with the Wolves,* first in this series, was published when Tiaja was twenty-two; I was forty-eight. Over those years, Tiaja saw me go through forty-seven rejections of this 2,200-page manuscript. She accompanied me as I worked three jobs at once to support us, saw me scrape, crawl, scrabble (these seemed usual in the lives of all the women I knew), and occasionally be forced to grovel (although I tried to cross my fingers behind my back on those occasions), saw me rise at 4 A.M. for undergraduate and for doctoral studying, stayed close through six years of psychoanalytic training.

Her life is different from the lives of those who have gone before, and for this I am deeply grateful. She does not carry the legacy of fear that permeated our family through sudden loss of home and livelihood because of war, unjust forced repatriations, torture in slave labor camps, and despairing flight as refugees—fears that make little sense to those who have not lived them. She has experienced some of the suspicious and negative projections by more than a few toward immigrants to America in general, toward those from the lower classes and from those who think those from a minority culture are somehow "less." Nevertheless, she has far less fear than her elders of being torn from loved ones, of intrusion by those in power, of an ongoing denial of freedom to speak fully in one's own words. But the family history is not lost on her. She knows that presently there are powerful educational, economic, social political cliques that she cannot hope to be invited into, layers of society that are powerful and yet look the other way with regard to accuracy about the issues of human suffering, ones who shunt aside the great potential of the spiritual. She well knows that the political climate of "We are moral, you are not" can be as dangerous and assaultive as one that teaches, "Amorality is best; do as you please."

But this child has the gift of the intuitive and understanding heart. She knows she must "go her own way," unconcerned by those who have put up walls against soul or mind. When she was small and her heart was in danger, I told her this rhyme paraphrased from Edwin Markham over and over again. *They drew a circle to shut us out,/things to ridicule, things to flout./But we had the will and the wit to win./We drew a circle that took them in.*

Tiaja is like a fierce young-adult bear—moving in the right direction to be a good mother, a fine wife and lover. She is already a solid daughter, an excellent artist. She has a caring regard for the family and for the greater world. Like myself and several others in the family, she has the gift of healing touch. I expect great things from her. She has already fulfilled many. Sometimes she tries to put ten pounds of mud into a five-pound sack, but this is all right. She is massively creative and doing just as she ought.

Righteous and necessary speech was handed down to me in my early life by the valiant singers and storytellers of the family, and I think it the most precious legacy for my offspring—to speak from deeply held and deeply examined beliefs, especially spiritual ones. My life experiences fueled my determination to speak out at every turn for those who are unfairly exiled, marginalized, those pushed out of the more safe and nurturant center. Though speaking before audiences makes me quake in my boots—if you took an X ray of me, all my blood would be pooled in my left leg only—I have worked and worked to overcome this. I have learned to speak out, even so.

Most recently I came to Washington, D.C., to testify before the Congressional Ways and Means Committee on welfare reform. Congressmen scornfully calling poor, hard-working women "welfare queens" was too much to take. I testified that twenty-five years ago I was on welfare for a year and a half. If food stamps and work-study meant that I was a "welfare queen" at that time, I wanted my crown now, for I had not received one back then. I spoke of mercy as one of the three basic "M's" of business—along with money and management. Some committee members were cold as stone, but in others you could see a decency: Shame passed across their faces as I spoke of *real,* not imagined, lives of deserving welfare mothers (and dispossessed factory and mine-worker fathers) and their children, and how the issues would be solved not by shaming people, as many congressmen seriously proposed, but by invigorating pride and spirit, by giving people a chance at, and a hand up to, a decent education. This subject is far from being closed; there is much more yet to be said.

The matrilineal and patrilineal goodnesses of family are like a hologram, the tiniest remnant contains the whole. I tell you as my grandmother Querida told me: "Only what is remembered with love is completely real." When I am gone, Tiaja will tell the story of my life on *El día de los muertos,* as I now tell the stories of elders who have passed on. When she is gone, her children will tell their children the stories. In this way, all we managed to become, both good and not so good; all we strove for, attained or not; all we believed; all we hoped to be, will be handed down from one to the other. In this way, the lessons of the battered heart, the doorway to death, the well of love, the gate of heaven, the frailties of the foolish, the fires of hell, the hard road, the one true song—all these will be carried into the future and never lost. What is the message I hope to send to the future?

Water can pierce through stone.

TIAJA KAPLINSKI PINKOLA DE DIMAS VILLAGOMEZ
A Daughter's Story

I grew up secure in my mother's love. When I was born, her strong arms held me, and still to this day, deep inside me, I feel held by her.

I began my life as a surprise to her. She conceived me while living in Guatemala. When I was ten years old, she told me that when I was conceived she had been wearing an IUD, that this stood for *intrauterine device*. I said, "No, IUD really means 'Incredible Unexpected Daughter.'" Even today, this still makes her laugh and laugh. I love to hear my mother laugh. She calls me her miracle child and says that babies come when they, not we, are ready.

My mother is my heart. It is as simple as this: When I speak of my life, I speak also of her and other family members who are my root-lines. My second groundnote is my mother's father, my eighty-five-year-old grandfather, who is a grumbly, wise immigrant tailor. I love him, and he has given me many insights about serving others in the old-country manner. Another is my maternal grandmother, an incredible Magyar cook and singer of the old songs.

My mother never taught me the word *feminist*. It just was not in our vocabulary. No one we knew used this word. She taught me, instead, the word *strength*. She taught me the word *fierce.* She taught me the word *devotion.*

The most feminist and feminine matters that come to my mind have to do with the strength of my mother's love—for family and for others. Through this I learned to stand up for equal rights for all humans, to keep *mi Guadalupe* close to my heart always, to love and care for the old people, to watch over all the little ones with a hawk's eye, to keep going no matter what. I learned to see that all humans have certain attributes and talents, that all humans are equal but sometimes different, that I don't necessarily have to like their ideas or beliefs but have to accept them as they are because they are human like me—even though sometimes I think a few people act like they're from the planet Mars.

First things first. In our family we are not only ourselves, but also derived from a mountain of the many lives of those who have gone before us. I know the women and men of our family back to my great-grandmothers' and great-grandfathers' generation. I know stories of *los viejos,* our old ones, and those from long before that—a long line of women and men poets, field workers, refugees, immigrants, war survivors, union scrappers, musicians, and so many more.

When I was very little, we were very poor. We moved through several tough neighborhoods. Where we lived, everyone needed a strong voice every day. The family teaching was that the little things in life take the most courage because although there is little excitement in the day-to-day tasks, they have to be done nevertheless.

I learned through the littlest things imaginable that trying to be tender is very important. I remember playing in the mud as a child and bringing a small "roly-poly" to show my mother. She said how beautiful it was and explained that because it was so little, it should be put back with its family. This and other similar events taught me to value life, many kinds of life. I think this is a feminist value.

When I was a baby, my mother smuggled me into her classes at university, and into all her workplaces, where her co-workers hid my mother and me in closets and cupboards for a few minutes whenever the big bosses came by. We were perfectly safe and my mother joked, "We are of the closet clan. We have a most elegant castle in the cellar room." We lived because she was dedicated to life.

I feel I know how to love even when people are making it hard. I think I know how to be strong, how to endure, even when I think it is not possible. I learned these things by example. I watched my mother suffer under Simon Legree types of bosses, and under several unjust and egomaniacal professor types. She gave opportunity to many; a few were greedy and tried to make her give even more, past her endurance point. I watched her stand it all and keep going. We had the strain of poor wages. Her heart's desire was to give us a better life through education. She struggled for her education. It was not handed to her. She called herself "the master juggler," with her two and three jobs at a time to put food on the table, pay tuitions and rent.

We laughed during all the years that my bedroom was in the kitchen of our three-room apartment, all the years her bed was also her writing desk. My kitchen bed did not trouble me. I thought it was cool to be able, in the middle of night, to open the refrigerator to get water without getting out of bed. She always joked about her desk-bed—that by age thirty she had slept with many of the great authors of the world.

Some people think poor people want to cross into the middle class for money. For us, it was to find sanctuary. I can testify that there are far fewer brutalities in the middle class than in the lowest classes. Injustice is not eradicated, but in the middle class at least there is a chance to correct injustice sometimes. Because most of our lives were spent in the lower class, even though we worked our you-know-whats off, we were shut out of many things, pushed out of many opportunities, given short shrift, ignored, passed over, uninvited, made to seem invisible. Anyone who says otherwise about the lower classes has not lived there long, nor good and hard, nor recently.

> My mother never taught me the word feminist. It just was not in our vocabulary. No one we knew used this word. She taught me, instead, the word strength. She taught me the word fierce. She taught me the word devotion.

When I was little, I lived with being taunted and mocked at school for being poor, for not being able to fit whatever was considered the "ideal girl" of the moment. Kids called me painful names about my heritage, our customs, our station in life. I'd run home to my mother, crying. She always comforted me. She taught me about changing prejudice, but she also taught humor. She'd say things like, "Tell me their names; we'll blow up balloons and tie them to their houses so that their houses will all float away. This is the way of our people." Then she'd say, "Just kidding." I would start giggling. I'd say, "They were mean." She'd say, "You don't have to live with them. You have to live with me. I'm meaner than they could ever be. So there." And I would just love my mother.

When I was eight, I was badly beaten up at school by a bully. My mother again surprised me. She bandaged my wounds and asked how fast I could run. My mother is a big woman, but she went out in the road and showed me how to run away, how to zigzag, how to call out loudly for help. She got down on the ground with me and let me practice on her how to kick and claw like crazy if I was ever caught again. Then she searched until she found a very gentle Japanese sensei who taught me Shotokan karate for many years. The spiritual discipline she and Sensei taught has stood me in good stead.

Small life events shaped my mind and spirit. When I was very little, I once had no gray crayon for a school project. The teacher said to just mix black and white. I remember coming home and asking my mother why when black and white people made a baby together, the baby did not come out gray. She explained to me that two people are not made of color but of love, that their baby is made of pure love. This is how I learned that people are not made of color, but of love. This has also stood me in good stead in my life.

When I was nine years old, my mother became desperately ill and almost died. I was *so scared*. She was my teacher, my friend, my playmate. I had other elders, yes, but this was my dear mother. She tried to reassure me, but I once asked the postman, "Do they have mail delivery in heaven?" After holding on to life by a little thread for many months, my mother slowly recovered, "by God's and Blessed Mother's will," she said. She made me laugh by saying, "My girl, bullets cannot kill you if it is not your time to die." I was so overjoyed that she had been spared. Yet to this day when I think that my life was almost without my mother, I feel weepy.

All my life my mother has been well known as a community activist, performance poet, and healer. She was internationally known for her audio work. When she traveled, she took family too if she could, but when family needed her, she canceled very important things to stay here. When her books were published and became known internationally, I felt no change in our relationship, because she became no different. She has not lost her shape over it all. She is strong; her head is not easily turned. The only thing that bothers me occasionally is when people intrude on her, or on us as a family, when we are in private moments, such as at Mass or at dinner. We all greatly cherish our family's privacy.

My outlook on life is as a woman who is oriented to my personal family and committed to helping other families too. We have gained a reputation for being *los abogaditos,* helpers of immigrants. We help *la gente,* our people, deal with strange customs and various contracts. Recently a friend bought a used car from a man who cheated him. My husband, myself, and my foster father confronted the dealer, making him return the money. The newly arrived, no matter how well educated, are often taken advantage of because they are not yet sophisticated in American ways.

We have had times that will live forever. The night before my wedding, for instance, my mother and I went away together, as is customary, for our last night together as mother and unmarried daughter. We exchanged gifts to demonstrate our esteem for each other and to show that we are both strong, that we will now be on equal ground. We talked almost all night, my mother saying, "Go to sleep now, my dearest daughter; tomorrow is one of the great crossings of your life." But I felt so filled up, I wanted to talk about every good and not-so-good thing that had ever happened to and between us since the beginning of time. She stayed awake listening to me all the while, until finally I ran down and fell asleep.

My husband, Juan, and I became betrothed in the old-country manner, with Juan's *padrino* and *madrina* (godfather and godmother) coming to ask my parents for my hand. For two days our elders consulted about our good and less-good attributes while we waited separately in rooms far away. After much explaining of Juan's good and not-so-good points to me, and mine to him, making sure we understood what give-and-take these would require in marriage, our elders finally agreed we were a good match. As Juan and I knelt to receive our parents' blessings, we felt encouraged that we would start our marriage with foresight. To us, our betrothal traditions were an invaluable process.

My husband loves my mother and foster father as much as I do. They love him as their own son. But as my mother says, even strong family ties cannot protect us from all things. On Christmas last, we announced to my mother and father that we were pregnant. They were so happy. They literally cried for joy. They hugged and kissed each other. They hugged and kissed us. But shortly after, I lost my pregnancy in the fourth month. My mother, my father, my husband, and I cried together again, but now for a very sad reason.

Many people tried to console my husband and me, but it was my mother who stayed by my side while I struggled emotionally and physically. There were complications. I had two surgeries in two months. Even though I am not totally emotionally calm about this subject yet, my mother, with her knowledge and kindness, made the situation better. She knew how to pray over my husband and me; she knew how to consecrate the fetus's body; she explained to us about how spirit and body sometimes miss each other and that there are many chances, not just a few, for a little one to come to life through our bodies. She knew how to make the funeral; she directed her husband and mine about how to dig the grave. She will reconsecrate my dear husband and me at the altar of Guadalupe when it is time. She stood by us at *La misa de los angelitos,* the Requiem Mass of the Little Angels. She comforted the family's men and helped them grieve. She was like a dog; she would not leave my side. No matter what misery and grief I had, she had words for it, could bear my pain and bear me up at the same time.

You might think this is going on about my mother. In our family we have praise-songs. This is one of mine about my mother, one that gives thanks to all those who helped her to become what she is—both the detractors over whom she rose and to our elders who have made her strong.

My greatest desire is to be a good mother. I have a certainty about how valuable life is, how to turn bad situations into good, or for good, or for at least a shred of whatever good can be had. I look forward to bringing children into our family. We have been taught in our family that bringing a child into the world also means trying to make the world a better place for *all* children. I am dedicated to the idea that there are ways to care for my family *and* to care for those outside my family, too. My mother is giving me guidance while I am close to finishing up writing two bilingual children's books that I have been imagining for a long time. Writing children's books is my first big step in the direction of reaching down into our family but also beyond family at the same time in order to help raise *all* the children. This is my goal.

What am I emphasizing in my books? Perseverance. If my mother said it once while I was growing up, she said it a thousand times: "God made people like us to demonstrate to others that the impossible is possible." I say this is both worthy and true. *¡Salud!*

Shana and Yolanda, 1976.

Shana and Yolanda, 1994.

Yolanda Moses
and
Shana Moses Bawek

YOLANDA MOSES, the first African-American woman to be chosen as president of the City College of New York (CCNY), was born in Los Angeles in 1946. A cultural anthropologist who received her PhD in anthropology from the University of California-Riverside, she says that she first decided to study anthropology because it was the only department that was interested in a women's studies program. Several years ago Moses transferred from her position as vice president of academic affairs and professor of anthropology at California State University–Dominquez Hills to become the tenth president of CCNY. City College is dedicated to providing first-rate education to children of poor, immigrant, and working-class people, and it was here, Moses says, that she felt she could make a difference. In her own words, "If we're talking about educational excellence, that's what we're talking about, and it doesn't have a color." She lives in Manhattan with her husband, Jim Bawek, and their younger daughter, Antonia.

SHANA MOSES BAWEK was born in Harbor City, just outside Long Beach, California, in 1976. She was seventeen years old at the time of her interview and had made the difficult decision to stay with her father in Claremont, California, until she graduated from high school, instead of following her mother to New York. In response to the survey question, "What do you do for a living today?" she responded, "Get good grades in school." Bawek says that her bicultural heritage—her mother is black and her father is white—has been a difficult legacy in some ways but also a wonderful opportunity for growth. She is now a student at Tufts University.

A Mother's Story

I never wanted a traditional relationship and marriage. The choices I wanted to make were not ones I had seen many married women making, and I was strident in my determination to be my own person. My hesitation wasn't so much about marriage but about having the sole responsibility for raising kids. You can't send a baby back.

One night our Lamaze class conflicted with a basketball game my husband, Jim, didn't want to miss. I was eight and a half months along and real uncomfortable, so I said, "You don't want to miss basketball one night, and I'm going through having this child for us? Your life is going to change, dear. There may be other times you're not going to get to play basketball, so you'd better get used to it." Basketball was Jim's passion, and he went from thinking I was unfair to realizing that I was absolutely right. A baby would change both our lives. It wasn't about his helping me; it was about working together. A dawning realization came over his face, like, "Oh, my God." He went to class that night.

Shifting his frame of reference early paid off. Since Shana's birth, Jim has been the primary parent two-thirds of the time. In addition, we had extended family to help. My sister, Johnnie, lived with us off and on for years, baby-sitting and keeping house. I felt comfortable going out of town and leaving her with the kids. Often on weekends my mother kept the children, so we could always get R and R when we needed it. That's how I've been able to do it.

My great-great-grandmother was a slave whose people were bought from the French Moroccans on the north coast of Africa. After slavery, she migrated from Mississippi to Louisiana. My light-skinned grandfather, sired by a white man who trained him as a mechanic, was run out of town for taking business away from white mechanics. Years

later we learned that he had gone north, passed for white, and sent for
his family, but my great-grandmother persuaded her daughter not to
join him. The women hung together, working for the same wealthy
white Farmerville family. My great-grandmother cooked, my grandmother cleaned, and my mother baby-sat and accompanied the family
on their travels. If eating places refused to serve her, they left. Thus her
experience was positive with at least one white family in that Southern
town.

My father was traveling with an African-American basketball team
when he met my mother, the Farmerville High valedictorian, in a local café. She had attended Grambling College until her money ran out,
and he was her ticket out of there. Joining the migration of blacks to
the West in the forties, they found work in the Briemerton, Washington, shipyards. My mother became a Rosie the Riveter, supervising
twenty people building ships. When the men returned from war, she
was let go.

Moving to Los Angeles, where menial jobs were available for
blacks, my father became a shipping clerk in a lumber company, my
mother a domestic. I was born in 1946, the first of four daughters.
Through the GI Bill, my father bought us a two-story house in the
working-class white community of Compton. We were the first black
family on our block. My parents cleaned buildings in the evening, so I
grew up thinking everybody's parents worked during the day *and*
evening and that you stayed with your relatives. When my parents
bought the vacant lot next door, my mother discovered a flair for real
estate, so she got her real-estate license. Her boss said she could "go
places," but my father, afraid of her success, told her to quit. She returned to being a domestic.

In our household people of different backgrounds came and went.
The white men and the Mexican man who rode to work with my father came over regularly to play poker. Each was prejudiced against
people of different colors as groups, but as individuals they were
friends. I learned that people can personalize relationships but still
have stereotypes about each other. If my father was tolerant about racial
issues, my mother was militant. She believed things should change and
that we should be agents of that change. She acted as the voice of conscience, urging the National Association for the Advancement of Colored People to do this or do that.

My mother's activism often focused around her children. When
Compton grew increasingly violent in the 1960s, we moved to Perris,

a small rural community east of Los Angeles. When my mother learned that most black or Latino students were automatically placed on the noncollege track, her militancy kicked in. Taking on the entire school system, she said, "My kids are going to be in college-prep classes because they are going to college." She was a tenacious mother. She joined the PTA, became a Girl Scout leader, and helped in the school cafeteria. At her retirement twenty-seven years later, she was supervising cafeterias in three elementary schools. In important ways she helped shape my notion of activism and community participation, of giving back and taking a stand when things are not right: "You can't be silent; you have to speak out—because if you don't, nobody else will." When the school guidance counselor refused to recommend me for a college scholarship ("You'll be a good secretary"), my mother said, "We don't need this," and showed off my work to the PTA. In the fall of 1964 I entered San Jose State College on a four-year scholarship from the national PTA.

My civil activism began when I joined the San Jose chapter of the Student Nonviolent Coordinating Committee and participated in fund-raisers, marches, and a voter registration drive. I wanted to go to Mississippi as a Freedom Rider, but my frightened parents said, "Don't do that; whatever you need to do, you can do right here in California." They promised me a car if I attended a community college at home, so I did.

My father and I did not have the best relationship. He was controlling; I was independent. When he was around, my mother pretended he was in charge and that she couldn't do things. I'd say to her, "Why do you do this?" and she'd say, "It's your father." I'd confront him, asking, "Why are you such a bully?" and he'd say, "It's none of your business; if you don't like it, you can leave." So I did. Shortly afterward, my father was stricken with cancer. Fortunately, we had a chance to reconcile our feelings before he died.

In my third year, I transferred to California State University—San Bernardino, the "Dartmouth of the West." I also married a fellow student; in retrospect, I realize I did it to escape my home situation. By the time I graduated, I knew the marriage was a bad idea. My husband, seeing that we were pulling apart, suggested that having a baby might calm me down. I did not want a baby at that time in my life, and his attitude fueled my determination to end the marriage after two years.

After graduating from college, I became a vocational rehabilitation counselor in Los Angeles but quit after two years because the agency refused to help those in real need. Around that time, my mother sent me a news clipping about a Ford Foundation survey showing that fewer than 1 percent of all PhD's in the United States were people of color. "Apply for it," she insisted. "What do you have to lose?" I applied and received one of 27 Ford Foundation Doctoral Fellowships for Minority Students awarded out of 750 applicants. In 1970 I began a PhD program in anthropology at the University of California-Riverside.

> I didn't hesitate to marry Jim because he was white. We share the same values and ideals; he is more committed to the issues I'm committed to than many blacks I've known.

I met Jim Bawek, my husband, in a group home run by the California Youth Authority in Watts, where we were both teaching. Jim grew up in a small Iowa town on the Minnesota border with a father who instilled in him the notion that people are people. I had expected to remain single, so when Jim proposed, I said, "Why don't we just live together?" He said, "Because I want the whole world to know that we are husband and wife and that we're committed to each other." I didn't hesitate to marry Jim because he was white. We share the same values and ideals; he is more committed to the issues I'm committed to than many blacks I've known. But I kept saying, "He can't be for real." My mother said, "He sounds like a good person to me. Besides, if it doesn't work out, you can always divorce him." That was her attitude.

The first time Jim's parents knew I was black was when they came to visit him and I was there. I could tell they were surprised. Afterward, Jim said, "But how did they do?" and I said, "Fine." Jim and I were married in 1972, at the height of the Black Power movement, in the county courthouse in Riverside, California. Afterward we had a party at my mother's house. When black friends asked why I married someone white, I said, "I married the person I wanted to marry." We've been married twenty-three years, and our parents ended up as good friends who share common rural values.

On June 16, 1976, I graduated from UC Riverside with my PhD and straight A's. There I was, nine months pregnant, leading the procession as graduate marshal. I tell Shana that she actually led the procession. Relatives from all over the state hovered around, pampering me because I was having the first grandchild. I was the only minority PhD graduate, and the ceremony itself was a turning point. After being hooded, I turned and hugged my male advisor. A display like that was unusual in such a staid ceremony, but other women graduates began doing it and the cheering crowd loved it.

Three weeks later, Shana arrived so quickly that Jim didn't make it to the delivery room. Most black babies have lots of hair, but Shana was bald and so white that when they brought her in, one nurse whispered to the other, "Are you sure this is the right baby?" After breast-feeding for two months, I decided it was time to return to my teaching job. One Friday I took Shana, with breast milk, formula, and bottles, to my mom's and said, "Here; we'll pick her up on Sunday." From that time on, she's been with my mother or sister on any given weekend. It has given Shana different perspectives on parenting, too.

We hesitated about having more children because of my career. But after several years of marriage I realized that child-rearing would not be just on my shoulders. Jim loves children and is good with them, and he insisted his share of the child care would be at least fifty-fifty. When Shana was three and a half, Antonia arrived—even more quickly than Shana. The doctor was mad because I cut it so close; I thought, "What's the big deal? *I'm* having this baby, not him." Afterward I had my tubes tied. With our full lives, I couldn't see how I could give any more children what they needed. It would have been too much.

I was a good technical mother when the kids were young. Everything was organized. That's the only way I could have my career *and* two kids. We hired someone to cook and clean, so when I was home I spent quality time with the children. They had to observe certain rules, however, such as nine o'clock bedtime. It was probably too regimented, but I needed downtime if I was going to be good for them. That was the only time I had for myself and Jim, or to do what I needed to do. They understood, and now they carve out their own time and space.

When we moved to Claremont in 1983, Jim sold real estate part-time, managed our income property, and took care of the kids. He chose real estate partly because when we were dating, his landlady asked him not to have me around because I was black. Jim was so angry that he went out and bought a house in Long Beach. After that, we began buying and renovating older places, so we had property in the early seventies, when none of our friends did. We weren't into materialism, but it was a way to level the field. If somebody had something to say to us about our liberal ideas, we replied as property owners.

We did not try to shelter our daughters from racism and sexism. You can only shelter them so long. We introduced racism and sexism as realities they would face in life. I began when they were young, pointing out items on the news and conveying in analytical terms what was going on. I explained the Ku Klux Klan, Jim Crow, and lynching. We tried to give them coping tools. Shana understood in first grade what racism was and has dealt with it ever since. She understands that she is bicultural, and that some people don't like others because of the color of their skin, and that sometimes someone says something about her because she's both black and white.

I don't separate racism from sexism because I don't separate my gender from my ethnicity. I conceptualize myself as a black woman, but sexism has been a more salient issue for me because of my profession as a female college president. When I became a card-carrying feminist, my husband began taking women's studies and feminist theory classes in order to understand the issues better. As he began seeing the world from another perspective, he said, "How do women put up with men?" Now he is a feminist himself. My friends say, "If you ever get tired of this man, send him over."

I'm not sure Shana calls herself a feminist, though she's been singled out by her classmates as feminist. She recognizes sexism in the media and says, "Oh, Mom's not going to like that" or "Did you hear that?" She and Toni play sports with a vengeance. I see sports as a way for girls to gain self-esteem without putting on makeup and glamorizing themselves. They're there to play, not to cheer the boys on but to be cheered on. Shana can sit down with a group of boys and talk about anything—politics, sports. What comes across is a self-sufficient young woman who feels good about herself. It's applied feminism.

I think Shana is concerned about my working hard. She and Toni were upset by my decision to come to New York, leaving them behind for the year in California. She says, "Mom, if being a successful woman is doing what you are doing, I don't want to be a successful woman. You work too hard." I understand that, but this is my future. I'm starting out in a new job, a new challenge, a new place. I want City College to become one of the premier urban public institutions in the country. Jim says I don't take care of myself, but I like being busy.

I have missed some important moments in my daughters' lives because of work. I regret that Toni took her first step without me, but at least Jim was there. I also regret not being present when Shana was a finalist for homecoming queen at her high school. I said, "Oh, God, it's a throwback," and pooh-poohed the whole thing, but she said the kids vote for those they consider the best all-around. She was shocked that so many students looked up to and respected her. Jim had planned to be in New York with me that week, so we asked a favorite teacher to escort her, but the night before, Shana called up, sobbing. She wanted us there, and we probably should have been more attuned to her needs. I felt bad.

I want Shana to have the tools to be a good global citizen. That means that she needs to have a strong sense of herself and to feel good about herself—all of her different selves. They deserve equal billing. She should never have to choose one of her heritages. I want her to be bilingual, to speak at least one other language in order to communicate internationally and in cities like New York. I want her to be strong enough to take risks and be out there by herself. The world I wish for her, a world of more understanding and less violence and hatred, will not happen overnight.

When the girls were small, Jim and I discussed whether to raise them as white or black. We finally decided to raise them as both, because they are both. They would be raised as *our* kids. Shana and Toni have grown up spending summers with white grandparents on an Iowa farm and the rest of the year with black relatives in urban Los Angeles. Blessed with bicultural backgrounds, they function comfortably in more than one environment. In our multicultural world, they will be the bridges and the leaders.

A Daughter's Story

Our family is different from my friends' families. I probably have only one other friend whose mother's job is equal to her father's. My friends say things like, "My dad does this, my dad does that," and the assumption is that the father is the one who is making the money and the mother is staying home with the kids. In our family it isn't like that—in fact, my father has been the primary parent. My parents decided together that if my mom was going to keep moving up in her career, someone would have to take care of us. With my mother gone, my father tries to be home for Toni and me every day after school. Whenever we can, we eat together. My father is completely supportive of my mother. He takes her work very seriously. I can't see him doing what she does, though. They are a lot alike in terms of their views and things, but the way they spend their time is different.

I respect my mother's will to work and change things. She will not go through her life without working hard to accomplish what she has set out to do. The way I see it, she's trying to be perfect, to have a good job and be a mom who is present all the time, but that's impossible. You can't be in two places at once. I know that she wants to have more time with us, but it doesn't work out for her. She stays up late and gets up early and works really hard, and I can't see her giving that up, since she does it for us.

I was born in Harbor City, just outside Long Beach, California, in July 1976. At the time my mother was an anthropology professor at California Polytechnic, and my father worked for the California Youth Authority. My mother stayed home with me for a few months before going back to work, then two of her sisters looked after me. My aunt Johnnie lived with us in Long Beach and cooked our dinner, which was important because my mom usually got home after dinner, around seven. We lived five blocks from the beach until I was in the second grade. I remember my mother taking me to the beach every weekend, and making sand castles. Then we moved to Claremont. I have lived in these two places my whole life.

As I grew older, I had nannies because my mother was so busy. My favorite nanny was a woman from Cambodia named Choitoi who took care of me when I was in first and second grades. We helped out her family because they didn't have much money. My little sister, Antonia, and I also had a lot of baby-sitters, some of whom were awful. We hated one baby-sitter because she ate all of our Halloween candy and was mean to us. As soon as Mom got home, we snuck down to tell her that the baby-sitter was mean.

One day we were in our Long Beach kitchen when my mother walked in and announced, "I am a dean." My dad started cheering. I had no clue what they were talking about. After we moved to Claremont, my mother became a vice president at California State University, which was closer to Long Beach. My father owned apartments in Long Beach, and he kept one empty so that she could stay down there two nights a week. The nights she came home she was often so late that we wouldn't see her anyway. Though both my parents were working, my father set his own hours, so he was home a lot more.

I would not be the same person if my father hadn't been around as much as he was. In fourth grade, when I was getting ready to run a track meet, my father ran with me every morning before school. I wouldn't have done it on my own. Now I love sports. My father also debates with me. When I argue, I argue passionately and idealistically. I can be obstinate and not look at every angle. My father forces me to see the logical point of view and clarify what I am saying.

Education is an important thing in our house. I've always loved school; I had good evaluations, and was motivated from the beginning. I learned to read early, and reading has always been one of my favorite pastimes. Even today, when I have free time I prefer to come home and read a book. My parents are smart, and we have discussions about everything from world news to moral issues. I am able to argue with them on their level. They respect me that way; I can say exactly how I feel.

My dad is white and my mom is black. My sister, Toni, and I look more white than black, and I am told that I look more white than my sister. I remember as a child wishing that I was all black or all white. It was strange to be hanging out with white kids and then to have my black mom come pick me up. I have to say, honestly, that I was embarrassed a couple of times, not because she was black but because I knew my friends would be shocked. I know about my black heritage because my mother has taught me a lot, but I feel neither black nor white. On an everyday basis, I would not be considered a black person from the friends I have and where I hang out.

I think racism goes both ways. It is hard being stuck in the middle. Last year I was at a party with friends when a guy we were talking to made a racist comment. I was embarrassed and didn't say anything. My friend spoke up and said, "You'd better be quiet; she's half black." It seemed so stupid to me that the reason not to make a comment was because I was half black. Some of my friends' parents are racists, and they tell their daughters, "You are not dating a black guy." I spend the night at their houses and eat breakfast with their families, and I know that they aren't against me or my mom, but that is only because they know us. It is scary that they are prejudiced against people they don't know because of the color of their skin. It definitely helps that my mother has a middle-class, professional job. Her status makes up for the fact that she is black—that's what I see my friends' parents thinking.

In world history class my sophomore year, an African-American guy I was friends with called me a "sell-out." I went home and cried to my dad and my mom's sister. They said that he was probably insecure with who he was. But what he said struck a chord. It makes me mad that you have to act a certain way just to fit in. I try not to fulfill any of the stereotypes. At the same time, everyone in history class knows I am half black because I feel I have to argue the black perspective. That part of me is viewed as lesser in status in our society, so I have to argue more for it; I have to prove that being black is more important. That's not how I feel, but because that part of me is a minority, that is what I have to do.

My mother and I sometimes have a formal relationship. When we are having a discussion, she argues by making points. It is difficult to prove her wrong. She has always seemed sort of perfect to me. She is a perfect role model. She is a thinker, and people respect her. She is also a good public speaker. It is strange watching the person you see at home in pajamas talking seriously to a crowd of people. Sometimes the little things I have done in my life seem so irrelevant in comparison to what she does. But she has always been there for me.

Sometimes I resent my mother's career. When she told us that she had an offer to be president of City College in New York, my sister and I were upset. We felt her career was the only thing that was important to her. I know this isn't true, because if it weren't for her career, we wouldn't have a lot of the things we now have. But I find it hard for her not to be around when I want her to be around. Earlier this year I was a finalist for homecoming queen. I made it through semifinals, and then I was a finalist. I didn't think I'd make it, so I told my dad to go ahead and make plans to go to New York that weekend, but it turned out that I did make it. I was supposed to have a father escort, and both my parents were out of town. It

> **Sometimes I think she is just too busy to enjoy her life.**

doesn't sound like a big deal, but at the time it was. One of my teachers served as my escort. My parents had someone tape the ceremony for them.

I know my mom feels guilty about being away from us. It is hard for her, but it is also hard being a kid because you can't always think with an open mind or see both sides of the story. Sometimes when I'm mad I say things that aren't nice. When we were first discussing the move, I said to my dad, "She doesn't care about us, anyway; she's just going to do what she wants to do." As it turns out, she has come home a lot more than she expected to. We have family meetings whenever my mom comes back from New York, which is about once every two weeks. When I was younger I enjoyed family meetings, but now that I'm older I don't think I need them as much. But even though I don't like the meetings, I know they are part of what keeps our family communicating.

My mother has influenced my political views. She is extremely feminist, and that rubbed off on me. When I was little, she read me fairy tales but changed the *he*'s to *she*'s. We also had a book of feminist fairy tales. I remember her telling me, "You can be the doctor; you don't have to be the nurse." In some ways I think this programming was bad. I was trained to look down on housewives, for example. As I got older, I realized that people are different, and however you want to run your life is okay. Some women don't want to have careers; they want to be housewives. I personally can't see myself being happy as a housewife, but I do think that if I really wanted to be one, my mom would kill me. My mom's younger sister, Eleanor, was a cheerleader, and my parents did not approve. I kind of felt that way with the homecoming event. My parents gave me a card and said, "Congratulations," but I felt that they didn't respect it that much. Actually, I didn't respect it much, either. Out of fifteen finalists, all of the girls were white except me; there were no Asians or Hispanics. I know that a lot of the votes I got were from African-Americans who voted for me because I'm half black.

My whole life I have been trying to figure out who I am and what my views are. During junior high, I was out to prove to the world that girls are better than boys, and I was dead serious about it. I played on the boys' basketball team. So I did internalize my mother's feminism. But I also rebelled by playing with dolls and reading romance stories. I loved Barbies, and my mother didn't like them much, though she let me play with them. Several years ago, one of my godparents' daughters gave me a whole bookshelf of romance novels, and I read every single one. I could just imagine my mother reading every line and finding fault with each part.

I don't know whether I want to have children. I am afraid of raising them the wrong way. I think I might stay home a bit longer than my mother did when we were little, and I wouldn't be quite as strict. We weren't allowed to get our ears pierced, wear makeup, or date until we were sixteen. Any dating I did before then I had to keep a secret, which wasn't difficult because my mom was gone a lot and my dad doesn't pick up on things so much. I can keep secrets from him more easily than from my mother. If I got a tattoo, for example, my dad would never know, but my mom would find out somehow. My sister shaved the back of her head when my mom was away, and weeks later my father still hadn't noticed.

My mother is totally nonmaterialistic. She didn't even have the right clothes for her new job. She had to hire someone to buy expensive clothes for her. She doesn't like to spend money on herself, and she's also too busy. Sometimes I think she is just too busy to enjoy her life. My parents don't drive really nice cars. They choose to put their money into our house and trips but not into material things. In that way, sometimes I think that I am different from my parents, because sometimes I really like those nice cars. I don't know if it's just a phase I will grow out of, or not.

My mother says that she only decided to get her degree in anthropology after meeting Margaret Mead. She knew she wanted to be better off than she was as a child, so she always had that goal. I don't know how I could do much better. I respect my mother a lot. She has always been strong. Of course, there are also a lot of things I would do differently, but that has to do with my personality. It may sound selfish, but I liked it when I had to get ready for the prom and she said, "Okay, let's go get makeup and shoes and get your hair done." I like it when she is doing things specifically with me and for me. I like my mother best when she is just being my mom.

Sayantani and Shamita, 1974.

Sayantani and Shamita, 1994.

Shamita Das Dasgupta
and
Sayantani DasGupta

SHAMITA DAS DASGUPTA was born in Cuttuck, Orissa, India in 1949, and moved to the United States at the age of nineteen. She earned her PhD in developmental psychology at Ohio State University in 1983 and now teaches psychology and women's studies at Rutgers University. The 1995 recipient of the Asian-American Legal Defense and Education Fund's Justice in Action award, she is a founding member of Manavi, a pioneering organization in the United States that focuses on violence against South Asian immigrant women. She and her daughter, Sayantani, have compiled a collection of Bengali folktales, *The Demon Slayers and Other Stories*. Das Dasgupta and her husband reside in Montville, New Jersey.

BORN IN COLUMBUS, OHIO, in 1970, Sayantani DasGupta received her BA in health and society from Brown University in 1992 and is now enrolled as a medical student at Johns Hopkins University. She plans to graduate in 1997. DasGupta is also a freelance writer; her articles have appeared in *Ms.* magazine, among other publications, and she coauthored *The Demon Slayers and Other Stories* with her mother. She currently lives in Baltimore, Maryland.

A Mother's Story

I believe strongly that you cannot give quality time if you don't spend quantity time with a child. My daughter, Sayantani, was a well-adjusted child, and I think it was because I was with her so much. I don't remember ever having to scold her or say no. I told my professors, "Look, if you don't let me bring my daughter to class, I can't take your course." I didn't want to stop my education because I had a child. By the time I was a graduate student, she either came to class with me when I taught or stayed in my office with other graduate students, who played with her and took her to movies and lunch. She attended my consciousness-raising group and accompanied me to antiwar marches and meetings. I never wanted to separate life's pieces. Sayantani was part of me, like my arm. I couldn't stick my role as a feminist in one compartment and my role as a mother and wife in another. Everything flowed together.

I was born in Cuttuck, India, in 1949, two years after India became independent from Great Britain. My father worked for the central government, often in remote areas without schools. I did not attend school until sixth grade and resisted my mother's attempts to teach me at home, preferring instead to be off in the jungle, walking through forests and climbing trees. My family was nontraditional in many aspects. They ignored the caste system and taught me that people are all the same. When I saw men doing interesting things that women were not allowed to do, however, I became conscious of gender.

My father came from a large feudal family. During the British colonial period he joined the nationalists and spent time in jail as a radical and Communist sympathizer. His revolutionary work put him in contact with many independent women. As a result, he treated me like an equal. If I wanted to do something and my mother said, "No, you shouldn't do it," my father said, "Let her do what she wants; she is strong and smart enough." He gave me freedom and affirmation, and he didn't need society's approval. He was nurturing and giving to everyone—except his wife.

My mother was socialized in traditional gender roles. She wanted me to succeed but feared I would get hurt if I wasn't "womanly." From the time I was twelve or thirteen, we fought. When a distinction was made between boys and girls, I refused to honor it, saying, "Why do I have to do it just because I am a girl?" My father was verbally abusive and angry toward her, but she fought back continually. When I was an adolescent, I encouraged her to leave him, but leaving would mean dishonor for her family and children. My brother, Subin, and I wanted to protect her, even though I loved my father. That was the biggest conflict in my life.

At the age of sixteen I graduated from high school. The same year I agreed to a marriage that was more or less arranged. My husband's and my parents had been friends for a long time and saw that Sujan and I had a lot in common. I didn't object to marrying Sujan, but I was already becoming political and had decided not to get married. Sujan says he was in love and wanted to marry me, and I gave in to pressure. A Hindu marriage is a collective event that goes on for three days and involves families, friends, and neighbors in the festivities. Like every Hindu bride, I wore red.

The day after the wedding, a Hindu bride and groom go off to live with the groom's family. There is no honeymoon. I found suddenly being married and moving to a different household terribly strange. I had known my husband's mother since I was five years old, but all at once my role was different. I was her son's wife. Between us there was difficulty and friction. My in-laws expected me to do certain things for my husband, but I refused, saying, "We are both human beings. We both have hands and feet. We'll share the work."

When my husband left India in 1967 to study engineering at the University of Cincinnati, I stayed with my mother in Calcutta and began taking college courses. A year later, I followed Sujan to Ohio. In order not to remain lonely and isolated, I immediately learned to drive. My visa barred me from working, so I volunteered at the university library. Next to our house was a small public library, where I read voraciously every morning. Soon the librarians were calling me when a new book came in, and before leaving Cincinnati, I had read almost the entire library.

I got pregnant four months before Sujan graduated. Fortunately, Sujan got a job with Bell Laboratories, and we moved to Columbus in 1970. Even without a community, I was happy preparing for the arrival of my baby. I sewed and knitted, making almost everything myself. Everyone said, "You will have a son," but I was convinced I would have a daughter. "If I don't have a daughter," I said, "I will have twenty kids until I have a daughter."

Sayantani was born the day before Halloween in 1971. In Sanskrit her name means "of the evening." The birth took many hours, and because I weighed only ninety-two pounds, I tore a lot. She was delivered by forceps, and one of her eyes was swollen shut for four weeks. It was not love

> "If I don't have a daughter," I said, "I will have twenty kids until I have a daughter."

at first sight. When I saw her I said, "Oh, my God, such a teeny-weeny thing. So much pain for this?" I brought her home having no idea how to handle a baby, and I was in constant pain. Sujan was nervous but supportive. After four weeks I felt better, and Sayantani began to look interesting. I breast-fed her for six months.

When Sayantani was three months old, I began taking courses at the local adult education center. In 1974 I began undergraduate courses and graduated from college in 1977. Wherever I went, Sayantani went with me. We were companions. I explained to her, "When you are in class, you cannot yell and run around, but when we come out we will play." In class she sat beside me and drew and ate her lunch; afterward we played and picked flowers. In the loose atmosphere, no one objected. Even the professors made friends with her. When she entered nursery school, I dropped her off and took a class, then picked her up and carried her back to school with me.

By the time I entered college, I was conscious that my skin color mattered. People reacted to me as someone from a different culture. Once a fellow student came up to me and said, "The girls from your country are so pretty, but why do you all look alike?" I replied, "Well, it can seem that way if you are not familiar with a culture. My mother cannot distinguish among white people; they all look alike to her." Offended, the man said, "What do you mean? We don't look alike! How can you say that?" I said to myself, "Oh, my God, there is a different standard here." That was a critical event in my life.

By the early seventies, I was aware of the women's movement and wanted to be part of it. I joined women's collectives and consciousness-raising groups and became active in the National Organization for Women (NOW). From the beginning, however, I felt that certain cultural pieces were excluded from mainstream feminism. For example, I thought that having children, though not necessary, was important because you need to pass things on to the next generation. Mainstream feminism, in placing so much emphasis on the individual, does not value children as it should. It is not enough for me to become all I want to be; all oppressed groups must come together for a better life.

This sense of the collective is part of my heritage. In India, identity means family, nation, culture, community. We refer to our cousins as "brothers and sisters" and our aunts and uncles as "different mothers and fathers." The danger in India is that the individual may get totally submerged in the collective identity, but the American emphasis on the individual is potentially detrimental in other ways. What gets lost is expansiveness—the sense that we are all here together. You cannot have a movement by yourself. Creating social change and breaking down the wall of patriarchy can occur only through a collective effort.

I remained connected to the mainstream women's movement for over a decade, but by the time we moved from Ohio to New Jersey, in 1983, I had begun to analyze how race and class were ignored within the feminist movement. I joined a committee working against racism within the National Organization for Women and even served briefly on the NOW board, but I found it impossible to continue. I raised all kinds of race issues: Why are women of color not within the mainstream movement? What is happening to include them? What is happening to include their agenda? But nothing happened. The mainstream was not yet ready to hear about women-of-color or class issues. Gradually I came to realize that the women's movement had become a mini-institution that defined and limited the parameters of what was acceptable within it. "This is the agenda within which you must work. If you keep raising these issues, then you are a traitor," I was told. So I left the mainstream movement.

In 1985 six South Asian women started a group of our own named Manavi, which means "primal woman." Manavi focuses on all forms of violence against women, not just physical battering or sexual assault. We define violence against women as any attitude, action, behavior, or condition (including poverty) that subjugates women in society. Lack of job opportunities and education constitutes violence because it is violating all of our rights. Manavi is a nationally recognized force. Culturally specific, we take a strong South Asian perspective, discussing issues relevant to women of color that are separate from the battered-women's and sexual-assault movements. Manavi encourages women to question patriarchal beliefs and to change situations within their own cultural backgrounds.

As I became increasingly involved in identity politics and women's organizations, I wanted to make a statement about claiming my own community. For fourteen years I wore Western clothing as well as traditional dress; often I wore jeans. Since 1984 I have worn only traditional clothing. It is important for all those I work with, in the mainstream and in other groups, to recognize that I am working from within my community.

For several years I was afraid that I had not raised an activist daughter. In high school Sayantani was busy trying to fit in. I watched her as she struggled to strike the right balance between her Indian heritage and American culture. From ages fourteen to seventeen she went through a period of rebellion when we screamed at each other constantly. "You are controlling me, and I am not going to listen to you," she said. Often our fights were about her wanting to go out, and I was very afraid. I saw her tremendous potential to do great things, and I didn't want her to get involved with somebody and just give it up. I think that men have the potential to kill everything in a woman, and I wasn't sure she knew that. I didn't want her to be squashed or thwarted by a partner who wasn't supportive of her, nor to marry early, as I did.

When Sayantani was young, I read to her all the time. Along with Sartre and whatever else I was studying at the time, I read and told her Bengali folktales. After she finished college, Sayantani said, "Mom, you should put together a book of Bengali folktales." When she suggested that we do the book together, I agreed. Many of the stories in *The Demon Slayers and Other Stories: Folktales Bengali* are from memory; others are from other collections.

Sujan and I have been married for thirty years. We fought and struggled, but we have emerged as strong, supportive friends who respect each other. I realized early on that men have the privilege of not changing because they are in a comfortable position. Sujan would have liked a wife who was content to keep house and cook. I did those things, but I also wanted to be an activist and challenge expected relationships. Change means risking and giving up things, and my husband did not accept change right away. As I learned about feminism, he learned with me. He saw that the world didn't crumble and that life could even become more exciting. Today he is a strong feminist and works with Manavi.

One of the things that comes with getting older is that I feel at peace with myself, my work, and the way I have brought up my daughter. I have given her a chance to see how women work. I have shown her that having children does not mean that you must stop your life. I have essentially raised her to be an activist. Many young activist women of color say they want to become policy makers in order to make changes, but being within a career often means accepting the system as it is. There may be more reason for the daughters of women of color to be attuned to activism today than for their more privileged sisters who have struggled to make gains but who don't have extra issues of color.

I am proud of Sayantani and happy that she is in my life. She has a wonderful intellect and a strong understanding of social change and oppression. She also has a warm heart. I would love to see her making substantial changes in people's lives, perhaps working in a women's clinic in the third world. I would hate to see her get distracted and give it up for something else, like making money. I don't want to see her leading a cozy, comfortable life and not taking risks. Sayantani is at a point where she knows where she is going, and I feel comfortable with that, wherever it may be. She has helped me appreciate life and the joy of struggle; she is my colleague and friend. I cannot even think of life without her. I see the world in her.

A Daughter's Story

Growing up, I was always with my mother. One of my earliest memories is of a Take Back the Night rally. I must have been four or five. I remember holding my mother's hand, turning around to see an ocean of candles, and feeling charged by the energy of all those women singing and marching together. Throughout my childhood I attended NOW rallies and meetings, and I sat in on a consciousness-raising group that met in our home each month. Sometimes I colored in the corner; sometimes I actively participated. From meeting all kinds of women, thinking about my own identity, and seeing my mother at work, I absorbed the message that women's issues are important and that inequities need to be challenged.

I was born on October 30, 1970, in Columbus, Ohio. When I was four my mother returned to college, and I usually went to school with her. Campus was fun because I got so much attention. I stayed with her all day, and when she went to night classes, I stayed home with my father. I had few baby-sitters. My parents scheduled their lives so that one of them could always be with me. I don't think they ever considered that the two of them might go out to dinner without me. My mother brought me into her life; she did not lose herself in mine. I was her little shadow; it was the nature of our relationship. We were and are very close friends.

My mother wasn't like the other mothers. She didn't bake brownies and she didn't belong to the PTA. She was a student. She didn't try to act like Mrs. Brady. When I was younger, I wanted her to be Mrs. Brady, but when I was older I didn't care. For that matter, I wasn't Marsha, either.

I grew up as the only Indian kid in a mostly white suburban neighborhood. My parents were involved in the Indian community, but not in the local community. As a result, I felt split. During the week I was

American; on weekends I was in a totally different world with my parents' Indian friends. My parents believed that language was an important part of our identity, so at home we spoke only Bengali. Sometimes I couldn't express myself well enough, and my parents made me repeat what I was saying until I got it right. At the time it was a pain. Now I'm glad because I know people who don't know their own language and wish they did. Sometimes when we went back to India, I forgot my English entirely and had to re-remember it when we returned to the States.

On the surface, my childhood in Ohio was happy and content. Underneath, I was full of self-doubt about my ability to interact with people and insecure about the way I looked. The memory is painful—one that I can speak about only because I now recognize it for what it was. Other kids made me conscious of my skin color. Sometimes their questions were technical: "Does your tan rub off? Why is your palm light when the rest of you is dark?" Sometimes their questions were lurid: "Do you live in a teepee? Do you eat snakes?" Sometimes their statements were mean: "Go back to where you came from. You are so weird." When you are a child you don't want to be weird, and I definitely had a sense of weirdness—of otherness. I thought the kids were making fun of me because I was brown, because I was ugly.

Those early years determined the way I thought about myself for years. When I was thirteen we left Ohio for New Jersey. It was the best thing that could have happened to me. The New York area exposed me to diverse peoples. It was a cosmopolitan area where there were more Asians and Indians. I now recognized the ridicule in my childhood that I had internalized so deeply as racism, and I finally began to separate from it.

My mother has been an activist for as long as I can remember. In 1985 she and five other women began the New Jersey–based South Asian women's group Manavi. Her activism was controversial in our Indian community, which is quite conservative. They asked, "Why is her husband letting her do this? What is her problem?" Even though my parents were deeply involved in the Indian community, there were still little jokes. The men said to my father, "We should start a men's group to oppose this women's group, because really it's the men who are oppressed." I think they feared that these troublemaking women would cause wives to leave husbands and encourage divorce in the community.

My politics developed alongside my mother's. When I was in high school, she began to do consulting work around workers' issues, so I started to think not just about race and sexuality but also about class. I began to see how all sorts of movements were connected. As she questioned whether NOW, her support group, or any other women's organization was working for her as an immigrant, a mother, and a South Asian woman, I began to recognize the racism around me and to question what it meant to be a daughter of immigrants and a young woman of color growing up in this country. Our politics evolved together as we questioned the nature of the women's movement.

In areas other than the political, however, my mother and I definitely had our share of conflict. In high school, dating was a source of tension between us. I had a boyfriend in high school (who was an idiot, now that I think about it) who at the time was important to me. Going out with him was a form of rebellion. I thought that I was mature enough, so I went ahead and did what I wanted. Now my mother tells me that she was afraid I would get married and not have a career. She wanted me to focus on my studies, and her experience as a sixteen-year-old bride who only went back to college after I was born obviously informed that perspective. Another conflict that I constantly had with my mother was that sometimes we would be having fun as equals, and then all of a sudden, when I would act up, she would become the authoritarian. That drove me nuts. I thought, "You can't do that. You can't punish me *and* joke around with me." I got through this period with my mother with lots of yelling and many verbal battles.

My father and I are very close now, but we went through a battling stage when I threatened to become an actress and he wanted me to do something more practical. Because he and my mother had been through a period of financial tension, it was important to him that I become economically independent. I ended up studying theater and pre-med—but not just to please my father. I was always interested in medical anthropology and different systems of healing.

In college, my political activism flourished. I had a leg up because I had thought a lot about my politics. Brown is an active campus, and I got involved with the Third World Center and the Women's Center. I was lucky to go to a place where institutions were already in place that I could join. I coordinated the Women of Color group on campus, I was a minority peer counselor, and I did workshops on race, gender, and sexuality for first-year students. In retrospect, I think the activist groups on campus were as vital for the growth of those involved as for what we accomplished.

I didn't have serious romantic relationships in college, but I dated a lot. My mother was aware of that and was fine about it. By then our relationship had evolved, and she recognized my newfound self-confidence and stability. She knew that she didn't have to worry anymore. As an adult, I don't need any authority telling me what to do. I have my own separate identity, so my mother and I can just be friends.

> Her activism was controversial in our Indian community. People feared that these troublemaking women would cause wives to leave husbands and encourage divorce.

Ideally, for a life partner, an Indian would probably be easiest, only because it is important that the person integrate into my family. But a lot of Indian-American men I've met have issues with self-esteem. Possibly that's because of the stereotype that they are less masculine than their American counterparts; Indian women, by contrast, are usually considered extra feminine, even exotic. A lot of Indian women I grew up with are progressive and outspoken in their politics, but few of the men are. One reason may be that the men are insecure in the larger community but extremely privileged inside the home. Indian girls, on the other hand, are not privileged within the home, so they are forced to examine their politics.

I cannot separate gender and race. Being a woman of color—a South Asian woman—has influenced the development of my politics, my self-confidence, and my self-concept. As a woman of color, it is difficult to call myself a feminist without a lot of explanation. The word *feminist* is usually too limiting. Someone recently asked me, "Do you consider yourself a South Asian woman or a woman of color?" And then, "Do you consider yourself a South Asian woman or a feminist?" It was so aggravating to be asked to prioritize or dichotomize myself like that. Those identities are integral to me and complementary and essential to each other.

The women's movement in the United States has been a movement for certain women but not others. There hasn't been enough room for women of various ethnic, religious, and class backgrounds to have their issues addressed. I can make alliances with the larger women's movement, and I can be friends with individual members, but it is not my movement. Mainstream feminism is still looking for one answer, one movement, but in reality there are many movements. Sometimes they work together; sometimes they don't. In these new movements, feminism sees gender as continuous throughout all spectrums of society and organizations—in labor organizations, in health-care work, in class-oriented movements. Different generations are working together and teaching each other. I have watched my mother do it: She works with women who are my age and younger as well as women her age and older.

The model of activism I have seen is women working for change for women. But it's important for men to be activists, too. In the last few years my father has begun working for Manavi, and that has been critical within our family. He became involved for his own reasons. I was proud recently when he said, "You can't be a man *and* a feminist and not be an activist, because if you aren't an activist then you are passively living off the status quo."

I came to medicine because it is one of the best routes to bring about social change in women's lives and in the lives of people in developing countries. A lot of my undergraduate work focused on Indian AIDS policy. The summer I graduated, I worked for AMFAR, the American Foundation for AIDS Research, in Washington, D.C. I've also done research in India regarding physician attitudes toward HIV and AIDS. HIV and AIDS seem to be my area because in them so many social issues come together: gender, race, class, sexuality.

I took a year off between college and medical school to try my hand at writing, and in that time my mother and I worked on several projects together. We wrote an article that appeared in *Our Feet Walk the Sky,* an anthology of works by women of South Asian descent, and separate articles for an academic book about South Asian women in America. I wrote a number of articles, including one about South Asian women and AIDS, and how the risk is being played out in the community. Now my freelance writing continues alongside my medical studies.

My mother and I have also written a collection of Bengali folktales together. Often when we had scheduled time for writing, she got tied up on the phone, and I'd become annoyed. It is difficult to keep a schedule with her because she leads a crazy life and doesn't say no to people. She has infinite patience. She is always willing to explain something for the hundredth time or do something for the hundredth time. I could never counsel abused women the way she does, because it frustrates me to hear women making the same mistakes over and over again. How my mother can be supportive and not judgmental or dominating, how she can be so gentle and giving of her time, is beyond me. I would lose patience and fly off the handle.

I am my mother's closest friend, and she is definitely mine. I like all sorts of things about her. She's fun, she's silly, she's an incredibly sharp, interesting ally, and she's a great person to discuss politics with. We respect each other intellectually and bounce ideas off each other. Now that I'm away from home, I worry that she has no one to talk to. She is a very private person. I know she talks to my father, but not about the nitty-gritty details of her life she tends to tell me. We talk on the phone every day.

The one thing we still don't talk about is my dating life. We talk theoretically about sexuality and identity and politics, but we don't talk about personal romantic feelings. Something in me wants to tell her everything because I have always told her everything, but when I have the opportunity, I hesitate. I need her advice, but I don't want to make either of us uncomfortable.

I would like a family, a stable family, that is integral to my work and my heritage. That means I will have to devise my career differently than mainstream medicine tells me to. Maybe once I have children I'll work part-time. I cannot envision having children and not spending as much time with them as possible.

I'm sure that my mother will continue to affect people's lives whatever she does, but I also want her to kick up her heels and have fun. I've seen my parents struggle economically and work very hard, and I'd love to see them spoiled. I'd like to see them in India with their friends—happy, pampered, doing the work they love to do because they love to do it, not because people are demanding it of them.

Miriam and Nguyen, 1976.

Nguyen and Miriam, 1993.

Miriam Ching Yoon Louie

and

Nguyen Louie

MIRIAM CHING YOON LOUIE, a third-generation Chinese and Korean woman and mother of two, was born in California in 1950. She works full-time for women-of-color organizations seeking to empower women at the grassroots level. Currently both media and research coordinator at Asian Immigrant Women's Advocates and project coordinator at Women of Color Resource Center, Louie has also been involved with the Third World Women's Alliance and the Alliance Against Women's Oppression. The first person in her family to go to college, she earned her BA in 1992 from the University of California–Berkeley. She lives in Oakland, California, with her husband and son.

NGUYEN LOUIE, born in Oakland, California, is the namesake of a Vietnamese woman warrior. In her mother's words:

Born Nguyen Thi Dinh Louie
March 6, 1975
Year of the Rabbit

Just your luck
To pop out 2 days before
A giant International Women's Day event
On your mom's way back from the printer
You always celebrate
Your birthday on the run
To an IWD conference/march/rally.

Louie is now twenty years old and a college student at Brown University. She describes herself as a Chinese-Korean-American girl who knows who she is.

A Mother's Story

My daughter, Nguyen, was born March 6, 1975, two days before International Women's Day. The Third World Women's Alliance was in charge of organizing a big celebration, and I had to drop off programs and files to another organizer en route to the hospital. My husband, Belvin, was there coaching and taking pictures during the birth, and I was so happy when Nguyen arrived. We named her after Nguyen Thi Dinh, the head of the women's union in Vietnam, who started the armed struggle against French colonialism. Twelve years later, during a women's peace conference in Moscow in 1987, I had the thrill of meeting Madame Nguyen Thi Dinh, by then a salt-and-pepper-haired grandmother. When I showed her a picture of Nguyen, she squeezed my hand and said, "I feel like she is my daughter, too."

I am a third-generation Chinese- and Korean-American, born in Vallejo, California, in 1950, the year the Korean War broke out. My maternal grandfather was a Methodist minister, educated by missionaries in Seoul. He was active in the Korean independence movement while Grandma raised their eleven children. My paternal grandparents came from Guangdong, a province in southern China, and did odd jobs in San Francisco Chinatown. My father upset his family when he married my mother, because she was Korean instead of Chinese.

Vallejo is a naval-shipyard town, and my father worked in the shipyard for over forty years. World War II broke the color line, opening up jobs for minorities in defense industries, but wages were low. To make ends meet, Dad also worked at a Chinese-owned gas station on weekends and moonlighted in a Chinese-owned grocery store at night. Mom took care of us five kids. While I was growing up, my parents fought constantly. As adults we gradually realized that Mom has manic-depression. One of my brothers drank himself to death at twenty-nine; another has had substance abuse problems and a hard time getting a stable job. Half my family can more or less function and get to where they are supposed to be in the morning, and the other half has a real hard time. I suppose we are your typical American working-class dysfunctional family.

After moving out of the projects, we were one of the first minority families to move into another neighborhood in Vallejo. After more black families moved in, some whites began to get hostile. I remember picking up the telephone party line one day and hearing, "Too many niggers are moving into the neighborhood." I thought, "Gee, are they talking about us?" That was my first encounter with racial discrimination. Our Irish-American playmates up the hill called us "Chinks" and "Japs." Mom told us different names we could call whites. One day when they called us "Japs" we called them "Limeys," and they got really mad and broke one of our windows.

When I was a high-school student, a Black Muslim tried to sell me a newspaper on the street, saying, "Hey, they're trying to kill your people in Vietnam." He was way ahead of me. Completely ignorant about Vietnam, I thought, "I'm not Vietnamese." Later my liberal civics teacher raised alternative points of view about the war, which started me thinking. When people at church said, "You know this is a righteous war because those people are Buddhists and we need to Christianize them," I thought, "This is wrong." That was it for me with the Christian religion. I quit going to church, which made Mom furious.

In 1968 I entered the University of California–Berkeley with scholarships and a Higher Educational Opportunity Program grant— the first person in my family to go to college. It was the height of campus activity at Berkeley. Students rioted in solidarity with the French student movement that summer. In the fall they boycotted classes when the school refused to allow Eldridge Cleaver, then a Black Panther, to teach. In the winter students of color organized the Third World Liberation Front to establish a Third World College, and in the spring others launched the People's Park action. When the police stormed the campus, gassing and beating students, I stopped going to classes, too.

I first met my husband in a freshman chemistry class at Berkeley. We were both trying to avoid getting F's for missing class during the Third World strike. Belvin is second-generation Chinese, and I asked if he had heard about the Asian-American Political Alliance, which later launched the larger Third World Liberation Front, which also included the Black Student Union, MEChA (Movimiento Estudiantil

Chicano de Aztlan), and the Native American group. He said, "Nope," and that ended the discussion. That summer we met again at the Third World Board office, where I volunteered as a secretary. My typing was pretty bad, but Belvin stuck up for me. In some organizations women complained about doing only clerical work. In the Asian movement women have always been outspoken leaders who did both the typing and the talking.

Eventually I became so involved in organizing activities that I lost interest in quantitative chemistry tests and premed studies and dropped out of college. When Belvin and I started living together, my mother and I got in a big fight about sex before marriage. We cried and screamed on the phone. Over the years Mom mellowed out so that by the time my sister Beth was in a relationship, Mom advised her, "Don't rush into marriage. Maybe you two should live together first to see if it's going to work." Coming from a family that was active in the Korean independence movement, Mom was open to our activism, whereas Dad, with his conservative Chinese working-class background, advised us, "Don't rock the boat; roll with the punches; don't fight city hall."

Belvin and I went to Cuba together in 1969 as part of the first Venceremos Brigade. (*Venceremos* means "we will win" in Spanish.) We cut sugarcane for two months during the big harvest and met with Fidel Castro. The Cuban Revolution, Vietnam War, China's split with the Soviet Union, student movements in Mexico, Japan, and South Korea—all were events that influenced and radicalized youth-of-color movements in the United States. Our racial identification with these movements opened our eyes to what the United States was doing in the third world and shed light on aspects of our own history as third-world people living "within the belly of the beast."

After Belvin and I had been living together for five years, I got pregnant. My mother said, "Miriam, you always do things ass backward. You're supposed to get married first, then have a baby." We had another big fight about that. In late 1974 I was four months pregnant when our friends and relatives helped us celebrate our marriage with a big lunch buffet at a Chinese restaurant. Nguyen likes to say she was there at the buffet, too, eating chow mein, roast pork, and wedding cake—from the inside. At the time we were under FBI surveillance because of our trip to Cuba. Once on our way to Lamaze classes with pillows under our arms, the FBI showed up on the stairs of our apartment, asking, "Do you want to talk about your trip to Cuba?" "No," we answered, and hurried to class.

When Nguyen was three months old, I took her to a baby-sitter and went to work as an administrative assistant at Asian Manpower Services, a job-training program for new immigrants. When Nguyen was two and a half, I took her to a child-care center in Chinatown that was pretty good. She cried when I left her, which made me feel terrible. Even in the third grade, when she started a new school, Nguyen still burst out crying, "Mom, don't leave me!"

> **A**fter Belvin and I had been living together for five years, I got pregnant. My mother said, "Miriam, you always do things ass backward. You're supposed to get married first, then have a baby."

I came into the women's movement by way of the Third World Women's Alliance, shortly before Nguyen was born. Our group did some of the earliest work in this country on the intersection of gender, race, and class, and took up issues ignored by the mainstream women's movement, such as infant mortality, sterilization abuse, abortion access for poor women, affirmative action, and special admissions programs for women of color. The alliance supported women with children because a lot of us had kids. At one point there was a Child Development Committee, and we always organized child care for meetings and events. When Nguyen was little, she got carted to everything. We took a spread for her to crawl around on at big conferences and demonstrations. When she was six, her brother, Lung San, was born.

My husband and I are pretty close, partly because our work in the movement has given us common experiences and reference points. But we also have had our share of ups and downs. We had a fight about my going back to work after Nguyen was born. He said, "We have to figure out if it's worth your going to work, because of the cost of child care. Maybe it's not worth it." We went back and forth until I said, "How come the price of a baby-sitter is deducted from my salary? How come the cost of the baby-sitter is not deducted from *both* our salaries?" After that I went back to work.

Belvin has always shared the housework and taken care of the kids. He is very responsible, partly because he grew up working in a family-owned Chinese restaurant. He chops vegetables super fast, helps when the kids are stumped on homework, attends parent-teacher conferences, and makes a mean dish of soy sauce pork. I have always worked for nonprofit organizations for low pay; he is the stable earner. He helps my various organizations with computer and campaign work, and lends a hand for special events and demonstrations. He got a Best Corporate Sponsor award for all the garment workers' campaign picket lines he walked. Now, like his father, Lung San helps me leaflet, put out bulk mailings, and inputs supporters on our data base. We brainstorm together on issues, and I badger Belvin to edit my writing. Some men are threatened by women who are active, but not Belvin. Rather, he sees me as a window into different experiences. Many of our friends are single or divorced, lesbian and straight, so as a straight married couple we are an aberration—a dying breed. Friends prophesying the end of the nuclear family call us the dinosaurs.

In 1983 I began working for Asian Immigrant Women's Advocates (AIWA), an organization seeking to empower low-income immigrant women who find themselves working for third-world wages. In 1989 I also started working with the Women of Color Resource Center (WCRC), which includes some good friends from Third World Women's Alliance days. Through AIWA I get to support Asian women workers' struggles for justice, while the WCRC allows me to work with and learn from feisty women-of-color organizers across racial lines. In 1990 I went back to Berkeley to get my BA and in 1991 I studied in Korea for a year while Belvin took care of the kids.

With all the running around we did, Nguyen grew up like a wild weed. If there were meetings at night, Belvin and I took turns taking care of her. Sometimes she would say, "Mommy, I don't want you to go," and I would say, "I have to go." Or she would yell at me as I went out the door. For a period after she turned twelve, we had big fights because she wouldn't do things as I saw fit. It took a while before it dawned on me that she wanted to be more independent. I had to realize that bearing down would only make her rebel against me.

I would have liked to spend more time with my kids while they were growing up. At the time I would not have considered giving up my organizing activities, but now I have some regrets. Nguyen still says, "Hey, Mom, where are you going? Who are you going with? When are you getting back?" Our relationship is something of a role reversal. I jump into things and end up being consumed by different activities, rushing from cause to cause and event to event. I probably get that from the Korean, manic-depressive side of my personality. Nguyen used to try to create some order to pressure me to stick around.

Nguyen has good instincts and is very independent. You can count on her to do the right thing and be at the right place at the right time.

Despite having grown up like a weed, she turned out pretty well. I wish she didn't have to agonize so much over her decisions, but she is a critical thinker; she works out things in her own methodical way. Her dad is pretty logical, whereas I am impulsive and often get myself out on a limb. Perhaps because her parents have such strong opinions, she works hard to come up with her own independent perspective on everything. In college she works so hard that she barely sleeps or eats. Sometimes her pop and I tell her not to study so hard, to try to get to more student conferences and demonstrations because that's also what a college education is about. Then we catch ourselves and laugh about the kind of parents we are. Nguyen went up to Boston for a training session for our Garment Workers Justice Campaign and demonstrations against manufacturer Jessica McClintock for corporate responsibility. That made her old mom happy.

I need to slow down because I am getting older. I can't get as much done now as I used to, and I can already tell that menopause is not going to be nice to me. Fortunately, a younger generation of women is coming up that is bringing in new points of view and different issues that we had not considered. I hope they can build on and take advantage of our mistakes and experiences.

I am hopeful for the future. Women in grassroots organizations need more resources and visibility. While the mainstream women's movement is considered to represent us in pursuing important electoral, legislative, and judicial battles, they don't deal with a lot of issues minority women face. The consciousness that the women's movement fought so hard for has filtered into different communities. Now women of color are creating distinct kinds of feminism and organizing relevant to their own communities and experiences. No longer do you have to decide whether your allegiance is to the minority community or to the women's liberation movement. That false dichotomy is absent from the organizations and activists of the new generation.

My definition of feminism has changed over the years. When I worked with the Third World Women's Alliance, I was emphatically not a feminist. I saw feminist ideology as placing gender above class and race, thus rendering working-class women, especially women of color, invisible. Now women of color have crafted feminisms that take into account the many oppressions and challenges they face. I've been in women's groups for over twenty years, and today if people call me a feminist I no longer get uptight about it.

Like anyone else, Nguyen has to deal with her identity and what she wants to be. But in terms of knowing who her people are, where she comes from, and what her culture is, she has a solid foundation. My husband and I handed down our values, either through osmosis at the dinner table or just by our kids' seeing how their parents function—what kind of work we do, whom we respect. Nguyen already has the kind of confidence in the way she looks at the world that took me years to achieve. What I had to fight for, she can assume. She takes for granted the principles of feminism and is secure in her ethnic identity. We've seen her stand up against arbitrary practices by authority figures in school and job settings even when fellow students and coworkers were afraid to speak out. The girl can hold her own.

It was rewarding to see how things had changed and developed when I went back to school and majored in ethnic studies. For all its ups and downs, that period of ferment in the 1960s was a turning point. Many of us who started out in those movements ended up forming ethnic and women's studies programs and new community-based organizations and campaigns so that this new generation can start from higher ground. I hope Nguyen can do something she really enjoys that will serve the communities and people who are struggling to get by. Whatever she chooses to do, I know she will put all her energy and heart into it.

A Daughter's Story

I am a Chinese-Korean-American young woman. It may be a mouthful, but that is who I am in my entirety. Each identity is an integral part of me that cannot be separated from the others. Because of this, prejudice is something that I have had to deal with all my life. Whenever I am made fun of or discriminated against, I say something and move on, so that I don't have a whole line of resentments following me. In high school this guy in my class would slant his eyes and ask me if he looked Chinese. One day I pushed my eyes together and asked him if I looked black. It became very apparent that he was being stupid. From that day forward, he treated me with respect.

I was born two days before International Women's Day (IWD), on March 6, 1975. This was always a hectic time of year because my mother was busy going to meetings and organizing programs for the IWD event. I resented the fact that it seemed to take precedence over my birthday. I always wanted a full-fledged birthday party with a dozen or so friends, junk food, and presents. Instead, I stayed in day-care with other children whose mothers were members of the Third World Women's Alliance. On my eleventh birthday I was allowed to be part of the IWD event; I gave a speech in front of three hundred people to raise money for a childcare center in Angola. My mother coached me and bought me a purple jumpsuit for the occasion. For the first time, I was actually doing something that might make a difference on the other side of the world. I think I grew more during that five-minute speech than I had during the previous year. That's when I realized why my mother did what she did and why it was important.

My parents were at Berkeley during the sixties. They agitated for the development of ethnic studies, dropped out of school, and protested against the Vietnam War. They were very liberal. They also gave me a lot of freedom to grow on my own. With that flexibility, I didn't feel the need to rebel. I don't really understand the kinds of relationships my girlfriends have with their mothers. Usually their mothers are overprotective, making my friends want to defy them even more. Although my mom and I are not equals, we are best friends. I can talk to her, confide in her, laugh with her, and cry with her.

We weren't always so close. As a young child, I remember telling her I hated her. I was resentful that she didn't have much time to spend with me. I felt closer to my father; he *did* things with me. We watched videos, ate potato chips, played board games, and went for walks together. When my dad brought his paperwork home, I would poke around and ask him what he was doing. My parents were probably gone from home the same amount of time, but I blamed my mother more. I guess it was because I thought my mother was supposed to be around.

When I was six, my mother became pregnant with my brother, Lung San. I was lonely and looked forward to having a sibling to play with, but I didn't expect my parents to spend so much time with him and not with me. Again, I blamed my mother. I tried to run away but made it only to the corner because I wasn't supposed to cross the street. Consequently I was forced to compromise with my parents and accept my new role as a responsible big sister, one who was too mature to have tantrums and run away. By age twelve I preferred to stay home from the conventions my parents went to and take care of my brother. We ate quick and easy meals, like Kraft macaroni and cheese and ramen noodles. After school and on the weekends when my parents were away, I rarely felt burdened with taking care of my brother or doing housework. I enjoyed being the "little mom."

Looking back, I realize that my mother always made sure we had quality time together. My father and I were content to bum around the house, but my mother insisted that we go out and do things. We went on excursions to the Berkeley marina, Golden Gate Park, and Chinatown, and we took family vacations in Santa Cruz and Hawaii. Although it may sound cheesy, my family is very trusting, loving, and closely knit.

At home we ate a mixture of ethnic and American food. Sometimes my father would fry pork in soy sauce and sugar, sometimes my mother would prepare soft tacos, and other times I would make spaghetti. Most meals were accompanied by rice and kim chee, which is a Korean pickled cabbage.

I used to feel pressure to be active in my mother's causes. I felt that I was letting her down if I didn't go to meetings. Being active was the morally right thing to do, but it wasn't always what I wanted to do. I wanted to be a "normal" teenager, to go to the movies or bowling with my friends. Often it seemed like my parents did not have any fun; they were always gone, and they came home exhausted. I wasn't able to see that their work was interesting or worthwhile. To me, it seemed oppressive. Also, I don't like to be pressured into doing things, even if they are "for the best." In a lot of ways I am more conservative than my mom. I often fight change. My mom wants me to get out there and be more active, and sometimes I just don't think I have the time or energy for it. I just want to be myself.

> I resented the fact that International Women's Day seemed to take precedence over my birthday.

I like the fact that my mom gets an idea into her head and carries through with it. For instance, two years ago she decided to learn how to speak Korean, so she studied abroad at Yonsei University. Sometimes I wish I could do that, but I have a lot of reservations. When I was thirteen my parents sent me to Cuba for a month with an international youth organization. My mother said, "It will open your eyes, and you'll learn so much." But I adamantly did not want to go. My body was changing and I had started to menstruate, and I was insecure and anxious about having to deal with guys or compete with girls on this trip. The mere thought of it terrified me. But my parents were firm; they put me on the plane, and I went.

My parents were right. It was an eye-opening experience. Delegations of young people had come to Cuba from all over the world: Angola, the Soviet Union, Nicaragua. I learned how impoverished some other kids were and the struggles they were going through. When I went home I felt I had a responsibility to do something, to use the information I had gained and become more active. I started out with good intentions, but my resolve dwindled when I went to junior high school. There were many cliques that required being popular and looking cute, and I wanted to be myself. I didn't want to change myself to fit into any clique. Instead, I stayed in the library, and everybody thought I was the nice little Asian girl. I was often lonely and miserable. I hated junior high.

In high school I discovered it was okay to be myself. In fact, it was cool to be an individual. I became secure and comfortable with myself and made a lot of good friends who accepted me for who I was. When I was a sophomore I was a founding member of the Asian Awareness Club. When complaints arose about Asian students getting beaten up and kicked in the hallways, we organized workshops on interracial relationships and Asian stereotypes. Part of what I liked about the club was organizing with my friends and deciding to do it on my own. My parents weren't telling me, "You are going to this meeting and will learn something from it." *I* planned the meetings and the different issues we discussed.

My parents both went back to college when I was in high school. It was hellish for them—having to work, take care of their kids, and maintain honor grades. But their experience made me see that going to college is an opportunity to learn, not just a means to a job. I decided to go to Brown because of its academic diversity and the fact that it offered the flexibility of creating your own major. Also, being at home with my parents was too comfortable; I needed to get out on my own and be more independent. Breaking away from my parents was the hardest thing for me to do. I knew that even though we would see each other in the future, the dynamics of our relationship would change. I would change. But my parents made the transition easier by flying out with me to the East Coast and giving me lots of support.

When I got to Brown, I went through a difficult time. Until I went to college I had never been so aware of my socioeconomic background, but at Brown it seems that the majority of the students have been through private East Coast preparatory schools, and I felt they had the upper hand. I also found it strange to meet so many students whose primary goal is to make money. It seems that many students aspire to be doctors not because they want to help people but in order to have extravagant lifestyles. I was disheartened by this attitude.

The first semester was a struggle for me. My parents stressed that although grades are important, they are not matters of life and death. They never made me feel as though I failed them by getting B's rather than A's. They just said, "Do the best you can." I have learned a lot from my experiences. I know my limitations and can balance my time and priorities better. I still feel the need to work, but the pressure is coming from within myself. And with my parents behind me, I am bound to be a success.

During my first semester, I tacitly went along with the "Asian gravitational pull." It was comfortable and familiar. However, many of the Asians I met grew up in predominantly Caucasian suburbs, and because I grew up in Oakland I found it increasingly difficult to relate. Over the course of the second semester, socioeconomic differences crystallized. I still have a lot of close Asian friends who are Thai, Chinese, Korean, Filipino, and Vietnamese. At the same time, though, I have a lot of close non-Asian friends who are Irish, Jewish, Mexican, and Dominican. I think part of this has to do with the fact that I am Chinese, Korean, and American, and because my parents' friends are of various racial and ethnic backgrounds. At Brown there is a lot of pressure to "stick to your own." But for me, commonalities and true understanding go far beyond race and have to do with cultural, social, and economic complexities.

I am a feminist by my own interpretation: I believe that men and women are equal physically and intellectually; therefore, they are entitled to equal rights, treatment, and respect. I take this for granted, and I immediately assume people are wrong for thinking otherwise. It's almost instinctive. Yet I would never introduce myself as a feminist; I am a Chinese-Korean-American young woman. As such, I must deal with more than uniquely feminist issues. Issues of race, class, and culture are equally important to me. Being a feminist is an integral part of who I am, but it is not all that I am.

At this point in my life, I can't see myself as being as much of an activist as my mother, but activism is definitely a part of me. It's in my blood. I'm not sure whether that's a blessing or a curse. I plan to tap into the activism on campus, but I don't want to devote my life to it. I prefer to deal with things on a personal level. What I want from life is to achieve my maximum potential, to be happy, and to be comfortable. I want to find a balance.

Eventually I would like to have the kind of relationship my parents have. They love each other, respect each other, and give each other support, but they are not joined at the hip. They have learned, changed, and grown both individually and "together as one" for the past twenty-five years, and they have encouraged me to do the same. When I went away to college I saw many parts of my mother and my father in myself: the discipline, the curiosity, and the ambition.

You can always hear and know what my mom has to say, whether it is through a bullhorn, a newsletter, or a poem. Her voice is strong, loud, and clear. She's wild; she's out there on her motor scooter. She's in the know. She has traveled around the world and back, working with different organizations and individuals and touching many lives. I am proud to be the daughter of Miriam Ching Louie.

Kianga, Nkenge, and Trina, 1990.

Kianga, Nkenge, Trina, and DeReco, 1995.

Nkenge Toure
and
Trina Stevens
and
Kianga Stroud

NKENGE TOURE was born in Baltimore, Maryland, in 1951 as Anita Beatrice Stroud. She later changed her name to Nkenge Toure. Toure grew up in a subsidized low-income housing development in Baltimore and remembers vividly her mother taking her at the age of twelve to hear Martin Luther King's "I Have a Dream" speech. In 1965 she enrolled in an all-girl's high school that was in the process of becoming integrated, and became part of a group called the Black Voice, which was committed to getting books by black authors in the school library and better communication between the black students and white faculty. She also attended political classes at the Soul School. Though she didn't graduate from high school, she applied to Antioch College through the Urban Studies Department in 1973 and was allowed to begin college while she earned her GED. Toure was a member of the Black Panther Party in Washington, D.C., when her children were born. She worked at the D.C. Rape Crisis Center and later became a director. Today she works for Potter's Vessel, an organization that provides services for needy children, and lives in Washington, D.C.

Trina STEVENS was born in Washington, D.C., where she still lives today. She is twenty-three years old. A student at the University of the District of Columbia, she lives at home with her son, DeReco. Stevens says she might like to work as a paralegal someday but has little interest in activism. She eventually wants to move into her own home with her son and is very concerned about providing him with an environment free from violence.

Kianga STROUD plans to be politically active, but not to the same extent as her mother. She has worked as a peer educator about AIDS and HIV, and testified before the Congressional Black Caucus, Congresswoman Patricia Schroeder's Select Committee on Children, Youth and Families, and the National AIDS Commission. Born in 1976 in Washington, D.C., Stroud attends an all-black high school. She would like to go into fashion merchandising.

NKENGE TOURE
A Mother's Story

I was covering the desk at Black Panther headquarters in Washington, D.C., the day my oldest daughter was born, in 1972. Her name should have been Tanya. My husband and I named her Trina Frelimo in honor of a woman—whose name the newspaper mistakenly printed as "Trina"—who was present with Che Guevara when he died. *Frelimo* stood for "Front for Liberation of Mozambique." Through the Black Panther Party I had met John Wesley Stevens, a Vietnam veteran who had received a dishonorable discharge following a racial incident involving officers. We got married in an African ceremony in Malcolm X Park, but we were never legally married.

The direction of my life was shaped largely by the Black Panthers. As a member, I worked to change the economic order and secure the rights African people are entitled to—to live free of oppression and fear and to make a living. The party, which attracted a diverse range of people, from professors to prostitutes, brought out the best in us. We saw ourselves making a difference. When my second daughter, Kianga, was born in 1975, I decided that since my daughters had Africa-related names, I should have an African name. My husband and I chose "Touré" in honor of Sekou Touré. *Nkenge* means "superior mind." My mother still calls me Anita sometimes. She says, "I already gave you your name."

I was born Anita Beatrice Stroud in Baltimore on March 5, 1951, and grew up in the projects. Crime, drugs, and teen pregnancy were prevalent in the neighborhood, but many people tried to advance themselves and to hold on to their values and principles. My father wasn't around, but brothers, aunts, uncles, and other relatives were part of my extended family. My mother, determined to provide as balanced an environment as she could, kept on top of our homework, activities, and friends.

My mother was on public assistance when I was young, but she got off as soon as she found a job. She took any work she could find. Working in a tomato-processing plant, she came home each day with bumps on her hands and between her fingers because she was allergic to tomatoes. At London Town Manufacturers she became a union shop steward. Staying on top of things at home became more difficult. I knew she worked too hard without enough support, so I started cooking dinner when I was ten. Nobody asked me to, but my mother got home at five o'clock and I knew she shouldn't have to cook dinner.

My mother, who was aware of larger events going on around her, made sure we were informed. She and her friends often talked about what was going on down South with the dogs and hoses. Martin Luther King was her hero. When I was twelve, she took me to Washington to hear his "I Have a Dream" speech. I never saw so many people in my entire life. She regarded the Nation of Islam highly and went to the mosque to hear Elijah Muhammad speak. She also encouraged me to read articles in the Muslim newspaper.

In 1965 I entered Eastern High, an all-girls school, previously all-white. With only one or two black teachers and no books about blacks in its library, Eastern was having a hard time with integration. School officials were anxious to protect their "high standards," and the atmosphere was strained and intense. Around 1967 the Black Panther Party arrived on the scene, and I heard about people in African countries for the first time. At Eastern we formed a group called the Black Voice to get books in the library and encourage better relationships between white teachers and black students. We asked the school to transfer a bigoted history teacher to an all-white school because she called black students names and graded them differently.

On February 12, 1967, this teacher told a black student to pick up trash off the floor. The student responded that her mother had not sent her to school to be a maintenance person, and the teacher called her a "black bitch." Word spread like wildfire, and the Black Voice made a plan. We came to assembly the next day dressed in black and sat up front. When the guest speaker was introduced, we stood and gave the Black Power salute. The bigoted teacher informed the main office that Black Panthers were taking over the school and locked herself in her classroom. School officials agreed to meet with us, and we seized the intercom and asked everyone to come to the auditorium to discuss the issues. Administrators closed off the auditorium where black students sat—in effect locking us in—and called the police. The SWAT team arrived, with helmets and billy clubs, releasing Mace and tear gas. They arrested the Voice leaders, and female students formed a chain around the paddy wagon. Eight of us were taken to jail.

Word spread, and a mass of students from other schools showed up in solidarity when we emerged from arraignment the next day. Needing a place to meet, we took over Murphy Hall at Morgan University and created a list of twenty-eight demands. Students went on strike for a month and demonstrated before the board of education, the city council, and the police department. Finally, under pressure from parents, most returned to school.

The ringleaders were not allowed back in school, however. I was one. School officials said I could attend summer school and graduate, but I didn't want to. My mother got a lawyer, who said they couldn't just throw me out of school, but I missed the hearing because I was trapped in Panther headquarters. Our offices had been attacked, and police surrounded the headquarters, so we couldn't leave. The siege lasted eight days. The community people who slept out in the street until the police went away saved our lives. I began attending political-education classes at the Soul School and learned about Africa and various struggles around the world. My mother believed the Panthers' cause was just, but she wanted me to finish school. In 1973 I was accepted to Antioch College through the Urban Studies Department and allowed to begin college while I earned my GED.

In 1970 the Panthers sent me to Washington to work with the D.C. chapter. I sold newspapers, worked on the breakfast program, and helped with accounting. We lived in Adams Morgan near the Panther printing presses on 18th Street. During the upheaval in the party resulting from the split between Eldridge Cleaver, Huey Newton, and Bobby Seale, I was sent to New York. I returned to Washington just two days before Sam Napier was found chained to a pole in our New York office, shot to death. Back in Washington I coordinated the People's Free Health Service (we screened fifty thousand people for sickle-cell anemia, hypertension, and diabetes) and worked on the prison program.

Panthers promoted the idea of equality among members and non-sexist behavior (though they didn't call it that). Women weren't Pantherettes; we were all Panthers. In some chapters a woman was the defense captain. But people are products of their environment. Women still wound up doing the cooking, extending sexual favors, and feeling taken advantage of. But the Panthers' influence has been far-reaching and profound. Many are leaders in their own communities today. A former Panther may be the one who starts the night basketball team, the one who gets the traffic light put up, the one who organizes the orange hats to patrol urban neighborhoods at night, the one who begins a mentoring program for young men, or the one who goes into public mental-health work rather than private practice in order to reach people in affected neighborhoods.

By the time Kianga was born, most Panther members had been called to Oakland to help Bobby Seale run for mayor. I stayed in D.C. to keep the newspapers and community programs going. I was a single mother by the government's definition, so during this time I was on public assistance. My husband and I started a bookstore called Education Through Liberation, and when some rapes occurred in the area in 1975 we held meetings at the bookstore for women to discuss the problem. After that I got involved in the D.C. Rape Crisis Center, one of the first in the country. We were among the first to name rape a crime of violence rather than of sex—a theory now widely accepted. We also promoted the idea that knowing the perpetrator does not mean a woman has brought the rape on herself.

Part of my motivation was personal. Growing up in the projects, I saw women battered by husbands and boyfriends. At the age of sixteen I was raped by my boyfriend while I was baby-sitting. I let him in, figuring, "He's home from basic training; he'll only stay a little while." But that's not how it worked out. I was a virgin, and the assault had a profound impact on me. For a long time I didn't tell anyone. I thought I had brought the rape on myself. I cried and grew depressed and introverted. I was completely disillusioned about sex and wondered, "Is this what they're writing the songs and poems about?" For a while I became sexually active by choice. Then, at seventeen, I had a painful miscarriage from an unwanted pregnancy. My bed was put in the dining room because I couldn't walk up and down the stairs.

When I went to work at the Rape Crisis Center, I became the wage earner, and John Wesley assumed responsibility for watching the kids. He cooked and did laundry, but he had self-esteem problems because I had a paying job and he didn't. He also drank. We were already married before I realized he was an alcoholic. He was not abusive, but his alcoholism was more than I could deal with, and the marriage ended in 1980.

The breakup was hardest on Trina because she spent more time with her father than Kianga did and her memories were more vivid. I regret that their father couldn't stay on the scene, because raising our daughters would have been easier and better. As it was, I dragged them to meetings until they were old enough to look out for each other, then I let them stay home. I didn't have baby-sitters, but a circle of friends helped out. I went to Africa for six weeks and left the girls on a scheduled rotation with my friends. Now I regret having been away so much.

Being a feminist or a political activist does not guarantee that your children will be like you. I do believe that certain things you instill in them will one day be useful to them. Sometimes they have to go their own way and do their own thing, but I believe that eventually they will embrace the values you have given them. I am happy that

> **Growing up in the projects, I saw women battered by husbands and boyfriends. At the age of sixteen I was raped.**

I have been able to instill a sense of self-reliance and independence in Trina and Kianga. Their sense of sexual politics (though they might not call it that) is keen. They refuse to allow themselves to be taken advantage of by anyone, particularly young men. They claim their own opinions and positions, and they speak their minds. I smile when I hear them telling girlfriends on the phone, "You don't have to take that."

Trina has a wonderful smile and a generous spirit. She also has incredible tenacity. During her last two years of high school I sent her to live with my mother because I thought she needed to be out of Washington. I would not have chosen for my daughter to have a child right after high school, but I think she is a good mother and I'm grateful that she graduated. I hope she will find a stable relationship. Because she and her son are living under my roof, her womanhood and my womanhood sometimes butt heads. She needs to be on her own—making her own mistakes and claiming her own victories.

Kianga has a kind heart. She's a natural-born cut-up, sometimes to the point where you want to say, "Look, this is not *America's Funniest Home Videos*. Would you please stop!" She is also strong-willed. Kianga is more open to new ideas than Trina. For several years she has been a peer educator about AIDS and HIV for teenagers. She testified before the Congressional Black Caucus, before Congresswoman Pat Schroeder's Select Committee on Children, Youth and Families, and before the National AIDS Commission before it was disbanded.

I envy my daughters their youth, confidence, and self-esteem. They have a better sense of who they are than I did at their age. But I regret all the violence they have to cope with. If they don't know directly somebody who's been killed, they know a friend of a friend who has been killed. I believe that everyone on earth is entitled to a good quality of life. Not just to survive but to live. People's basic needs must be secured before they can pursue the needs of the human spirit.

Frederick Douglass said, "People want to pull up the crops, but they don't want to plow the field." We have to address the idea of instant gratification in our society. You put food in a microwave, or pop in a video for an immediate story. Our children have learned to want things right away. They don't want to toil. With every struggle there is sacrifice, however, and without struggle there is no victory. It is the parents' job to instill certain values in our children. Some attitudes and activities in our schools need to change. Communities must become more actively involved in providing an ethical framework for children.

I hope to live long enough to see a significant change for people in our society. In a grassroots way, I am doing what I can to bring that change about. In 1989 I began working at Potter's Vessel, the social-service division of an organization called TERRIFIC—Temporary Emergency Residential Resources Institute for Families in Crisis—which provides services for needy D.C. families. The group, which works to restore broken families, takes its name from the biblical parable about a potter who used the pieces from a broken pot to form a vessel more beautiful than before. Grandma's House, another division of TERRIFIC, started the first homes in the nation for HIV-positive infants. We began with one house; now we have seven. Grants fund our salaries.

Occasionally I call myself a feminist, but I consider myself African-American first. I prefer the term *womanist* because I think women of color more easily identify with the term. In fact, one weakness of the women's movement has been its failure to be more encompassing, to understand what drives women of color. The gap continues between women of color and white women in terms of what they see as important and interconnected. Certain issues unite all women, but within the general women's movement there exists a separate movement of women of color.

It takes a long time to think of ourselves as wise women who have answers and knowledge to share with others. The fierceness of what we know and what we've done boggles the mind. Someday I hope to collaborate on a book about the history of women of color in the women's movement, particularly addressing the issue of violence. Most people don't realize that in terms of rape, sexual harassment, and domestic violence, almost all the major cases that have seized the country's attention and served to direct change involved women of color. I want to write that herstory.

I believe there is a hero, or a "shero," in everybody. Fannie Lou Hamer, a woman with a sixth-grade education, changed Mississippi politics. Ella Baker started many chapters of the NAACP. I also draw a lot of strength and inspiration from Septima Clark. These are my "sheroes." Sweet Honey in the Rock says we are "still on this journey." For me it's not so much the destination but the journey.

A Daughter's Story

I admire my mother because she works hard every day to raise her children. I could have ended up a lot worse off than I am now, twenty-three years old with a baby and living at home. I could have ended up using drugs; I could be dead. I have never used drugs; I don't really even drink. I am terrified that I might be an alcoholic like my father.

When I was born, on April 15, 1972, my parents were active in the Black Panther Party. They owned a radical bookstore, where they served free breakfast to the YSB (Young Sisters and Brothers)—the children of the Panthers and children from the community. One of my earliest memories is of my parents taking me to a rally to impeach Nixon.

When I was small, my mother took me to live in Baltimore with her mother for a year. Then we moved back to Washington, where she stayed active with the Panthers. I went to a baby-sitter for a while, but my mother thought the baby-sitter was spoiling me because I threw temper tantrums when I didn't get my own way, so she kept me at home. My mother taught me my ABC's, my shapes, and my colors. By the time I was three, I could write my whole name, my address, and my telephone number. When I was four, too young to go to school, my mother taught me how to count and to read. By the time I got to kindergarten, I was doing first-grade work. I have always been able to read and write above my school age.

When I entered school, my mother began working full-time as director of the Rape Crisis Center, and my father stayed at home. He used to play with me all the time. My grandmother didn't like it when he played rough and threw me in the air. He made jewelry—earrings, necklaces, bracelets—which he sold on the street. My father left us when I was seven and Kianga was three. We became latchkey children. We went from school to the after-school program, where we learned sports, and they taught us prayers and took us on trips. Dinner was served there, too, but the food was nasty. Most of the time my mother picked us up after dinner. When I was nine or ten, I learned how to heat up food at home. Kianga and I didn't much like staying home alone. I told my grandmother, "Mommy works too much; we don't ever see her." She told my mother to stop working so hard, and my mother cut down her hours. But we were still latchkey kids because she couldn't ever seem to get home before six.

I missed my mother, but I wasn't lonely or scared. I understood why she had to work, and I didn't feel neglected. My father was gone and somebody had to provide for us. Our bills had to be paid so we wouldn't be out on the street. It wasn't as if we could go over to our grandmother's house; she lived in Baltimore. Besides, it would have been impossible for her to take care of two little girls. She herself worked hard until she was sixty-two.

For a long time I hated my father. I couldn't see how anyone could make children and then not stick around to take care of them. My uncle said, "You can't hate your father. To hate your father is to hate yourself, because that is part of you." So I put that out of my mind. Now I think my father is lonely, because he calls us at least two or three times a month. I couldn't tell you if he is working or not. But I don't feel sorry for him. He has another daughter who is older than me whose name I don't even know.

My mother was strict with us. I thought everybody had more freedom than I did. There were all kinds of rules: We had to come into the house before dark, eat all our vegetables, and do our homework every night. She taught us that education came first. We had to do our homework before we were allowed to do anything else. For a long time we didn't have a TV.

When I started St. Paul Junior High School, I began to get into trouble. In the seventh grade I got suspended for a fight. In eighth grade I challenged my teachers; they would say something to me, and I would say something right back to them. Then they'd send a letter home to my mother. I don't back down from anybody, and I don't let people talk to me with disrespect. I lose my cool; I holler. My mother stays calm. You cannot get her to holler at you; you cannot get her to lose her cool. She handles things better than I do and gets a better response. She's always been like that. I think I might be more like my father.

In elementary school I didn't have to work hard. In junior high I did, but I didn't want to put forth the effort. I barely made it out of tenth grade. All my grades were C's. I thought I was so smart; I could go to school for two days instead of five and still get all C's. I was learning how to be a court reporter, which meant you went to trade school for two days and academic school for three. I went to trade school, but I wouldn't go to academic school. Instead, I came home, watched TV, and slept. My mother finally found out because they called her at work. The school placed me on probation, but I just found someone to sign my teacher's name in order to show my mother. I still went home; I hated school.

My mother probably thought I was having sex before I actually was. The first time I had sex it was my own decision. I was sixteen, and it was with a guy from my high school (who later ended up getting shot). I had known about sex for a long time; my mother had bought Kianga and me a book called *Our Bodies, Ourselves.*

During high school my mother took me to a therapist because I would not interact with my family. I told my mother I wasn't going to say anything to her because we argued all the time. Some people said the reason we argued was because we are too much alike. Both of us are stubborn. I always wanted to have the last word, so we bumped heads. And sometimes she can be cold. You'll go in to talk to her and there will be something wrong, and you'll say, "What's wrong?" and she'll say, "Nothing." I don't press the issue. If it's nothing, it's nothing.

I didn't like therapy. The lady tried to make me think I was crazy for real. She asked me stupid stuff: "Are you acting like this because your father is not here?" "No. What do I need my father for? My mother can take care of me." The therapist always used to say it was my father. And she told my grandmother, "Next time Trina calls, you tell her that you don't want to hear." I told the therapist, "I don't know where you got your degree, but you don't tell people they can't talk if they have a problem and they can't find someone to talk to. If you are going to tell her she ain't talking to me, then I ain't talking to you, and I ain't coming here no more." So I stopped going.

All my friends were older than me and I wanted to stay out late like they did, but my mother wouldn't let me. We fought all the time. Finally I decided that I wanted to leave home and go Baltimore, and she agreed that I could go. I think she thought I would be safer there. So I went to Baltimore and stayed with my uncle, his girlfriend, and their three children.

I didn't tell my grandmother when I got pregnant the first time, but she just knew. So she told my mother. At first I denied that I was pregnant, but then I admitted it. It was not a difficult decision to have an abortion. I talked my way through it. I was telling the nurse about how I wanted to be an accountant, and the next thing I knew, it was over. I was not depressed at all. I didn't want to get married. I was going to get an abortion the second time, too, but my boyfriend, Calvin, wanted me to have the baby. Most of my friends got pregnant and had children before I did. They didn't finish school, and they don't have jobs now. At least I finished high school and I'm enrolled in college.

> I had known about sex for a long time; my mother had bought Kianga and me a book called "Our Bodies, Ourselves."

I am not having any more kids. It's hard enough taking care of one, and the world is too crazy to be trying to raise somebody's kid by yourself. But I will never get married, because I think marriage is overrated. This is how I see it: You can live with somebody, use their money, have them pay your bills, have sex, and take care of your children, and you don't have to be married. And if you decide that you don't want to be married, you don't have to go through a divorce.

Right now I don't want to be tied down. I want to do what I want to do. I had a boyfriend, but he's gone. He was jealous and possessive, and my mother said that when people are jealous and possessive they'll hit you. She told me and Kianga to let no man beat on us, because we aren't punching bags. So I decided that if I had to fight him, I didn't need to be with him. I am not going to be in an abusive relationship. He never hit me, but he pushed me one day.

I guess I would call myself a feminist. I've never called myself one because I never knew what a feminist was. I used to hear the term, but I didn't know what it meant, so I asked my mother. If a feminist is a person who believes that women and men are equal, and that a woman can do what a man can do and should be paid for the same thing a man can do if she can do it, I believe in feminism.

When DeReco visits his father in Baltimore, I get nervous. It is drug-infested there. People get shot in the neighborhood; it is a common occurrence to hear gunfire. DeReco's father will not let him go outside. It worries me that he is exposed to so much violence. Most men I know have guns, and there is so much violence on television. I try to monitor what DeReco watches, but it is kind of hard for me with him still seeing his father.

I am concerned about my son's future. If he makes it to eighteen, I will be so happy. I do fear for his life because he is a black male. Everyone knows that to be a black male and to make it to twenty-one is an accomplishment in itself. I would like to see DeReco graduate from high school and go to college.

Not too many people from my high school went to college. Before I graduated from high school, half the girls in our class were pregnant, and after I graduated, it seemed like everybody had a baby. My mother wants me to finish college, but I have mixed feelings about it. I know she is disappointed that I temporarily dropped out of the University of the District of Columbia. She said one day, "I know your life could be different." I could go back this semester if I had the money. I know that you need more than a high-school diploma to get a job; I've been trying to get one, and it's hard.

I do like to read. I read anything interesting: Terry McMillan's *Waiting to Exhale,* or *I Know Why the Caged Bird Sings, Disappearing Acts, The Autobiography of Malcolm X.* I liked *Waiting to Exhale* the best. I liked the character Savannah, who was so independent; she was like, "I don't need nobody for nothing." I read *The Color Purple* and *Their Eyes Were Watching God.* My mother read them first, and that's why I read them. I read to my son sometimes when he hands me a book. I am not teaching him to read yet. Me and my mama buy books for him.

DeReco and I are living at home with my mother and Kianga now, but we are planning to move when I can get the money together. My mother makes me cook, but I don't feel guilty about not helping around the house more. I am not home a lot. My mother will tell you, when Thursday or Friday comes, I am gone from this house and she and Kianga don't see me until Sunday. I'll take DeReco to my girlfriend's house.

Before I move, I have to get a job, or I'll have no way to pay my bills. Right now I get three hundred and thirty dollars a month from unemployment, and I'm not going to take my son into public housing. I refuse to raise him in the projects. I would like to be a paralegal. Who knows? If I finish college and get a degree as a paralegal, I might go back again to be a lawyer. I have never wanted to be an activist because that is just not me. If I did anything, I guess it would be something like AIDS work.

I think my mother's activism work is great. It keeps her busy, and it is a job. She went to college, but she didn't graduate. Even without a degree, she got a job and she makes money. Sometimes I worry about her health. She is so busy. Aside from her job, she is in about five or six organizations. I tell her not to work so hard, because it gets her stressed out and it affects her health. Nobody has to work that hard. She says she has her future planned: After she stops working, she is going to travel. I hope she has money saved up for that.

KIANGA STROUD
A Daughter's Story

My mother always wanted us to know about black history, about pride in women. When I was in elementary school, she used to embarrass me. She wore African prints and dreadlocks, and the jewelry. My friends would ask, "Why does she have on that African stuff?" and I would say, "Because she wants to." I defended her, but I was still embarrassed. It changed when I got into junior high school. Now I feel like it's her life; she can wear whatever she wants to wear. I don't wear African dress because I haven't found anything that looks good on me. I'm not saying I'm ruling it out.

My mother was not like the mothers of my friends. She had a different kind of job. Every job that my mother has ever had has been community-oriented or helping women. Other people's mothers worked in office jobs or government jobs; my mother worked at the D.C. Rape Crisis Center. We used to go to a lot of events, like Take Back the Night rallies.

I was born on March 29, 1976. The first apartment house I remember living in was across from Malcolm X Park in Washington, D.C. We lived there until I was eight or so. Our apartment had two bedrooms; my sister and I shared a room. After I was three or four years old, my father didn't live with us anymore. Sometimes we would go to stay with him, but I don't have a lot of memories of him. We didn't see him often. My father was unreliable—saying he was going to come and he wouldn't come, drinking. When he was drinking he would be in a different kind of mood. He didn't act violently or treat us bad. We just couldn't count on him. It made me sad. I don't see him now, but he calls us a lot. I don't really want to see him, because I don't have a lot to say to him. He didn't help support the family at all.

Whenever Trina or I wanted anything, we went to my grandmother. When we were younger, my mother didn't want us to get our hair pressed, but my grandmother got me a Jheri curl. I relax my hair now and dye it black; my mother finally gave up. I think it looks better this way, and everybody teased me before. I was the only one at my school with nappy hair.

A lot of times my mother was not at home because of her hours. We had to let ourselves into the house and cook for ourselves; we were latchkey kids. This started when we were around ten and six, from the time when my sister could—I won't even say "take care of me"— be responsible for me. We watched TV, did homework, ate. We did have people who checked on us, like friends or neighbors in the building. If my mother wasn't home by the time we went to bed, then somebody would check on us or call and make sure that we got into bed. A lot of times I wished my mother had been at home. I resented her for being away at meetings. I felt neglected some, and I missed her.

My elementary school was a public, all-black school in the Adams Morgan area. In every class I was in, I was the smartest. I won spelling bees and essay contests. I learned to read early, which is one reason I was the smartest. I think it was because my mother read to us a lot.

Sometimes I did my homework at the Rape Crisis Center. I would answer the phone and help out. I was aware of the concept of rape at an early age. My mother taught us about sexuality, little by little, from pre-kindergarten on. The first things she taught us were, "If someone is touching you, let me know" and "Nobody should be touching you somewhere you don't want to be touched." Then she taught us about rape, then we learned about periods. There were times when either she or someone she had appointed would come to my school and talk with us about those subjects. I wasn't embarrassed; I was kind of proud of her.

I didn't particularly like junior high school. There was a lot of peer pressure to be like everybody else. I got a lot of ridicule about my nappy hair. I didn't read much. I watched TV and went shopping on the weekends. Before, I had always been studious, but in junior high my grades went down because I thought it was cool not to do homework. Math seemed difficult, so I didn't want to learn it. My mother wasn't going for that, and I got in trouble. I had to go in early in the morning or stay after school to meet with my teachers and be tutored. After I started going in early, I began liking school and making good grades again.

Education is important to my mother. I have always been studious, but I am a procrastinator; I wait until the last minute to do assignments. I sit around. As soon as I get home, I watch TV almost until I go to bed at ten o'clock. I talk on the phone and take an hour or so for homework. But my mother doesn't say anything about the TV because I get my work done.

When I was twelve my mother got me involved in a program called Peers, which was a group of teenagers who went around and talked to other kids about HIV and AIDS and how to prevent it. I was a Peer until I was seventeen. It helped me with my public speaking and self-esteem. I would like to do something like that for my own children someday.

My mother taught us values. She is loving, but I wouldn't say she is warm. She smiles and jokes, but not too much. She hugs us, but I see my mother as too serious. When people come over—my friends or boyfriends—they don't always feel welcome. One reason for this, she says, is that she's the mother and the father and she needs to let them know from the beginning that they won't be disrespecting us. She can't joke around with them, exactly.

I was fourteen or fifteen when Trina got pregnant. It has been hard for her. I think the hardest thing is that she doesn't have a steady job. It isn't easy to get a job anyway, and when you have a child, you definitely need some kind of employment to provide for it. DeReco doesn't want for anything, but it is still hard. If Trina had waited, things wouldn't be so difficult for her. She doesn't get to go out all the time like I think she probably wants to. I'm not a baby-sitter, and a lot of times my mother doesn't want to watch DeReco. I'm not going to be used for that—for Trina just going out. If she was going to a job interview or something productive, I would baby-sit for her.

I don't think anybody knows how hard it is to take care of a child until it happens. I watch DeReco in the morning when I wake up, from six o'clock to maybe eight-thirty, and then when he gets home from daycare in the afternoons. When Trina first came back to live with us, I was happy. I was one of the ones who helped my mother make that decision; I was on Trina's side. But it has been almost three years, and she is still here. I feel like right now it should be just me and my mother. I resent that this is my time and Trina has come back with a baby.

It would be nice to be married before I have a kid. One or two of my friends have babies. There are a lot in my school. Right now I am not prepared to have a baby. If I had to make a decision, I would get an abortion, because I don't have a job and I'm not out of school. I'm not financially ready to raise a child.

I lost my virginity when I was fifteen. I didn't tell my mother. It was somebody I liked a lot, so I just did it. We used a condom. After that, he was my boyfriend. The only reason we broke up was that he got locked up. That was two years ago, and he is still locked up. I'm not glad that I began having sex. When I look back, it wasn't really needed. It didn't better my life; it didn't feel good. I am not exactly happy to be sexually active now. My mother knows I am having sex, but she doesn't want me to have it at home. She is strict. When I have a male visitor, he can't go in my bedroom.

I have had a lot of boyfriends, but I haven't had a lot of real relationships. I feel a void, and I know something is missing. My father should have been there. I had one boyfriend for almost a year and a half, and twice while I was going with him he got shot. Looking back, I think he was a drug dealer. I myself don't worry about getting shot. Usually the people who get shot are involved in certain things, and I'm not involved in any of those things. I have never used drugs. Unless I am in the wrong place at the wrong time, I don't think I have to worry.

Even if my father is not with us, he should help support us. Now that my mother is trying to buy a house, she doesn't have money just to throw away. We all have to make sacrifices for that. There are times when she will say that we have to eat certain things because she does not have the money to get other foods. I am mad because economically it is a burden on my mother to do everything by herself. This school year itself is very expensive, with senior-class fees and the class trip and the prom. I have been trying to get a job, but it's difficult.

I want to go into fashion merchandising. If I don't succeed at that, I'll be in trouble, because that is the only thing I really want to do. I hope to go to one of the institutes that are set up just for fashion. Maybe I will go to a two-year college first and then another school for four years. That way I won't get off track. I don't know where I got my interest in fashion. Not from my mother. She respects my interest, as long as it is not just a phase I'm going through. Whatever I want to do is okay as long as I succeed in it. At one time I wanted to be a hairdresser, so I was planning to go to cosmetology school for half a day and high school for half a day. She didn't let me do it because although I would learn a trade, I wouldn't learn basic skills that everybody needs. I don't think she valued cosmetology much.

I attend Eastern High, an all-black high school in D.C. I feel different from most of the people in my school. It isn't the type of school that people who are into political issues go to. Everybody just worries about looking good; they don't worry about real issues, from what I can see. No girls in my school call themselves feminists. Another high school, Wilson, might have been better for me. It is culturally and economically mixed, and students there are concerned about political issues. A lot of people who go there come from good homes. But Eastern is my neighborhood school, and I was tired of traveling.

> **Sometimes I don't think I am doing enough to help her, but she needs money and other things I can't give her.**

I think that I will be politically active when I am older, like my mother, but not to the degree that she is. It doesn't interest me as much. I don't want to compete with my mother. I'm not out there with NOW or the ERA. I'm not saying that I don't think women should be equal and successful, but I don't think I'll work toward that exactly. Right now I am not working for anybody. I am working for myself, for my own selfish reasons.

I am a lot like my mother—in good ways. Sometimes I'll say something and I sound just like her. For instance, my mother taught me how to help my friends. If somebody is my friend, or if I like a person, I listen to them if they need me. When my friends have a conflict with their parents or anybody, they'll come and tell me. Usually your friends will be on your side, saying, "Yeah, you're right, you're right," but I'll give them the opposing side and really make them think about how it is. My mother does this with me. So I learned that from her.

My mother has a sense of humor, but she doesn't show it very often. I am funny, and I like to make people laugh. She is trying now, because I talked to her about it. I told her she needs to open up, loosen up a little. Sometimes I don't think I am doing enough to help her, but she needs money and other things I can't give her. I would definitely like for her to find a man. Not that she sits around moaning, "I need a man," but I think she would be happy if she had one. It's good for most people to have a mate or a companion. I think she would lighten up a little.

My mother dedicates her life to activism. I can see that she is helping people. I have met a lot of people who tell me, "Your mother helped me tremendously. I admire your mother." I am proud of her and her accomplishments.

Joy and Rainy, 1974.

Joy and Rainy, 1993.

Joy Harjo
and
Rainy Dawn Ortiz

Joy HARJO, a member of the Muscogee (Creek) Tribe, was born in Tulsa, Oklahoma, in 1951. She attended high school at the Institute of American Indian Arts in Santa Fe, and she says that this early encounter with a generation of Native American artists has shaped her path. Harjo earned her MFA in poetry at the University of Iowa in 1978. She is a poet, writer, and musician as well as a professor in the Department of English at the University of New Mexico, Albuquerque. She resides in Albuquerque and tours the country with her band, Poetic Justice. Her books include *She Had Some Horses* and *The Woman Who Fell From the Sky*.

BORN IN ALBUQUERQUE, NEW MEXICO, in 1973, Rainy Dawn Ortiz is of both Muscogee (Creek) and Acoma descent. She now lives in Albuquerque, where she is a student at the University of New Mexico and raises her young daughter, Krista Chico. Like her mother, Ortiz has a gift for poetry:

Every day it is always there
Whether in mind or body
Whether I want it to be or not—
Sometimes it's like being haunted
By a constant presence
Of sometimes happiness
Sometimes anger—
But it is always filled with love.
That love is my protector
That protector is my mother.

A Mother's Story

My daughter, Rainy Dawn, was born in Albuquerque, New Mexico, on a hot July afternoon, when everyone was wishing for rain. Rain is important in the Southwest, and her birth meant regeneration for our family. Rainy had come to me in a dream, a dream in which we laughed and talked, and I agreed to make a place for her. Before that dream I did not plan to have another child. I already had a son, Phil, and knew the struggle to raise children with grace was difficult, especially without the resources of close family or money.

When I was growing up, girls were expected to become nurses, teachers, or brides. Even at a young age I was horrified that most of my peers saw marriage as their life goal. I wanted to be an artist and had no intention of becoming a wife or mother. To be married and have children signaled the end of a creative life for most women. It did for my mother. She used to write songs on an old Underwood typewriter in the kitchen after she'd cooked and cleaned the house. That was during the few years before she went to work more than forty hours a week as a cook and/or waitress.

My father's people are of the Creek Tribe, or Muscogee. (*Muscogee* is the more accurate name; *Creek* is the more widely recognized name, given to us by others.) Their homeland is in what is now called Alabama, but the family was moved to Indian Territory (now Oklahoma) in the mid-1800s during the forced march known as the "Trail of Tears." My great-grandfather was allotted land over what turned out to be one of the largest oil pools on the continent, Glenpool, so his family became wealthy. My father was born in a twenty-one-room house, later lost through a swindle.

Indian women don't tend to follow the traditional roles of Christian Euro-American cultural values. We are often independent, yet work hard for our peoples. We aren't misty romantic figures, all-knowing spiritual gurus, or grunting squaws, as the stereotypes would have us. My father's mother, Naomi, and her sister Lois both obtained BFA degrees in art in the early 1900s from a university in Oklahoma City. My grandmother died when my father was young, so I only knew her through stories and photographs. My aunt Lois and I are similar spirits. She painted and was involved in the arts. Our paths have led in the same direction—west, toward New Mexico. I have missed her terribly since her death in the early 1980s.

My maternal grandmother was half Cherokee and half Irish. Orphaned when her mother died of childbed fever, she was raised by full-blooded Cherokees in Oklahoma. A gifted storyteller, she used to keep her children entranced for weeks with her tales. My mother was the only daughter in a family of six sons. Her mother resented the attention she received from her father, and treated her badly. How difficult it must have been for her mother to have such imagination and nothing else of brightness in the world, only the relentless struggle for the bare essentials. Her few possessions of value, a silver hairbrush-and-mirror set, were kept in their original wrappings in a dusty drawer—reminders of distant beauty. When my granddaughter Haleigh was born, I felt the spirit of this grandmother in the room. She was happier, had a grace and lightness not possible for her in this world, and blessed this new child.

My parents married during the post–World War II boom, the great arc of the American dream, and they tried to assimilate. My dad worked in manufacturing. His mother died when he was young; his father beat him, then sent him to the Ponca City Military Institute. My father was a sensitive man who had built a shell around himself. Seeing through his shell, I felt close to him. My mother, a homemaker, had grown up in poverty. As a mixed-blood, she lacked self-esteem and felt powerless. Her in-laws, a prominent Indian family with money, looked down on her, she said, because she came from nothing. I was frustrated by her inability to act on her own and our behalf. Now I realize that she did the best she could.

I was born in 1951 in Tulsa, Oklahoma, the first of my mother's family to be born in a hospital. During the birth my mother and I almost died, and I was kept alive on a breathing machine. Three siblings followed, each two years apart. Our house began to topple when my father became a violent alcoholic and beat my mother and us children. He brought other women into our home. I encouraged my mother to leave him because of his growing violence and disrespect. I was my mother's confidante and felt responsible for taking care of her, but I also felt that I was betraying my father.

My parents divorced when I was eight, and I thought it was my fault. Divorce was a stigma in our lower-middle-class community. As it was, I used to get into fights on the street because other kids taunted me and called my family "dirty Indians." School became my refuge, and my attendance was near-perfect. Reading became my escape, yet reading wasn't valued in my home. I loved art and constantly drew and painted. Poetry came later, though at a young age I loved the sound sense, the music inherent in poetry.

My mother soon married my stepfather, a non-Indian who hated Indians. He did not love us and was terribly jealous of my mother. Once, in a fit of jealousy, he forced her to play Russian roulette with a loaded gun. We begged her to leave him, but she was terrified of being without a man, especially with four young children. She had seen too many women with children left destitute. He threatened to burn the house down with all of us in it if she left him, and we believed him. Though emotionally sick, he was respected by the community because he was white and belonged to the Elks Club. I said nothing: Nobody would believe the word of an Indian girl-child against that of a white man who had stepped in to raise four mixed-blood children not his own.

When I was fifteen a chance occurrence altered the current of my life. I was preparing to go away to Indian school, excited about the prospect of being with other Indian students and out of my turbulent home. As we were leaving the Bureau of Indian Affairs, my schooling arranged, my mother added, "And she's a very good artist." The BIA representative then told us about an experimental school in Santa Fe that stressed the arts. I was accepted.

The Institute of American Indian Arts in the late sixties brought together Indian students from all over the country to create art—music, poetry, painting, sculpture, and drama. We used both traditional techniques and more modern European-inspired methods, often a combination of both. I became involved in creating an exciting show, "Deep Roots, Tall Cedar," which blended traditional tribal motifs with contemporary drama. Treated as professionals by director Rolland Meinholtz, we performed professionally. Many celebrities came to our performance and offered support. We took the show on the road, performing along the Northwest Coast. Being part of such a creative endeavor was an awakening for me. It stirred my pride. It was about being proud of my people and my history instead of ashamed.

At sixteen I became pregnant by a fellow Cherokee artist. I began working at a pizza parlor in Tulsa when my son was seven weeks old, and I married his father on my eighteenth birthday. I didn't love him, but I wanted my son to be legitimate, a major concern in those years. During the marriage I worked at several jobs, from cleaning hospital rooms in Tulsa to pumping gas in a miniskirt at the Shell Gas Mart after moving back to Santa Fe. Half my paycheck went to child care. My husband was supposedly looking for a job, yet he never seemed to find one. Besides my son, I was also raising my husband's young daughter, Ratonia. I hired a baby-sitter to look after the children. Apparently she looked after my husband, too. After three difficult years I left. I only regret not taking Ratonia with me.

On the University of New Mexico campus I joined the Kiva Club, the Indian student club, which provided a warm environment of support. We became a major force for change for tribal communities. I worked on a project to put Indian history into textbooks and returned to my first love, painting. Through the Indian movement I became aware of the larger struggle, which was also my personal struggle. The civil rights movement encouraged us to proclaim beauty in our difference. As we began to understand that oppression had become our eyes, ears, and tongues, we rose up together with pride and a greater love for ourselves.

I have called myself a feminist and practice feminism, but I prefer Alice Walker's term *womanist.* In the early days of the women's movement I felt excluded. I was an Indian woman and a mother, and feminism did not particularly address my concerns. Today I call myself a worker for human rights, but women's rights are a central and crucial part of my work. Each of us is born of woman, and women are the central transmitters of culture; yet women still are not valued in the dominant culture.

My first year at the University of New Mexico I met an Acoma poet—the first Indian poet I ever met. I was excited to discover that poetry can be constructed of things that make up everyday life. Through his influence I rediscovered my love of words and language. I began to write poetry seriously for the first time. We were together for only a short time, however, before I realized that he had a serious drinking problem. It was a dreary time, dealing with the erratic behavior of a binge alcoholic as I raised my son (and then daughter) and attended the university. Now I have to wonder what I was thinking then. I wouldn't put up with such behavior from anyone now. My only explanation is that because I was raised in a home with an alcoholic father, I was still acting out of instinct.

Rainy was born in 1973. Like her brother, she came into the world under difficult circumstances. The consequences have reverberated through the years, sometimes quite painfully. Such experiences either become useful knowledge or destroy you. Whether a woman wants to or not, she often acts out her mother's struggle in some manner. Caught up in mere survival, I lacked the perspective needed to work it out at the time, and I left Rainy's father when she was still an infant.

> **Each of us is born of woman, and women are the central transmitters of culture; yet women still are not valued in the dominant culture.**

Often the worst pain women endure is over our children. At fourteen my son was desperately searching for a father. We lived in a Chicano neighborhood in Santa Fe, and he began to model himself after gang members. To be initiated he had to commit a theft. He did and was caught. Other families watched behind the safety of their windows as my son was handcuffed and taken away in a police car.

Rainy was quieter, seemingly more complacent than her brother. A beautiful and intuitive child, she carried within herself a deep wisdom as well as the pain from all the shuffling between apartments and houses in our moves related to school, jobs, and relationships. But she also missed the steady presence of a father. Her rebellion near the age of fourteen was unexpected and therefore deeply disturbing. I think when children are raised by one parent, that parent becomes the focus of all rebellion, rage, and anger. Without the safety net of an extended family, we all fell for a while.

Rainy wanted to attend school with other Indian students, especially after her experiences with racism in public schools, so she entered an Indian boarding school outside Gallup. Because students didn't board over the weekend and I was living in Colorado, we arranged for her to stay with a favorite uncle and aunt and their daughters. It was a difficult period. I was trying to give Rainy what she needed, but she really needed me. Feeling abandoned, she clung to this "real" family of mother, father, sisters.

When Rainy was sixteen there were more rumblings of trouble.

She became obsessed with a Navajo boy who had carved her initials on his hand. He resembled her father at that age and had already been kicked out of school once for misbehavior. I sensed they were doing drugs and drinking, so I showed up at the school unannounced to bring her home—something I should have done sooner. But before I finished signing her out, before I'd even seen her, she left on the back of a motorcycle with her boyfriend. For two months I didn't know her whereabouts, though she was rumored to be on the streets of Gallup, a border town notorious for its cruelty toward Indians. These were the worst months of my life.

When Rainy returned with her boyfriend, she was pregnant. My granddaughter Krista was born in July 1990. Rainy had some difficult times with this boyfriend, who was dangerous and violent. Once, just before Christmas, I had to rescue her and the baby from the street in the middle of the night. It was a dangerous area; the baby had no shoes, and they were wrapped in a blanket.

Fortunately, circumstances have improved for all of us. Rainy is now a full-time student at the University of New Mexico, studying creative writing. She gave her first poetry reading recently and has the makings of a fine poet. The man she is with respects her. My granddaughter Krista is quite a storyteller and is constantly making art. My son works on the railroad in Wisconsin. His daughter, Haleigh, is also a vivacious storyteller. We miss them, being so far away.

Rainy and I have a symbiotic tie. Her life in many ways has followed the pattern of my own. This connection has been a blessing, although it has complicated our relationship. Rainy had to struggle to make her own place in the world, just as I had to struggle to make mine. When my children were young, we were surrounded by conflict. I didn't want to deal with it, so I closed myself off emotionally. I hadn't come to terms with my own terrors, and anything resembling anger evoked fears. I was so often absorbed in my own problems, I didn't know how to reach out to make our relationship work.

I regret not being more present for my children. I missed them terribly during the years I had to work so hard, attend school, and make sure they were taken care of in basic ways. I cooked for them—we didn't eat junk food—and made most of our bread. They had new clothes for school and whatever I could buy with my often-meager scholarships, grants, and jobs. I was the only person steadily there for them, and I deeply loved them. But what they really needed was more of my attention, a sense of family. It took many sacrifices to become a writer in a culture that does not value artists or women. I think Rainy understands that.

I want Rainy to feel her own center of power, born of her sense of compassion, her great love for the children of this land, and her creativity. She's beginning to, the way I knew she would. These lines from "Rainy Dawn," published in *In Mad Love and War,* express my love for her: "And when you were born I held you wet and unfolding, like a butterfly newly born from the chrysalis of my body. And breathed with you as you breathed your first breath. Then was your promise to take it on like the rest of us, this immense journey, for love, of rain."

Life is precious and it goes on. I see it in the gifts of my children and their children. Knowing this restores me, restores all of us.

A Daughter's Story

I was born in Albuquerque, New Mexico, on a hot July afternoon. At the time, my mom was a student at the University of New Mexico. My dad's occupation was somewhere between poet and alcoholic. Due to my dad's drinking, my mom left him when I was about eight months old.

We have lived in all kinds of places. I have gone to at least five different elementary schools and to just as many high schools. It was hard moving around so much. I was not able to make many friends in elementary school. Most of the kids there had been friends since they were really small. I was not very outgoing, and I usually ended up talking to the teachers. The other problem seemed to be that I was a Native American. I was usually the only one in my class. My classmates would make me feel alienated by dancing around me to a fake Indian beat, or they would yell like the Indians they saw on television. In one instance, while I was going to an after-school program in Denver, Colorado, the kids there asked me what kind of food I ate and if I lived in a teepee.

My mom was not like your average mother, nothing like June Cleaver or Mrs. Brady. She always seemed more hip than all the other mothers. Many of my friends told me that they liked her better than their own mothers. Her clothes are always in the style of the times. My mom likes to go out and have fun. Other mothers, including my grandmother, seemed to be more intent on pleasing their husbands and taking care of their children, to the point where they would rather risk their sanity than disapproval from their husbands or kids or even other parents. They always made sure that their husbands were pleased, rather than making themselves happy.

My mom went on trips a lot. I know that it was a part of her career, but it was rough at times. I would have liked her to spend more time at home. She was a very affectionate mom. She was always willing to hold me when I needed a hug, and she told me she loved me all the time, so that I never forgot, no matter how distant we got. There were times, however, when I wished she had been there to help me or could have seen what I was going through.

There was one significant time in my life when I really needed her. When I was nine we lived in Santa Fe, just off Cerillos Road, across the road from Santa Fe Indian School. It was in this house that a relative started to mess with me. At first he just kind of kissed me, but soon the fondling escalated to more. My mother was not at home most of the time this was going on. He always told me that it was so he could know what to do when he was with another girl. I was trusting of him because he had always been there to protect me. I thought he must have known what he was doing. I knew that what he was doing probably shouldn't have been happening, but I didn't want to go against his judgment. A couple of times my mom was in her room right next door while this was going on. Once she almost walked in on us, but we heard her in time for me to get covered with a blanket and sit in a corner of the room and pretend that I was watching TV. I was scared to death that she would see me and get mad and blame me, but I was more scared that she would get mad at my relative and then he would stop caring for me.

For some reason I used to feel that it was my fault. I never actually told him, "No, I don't want to do it." I rationalized that maybe it was not so bad because he had not actually fully penetrated me. But a good friend, Tim Chee, helped me see that it wasn't my fault. I was just a little girl, and this relative of mine had manipulated me. Tim also helped me to decide that it was time to tell my mom. It was a very hard decision for me. I was fearful that she would be angry, though I know that she is very understanding.

My mother is a very special person. She is strong. She has been through a lot of hard times but has managed to make it through. I admire her very much. She has taught me that I should respect myself as a woman and not be ashamed of myself. My mom is a well-known and respected poet, and I am very proud of her. I am proud of her success in her writing and in her music. She is a talented saxophone player, and I know she will go far in her career.

Both my mom and I had a child at a very young age. She had my brother when she was seventeen. I had my daughter, Krista, three weeks after my seventeenth birthday. At the time I had a lot of mixed emotions. I was scared of becoming a mother, since I had not grown up all the way yet myself. But I was very happy with the little girl I had. I was proud that I had brought someone so beautiful into this world. Her father was there with me during her birth, and he also seemed very proud of her.

I went through some rough times with her father. We never really got along, and we fought a lot. The relationship was never healthy for either one of us, nor for our daughter. I finally decided to leave him, which was not an easy decision, as I had already grown to be co-dependent on him. Tim helped me realize that love does not have to be so hard; you should not have to fight for what you need and deserve. I am now living with Tim, and we have a good, loving relationship.

> At an after-school program in Denver, Colorado, the kids asked me what kind of food I ate and if I lived in a teepee.

I know that I have gained a lot of good qualities from my mom. I am strong like her, although at times I think not as strong as I would like to be. I like to write short stories, but I don't think I'm that good at poetry. Then again, recently I had my first poetry reading for my creative-writing class.

My mom and I are also different in a lot of ways. She takes everything too seriously. Like in the movies, when something is not done the way it would be in real life, she gets all upset. Of course it is not the same—that is the whole reason for movies. Krista has inherited my mom's quality of overreacting. But I love my mom and I would never trade her for anyone in the world.

I have never thought of my mom as a feminist, although in her own way I know that she is. She does not go all out and rally for feminism. She has her own battles to fight in her own life, and each one she wins is a small step toward rights for women. I think that if the cause was strong enough, she would go out and protest. But I think that in her writing and her music she makes her statement about feminism.

As for me being a feminist—just like my mom, I think that I am, in my own quiet way. I think that if we were all meant to be the same, we would all have been born exactly the same. But that does not mean that women are worth any less than men. Nobody should be superior over anyone because of what sex they are.

Watching Krista grow up, it is interesting to see what qualities have come out. She is really into makeup and not wearing "boy clothes" and not playing with "boy toys," something she has learned at her daycare. But usually she is an instigator in rough-and-tumble play, and she loves to jump and roll around in the dirt. Recently I saw her go up to a boy in line in front of her and push him out of the way, telling him, "Girls first!"

I have high hopes for my daughter. She is very outspoken—maybe sometimes too much. I believe that she is going to be a leader in her class. I hope to be able to teach her to choose how to fight for the right causes. She likes to talk a lot, and I know that she will be a great help to whatever cause she fights for. Krista has gained a lot of these qualities from both my mom and me. I am very proud of that. I hope that she produces another generation just as strong.

Appendix

INTERVIEW QUESTIONS

I. *GENERAL/OVERVIEW*

1. What kinds of mothers have leading feminists been, especially as role models for their daughters?

2. By what specific means (e.g., conversations, friends, books, media) has feminism been passed from one generation to the next?

3. What regrets do feminist mothers have about the way they raised their daughters?

4. How do women raise strong daughters?

5. Are the daughters of active feminists usually themselves feminist?

6. What do they believe have been their greatest successes?

7. What is it like to rebel against a rebel?

8. Would the daughters be willing to make the kinds of sacrifices their mothers did?

9. What roles do men play in the mothers' and daughters' lives?

10. How does the theory of female empowerment translate into practice?

11. How do feminist mothers mentor feminist daughters?

12. What battles do the daughters believe their mothers have won?

13. What remains to be done?

14. What do the daughters take for granted? What do they assume that their mothers never could?

15. What are the daughters teaching their mothers?

II. *SPECIFIC QUESTIONS*

A. *Feminism*
1. Do you define yourself as a feminist?
2. When did you become a feminist?
3. Why did you become a feminist?
4. How did your feminism develop?
5. What is feminism to you? How do you define it?
6. What radicalized you?
7. What did your mother or father give—or not give—you that caused you to look deeper?
8. How did you come to the realization that you deserved more than the dominant culture had led you to believe?
9. What was the first manifestation of your rebellion?
10. Did you get squashed?
11. How did you cope with the squashing?
12. In what ways did your mother/father encourage the rebellion? In what ways did she/he discourage it?
13. How has feminism affected your marriage/relationship(s)?

B. *Motherhood*
1. Do you remember the day that your daughter was born?
2. What was going on that day in the world?
3. Was this your first pregnancy?
4. Did you choose to become a mother?
5. Were you happy to have a daughter?
6. How has motherhood affected your marriage/relationship(s)?
7. What is your daughter's relationship like with her father? What is your relationship like with your own father?
8. Do you have any misgivings about the way you raised your daughter?
9. How do you feel in general about the way you have raised your daughter?

10. What kind of parent were/are you? Were you strict, permissive, reflective, or reflexive?

11. Did your own mother model or instruct?

12. Did you raise your daughter the way you were raised?

13. In your mind, was the time you spent with your daughter compromised by your work? Did your work keep you from parenting?

14. What was the cost of your double role? To you? To your daughter?

15. What good came out of it for you and your child?

16. How is your relationship with your daughter similar to or different from your relationship with your own mother?

17. What has your daughter rejected that you hold dear?

18. What kind of relationship did you have with your daughter when she was a teenager? And now?

19. What compromises, if any, have you made that your daughter is unwilling to make?

20. What choices, if any, have you made that your daughter is unwilling to make?

21. What compromises, if any, has your daughter made that you were unwilling to make?

22. What choices, if any, has your daughter made that you were unwilling to make?

23. What do you wish for your daughter in the future?

24. If you had it to do over again, what would you do differently?

25. What advice would you give your daughter when her daughter is born?

26. How do you think your daughter will parent differently?

C. Feminism and Motherhood

1. Were you a feminist when your daughter was born?

2. Did becoming a mother change your definition of feminism?

3. How did raising a child change or reinforce your concept of feminism?

4. How has feminism affected your child-rearing?

5. To what degree did your personal life suffer because of your political involvement?

6. Has your motherhood ever been a source of conflict for you as a feminist?

7. Has your feminism ever been a source of conflict for you as a mother?

8. Do you feel that you have reconciled motherhood with feminism?

9. Has your daughter's experience changed your own beliefs? If so, how?

10. Did your daughter, in any way, encourage or direct your social activism?

11. Does your daughter consider herself a feminist?

12. Are you optimistic about the future of feminism as displayed in your daughter, or are you pessimistic?

D. For Daughters Only

1. Do you remember when your mother first became involved in feminism?

2. To what degree did your mother's growth as a feminist determine your own?

3. Have you claimed the feminist cause as your own?

About the Authors

CHRISTINA LOOPER BAKER, professor of English in the University of Maine system, teaches women's studies and is the author of *In a Generous Spirit: The Life of Myra Page.* She is the mother of four daughters and lives in Bangor, Maine.

CHRISTINA BAKER KLINE is the author of the novel *Sweet Water.* Living in New York City, she teaches fiction and nonfiction writing at New York University.